The Picturesque Garden in France

The Picturesque Garden
in France

DORA WIEBENSON

Princeton University Press   *Princeton, New Jersey*

Copyright © 1978 by Princeton University Press

Published by Princeton University Press, Princeton, New Jersey
In the United Kingdom: Princeton University Press, Guildford, Surrey

This book has been composed in Linotype Granjon

Printed in the United States of America
by Princeton University Press, Princeton, New Jersey
Illustrations by the Meriden Gravure Company, Meriden, Connecticut

Designed by Glenn Ruby

Frontispiece: Philosopher's Pyramid at Ermenonville, also reproduced figure 59.

Library of Congress Cataloging in Publication Data:

Wiebenson, Dora.
    The picturesque garden in France.

    Bibliography: p.
    Includes index.
    1. Gardens, English—France.   2. Gardens, English.
3. Gardens—France.   I. Title.
SB466.F8W53   712'.0944   77-22704
ISBN 0-691-03930-5

Contents

List of Illustrations

Archives Nationales, Paris: 5, 6, 22, 32.

Archives Photographiques, Paris: 73, 76, 84, 138, 150, 151, 154.

Archives Seine-et-Marne, Melun: 159.

Bibliothèque Nationale, Paris: 2, 3, 4, 17, 18, 19, 20, 21, 23, 25, 26, 28, 30, 31, 34, 72, 81, 98, 99, 107, 108, 109, 110, 124, 127, 128, 130, 136, 144, 145, 148, 152, 156, 158, 164.

Bowes Museum, Barnard Castle: 33.

British Museum, London: 139, 141, 162.

Bulloz, Paris: 29, 52, 53, 56, 71, 75, 78, 113, 131, 140, 149, 163.

Devonshire Collection, Chatsworth: 39.

Didon, Lunéville: 14, 15.

Documentation photographique de la Réunion des Musées nationaux, Paris: 44, 45, 46, 47, 48, 49, 50, 51.

Giraudon, Paris: 105, 106, 137.

The Henry Francis du Pont Winterthur Museum, Winterthur: 165.

The Metropolitan Museum of Art, New York: 36, 41.

Musée Historique de Lorraine, Nancy: 13.

Musée de Lunéville: 11.

Nationalmuseum, Stockholm: 115.

Public Record Office, London: 166.

Royal Institute of British Architects, London: 161.

Acknowledgments

Many people, who have been charmed as I have been by the picturesque garden, have aided my work on this study. Among these enthusiasts are: Jacqueline Bougon, who has kindly shown me the remains of Le Raincy; George Clarke, who gave of his time and considerable knowledge to guide me through Stowe; Jean Cailleux, who has shared his extensive acquaintance with Moulin-Joli and Méréville with me; Olivier Choppin de Janvry, to whom every lover of French eighteenth-century gardens is indebted for his devoted restorations of the Pavilion at Cassan and the Désert de Retz; William Holden, who knows all about Woburn Farm; Denis Lambin, who introduced me to Ermenonville; Susi Lang, who has done considerable research on the iconography of the early eighteenth-century picturesque garden; Agnieszka Morawinska, who has introduced me to Polish articles on Lunéville and provided translations of them; Monique Mosser, who has shared with me her considerable information on the French picturesque gardens; Peter Willis, who has been helpful in introducing me to English picturesque garden enthusiasts; and, above all, Kenneth Woodbridge, to whom I am deeply grateful for many discussions on gardens, for showing me Stourhead and Rousham, and for including me on trips to French gardens in the vicinity of Paris.

Allan Braham, Robin Middleton, and Damie Stillman all have been kind enough to look at versions of the typescript, and I am indebted to them for suggestions and corrections. I am, of course, responsible for any errors. Mary Laing has been a sympathetic and enlightened editor.

Among the institutions to which thanks are due are the Courtauld Institute, which demonstrated early support of the picturesque garden in its colloquium on eighteenth-century gardens held in August, 1973, and the American and British Societies of Architectural Historians, which invited me to read excerpts from drafts of this book at three consecutive annual meetings: 1973, 1974, and 1975.

Libraries, archives, and museums that have been of help in the research for this book are, in London, the British Library, where I am overwhelmingly indebted to the staff for its unceasing and courteous help in supplying me with massive amounts of material during the many months I used its resources; and the Library of the Victoria and Albert Museum, which was a supplemental source of information. Those in Paris include the Bibliothèque Nationale, and in particular the Cabinet des Estampes; the Musée Carnavalet, where research on this book began many years ago and where I am indebted to Michel Gallet for introducing me to the collection of material on Paris; the Musée Marmottan, where the Carmontelle drawings of Le Raincy are located; the Bibliothèque des Arts Décoratifs, where Comte Ernest de Ganay's indispensable thesis on the *jardin anglais* is deposited; the Bibliothèque Historique de la Ville de Paris; the Bibliothèque de l'Arsénal; and the Archives Nationales. In the environs of Paris are the Musée de Sceaux, where material on gardens around Paris is located and where I am indebted to Maddy Aries for her help; the Musée Jacquemart-André at Châalis, where Pierre

Marot with extreme kindness has located material on Ermenonville and permitted me to see it; and the Musée Condé at Chantilly. In France I also have used the Musée at Lunéville and the Musée Historique de Lorraine at Nancy, where the bulk of material on the gardens of Stanislaus is located; the municipal libraries of Lyons have engaged in a fruitless search for the missing Moreau publication on Chinese gardens. In the United States the following have been helpful: the Garden Library at Dumbarton Oaks, where Elisabeth MacDougall has kindly permitted me to use the resources; Avery Library, the New York Public Library, and the Library of the Metropolitan Museum of Art, which have all been of help in the later stages of work.

It would have been impossible to proceed with this work without the assistance of grants from the University of Maryland General Research Fund for travel and photographs, the American Philosophical Society, and a combined grant from the National Endowment for the Humanities and the Samuel H. Kress Foundation. In particular, the last grant permitted me to devote one year exclusively to the researching and writing of this book.

Foreword

Gardens are one of the most important artistic manifestations of the eighteenth century: they draw upon all the arts and even some of the sciences and they were at the time of their design a testing ground for new gardening concepts, theories, and styles, which often foreshadowed later developments. But gardens are among the most fragile of artistic creations. They are subject to the continual encroachment of nature and they demand constant maintenance. All but the most revered are doomed to disappear. Moreover, gardens are the product of ever-changing fashion—in style, cultural taste, politics, and social attitudes—and are thus constantly being altered or replaced. The task of establishing a pattern of garden development is therefore a difficult one. Even the recording of a single garden may meet with overwhelming obstacles.

Added to these facts, knowledge about the French picturesque garden is far behind that of the English one, on which interest was focused as long ago as 1927 with the publication of Christopher Hussey's *The Picturesque*. In the case of the English garden, its history has been subdivided into three chronological phases—heroic, artificial, and natural—and, more recently, has been well enough investigated so that the earlier oversimplifications of its development are now being corrected. On the other hand scholarly research on the French picturesque garden has barely begun. There is only one comprehensive authority, the Comte Ernest de Ganay, and his encyclopaedic work of 1923 exists only in manuscript form. Sections from this work were later published in article form by Ganay, but no general pattern of garden development was established. It is generally believed that the picturesque garden came into being in France only in the 1760s, and that it was a product of English influence, not of French tradition; development from an experimental to a perfected stage is considered to have been minimal.

Moreover, French picturesque gardens, in contrast to the English ones, are less fortunate in their preservation. The type is not in the mainstream of the French tradition, and, as a product of private rather than royal patronage, it has been of little interest to those institutions concerned with the preservation of the French heritage. In addition, because they were created in the period just before the Revolution and were a symbol of the aristocracy, they were often destroyed or fell into ruins when the owners abandoned their estates. Finally, records of the designing of these gardens are in the main restricted to occasional and partial contemporary descriptions, a few illustrations, and, in rare cases, documents, which are often preserved in local archives or are in private hands, and have all but disappeared. In one notable case, Ermenonville, most of the documents seen by the Comte de Ganay less than fifty years ago are at present hopelessly lost.

These facts have determined both the scope and the topic of the present study. By devoting research to a new aspect of gardening history, that concerned with the French picturesque garden, it may be possible to gain a clearer idea of the general type, picturesque garden, and how it developed. With this in mind, the book is divided into three sections. The first is concerned with the relation of the French picturesque garden to its own national tradition and to that of its English counterpart. Second, in order to establish the motivation and philosophy underlying the garden, English and French picturesque gardening theories have been considered. And, third, several of the major picturesque gardens are analyzed in an attempt to differentiate sub-types and to indicate their development.

It is, however, clearly an impossible task, given the present state of research and the lack of source material, to produce a definitive study. The present one is intended, therefore, to be introductory. I have attempted here only to provide a coherent framework from which to view the field of eighteenth-century gardens in France, one on which more detailed studies may be based, or from which scholars may depart. As comprehensive a bibliography as possible of existing literature on French gardens and relevant publications on English gardens and related fields has been provided. It has also seemed best not to attempt to present a firm set of con-clusions, but instead to suggest a number of directions into which further study might lead. Finally, and regretfully, it has been necessary here to limit detailed studies of the gardens to a few key examples, for which at least some certain documentation exists, and which appear to be illustrative of major trends in the development and typology of these gardens.

The Picturesque Garden in France

CHAPTER I

The French Picturesque Garden
before 1760

The history of the early development of the picturesque garden in France has only begun to be recorded.[1] Recent scholarship suggests that its origin and growth were not dependent on the English picturesque garden, but that there were many parallels to, and even advances on, the better-known counterpart. It is not, however, the purpose here to attempt to determine the priority of either France or England in the development of the new gardening style, but rather to sketch the known stages of French development, and to point out relationships to the English one.

French interest in picturesque gardening, like that of the English, had roots in literature. But where English interest was a reflection of the importance of agriculture in the development of the national economy and of the role of the individual within this context,[2] French interest reflected the retreat of the individual to nature and to the rural life in a period of political and economic decline. This retreat has been documented in French literature,[3] although, as in England, direct influence of literature on gardens seems to be rare. However, one of the lesser-known but important literary works associated with the retreat, the pastoral novel *Astrée*, written by Honoré d'Urfé in the late fifteenth and early sixteenth centuries and published between 1608 and 1628,[4] deserves some discussion because of its special relevance for later French gardening developments.

Astrée is a long-winded, archaic, and moralizing story of the adventures of shepherds and

[1] E. de Ganay has made a comprehensive contribution to the French picturesque garden in his dissertation *Les Jardins à l'anglaise en France au dix-huitième siècle.* The early eighteenth-century French garden has been considered by Ganay, *Les Jardins à la française en France au XVIIIe siècle;* A. Marie, *Jardins français classiques des XVIIe & XVIIIe siècles;* and, most recently, I. Dennerlein, *Die Gartenkunst der Régence und des Rokoko in Frankreich.* For complete references to these works, see Bibliography.

[2] For the English literary background, see S. Røstvig, *The Happy Man: Studies in the Metamorphosis of a Classical Idea*, 1: (1600-1700).

[3] For the concept of nature in France, see A. Monglond, *Le Préromantisme français*, Grenoble, 1930

(2v.); J. Ehrard, *L'Idée de la nature en France dans la première moitié de XVIIIe siècle*, Paris, 1963 (2v.); G. Atkinson, *Le Sentiment de la nature et le retour à la vie simple: 1699-1740*, Paris, 1960; and the still unsurpassed D. Mornet, *Le Sentiment de la nature en France*, Paris, 1907. For bibliography, see Paul H. Johnstone, "Turnips and Romanticism," *Agricultural History*, XII, no. 3, July 1938, pp. 224-255, esp. pp. 226-230, 241-244.

[4] For *Astrée*, see C. O. Reure, *La Vie et les oeuvres d'Honoré d'Urfé*, Paris, 1910. Only the first three books were written by d'Urfé, the remaining two volumes were written by his friend and secretary Baro, from manuscript notes by d'Urfé.

shepherdesses, set in the simple rural countryside of d'Urfé's native Forez. The work was out of fashion after the mid-seventeenth century, although it was well thought of past the mid-1750s.[5] At least six biographies of its author or discussions of the work appeared by the mid-eighteenth century: many were based on the short but definitive 1711 biography of d'Urfé by the Abbé Huet, who considered the novel to be the most ingenious and polite work in its genre ever to appear.[6]

In the early eighteenth century the novel was, along with the *fêtes galantes* of Watteau, a symbol of idealized life, and it represented—like Watteau's paintings—a nostalgic return to the simple life associated with the period before the reign of Louis XIV. Indeed, d'Urfé's name later was coupled with that of Watteau in Horace Walpole's biography of the painter: "The genius of Watteau resembled that of his countryman D'urfé; the one drew and the other wrote of imaginary nymphs and swains, and described a kind of impossible pastoral, a rural life led by those opposites of rural simplicity, people of fashion and rank."[7]

The form of *Astrée*, and of all pastoral romances, was based on an Italian tradition which had its roots in Neoplatonic philosophy.[8] D'Urfé's romance was considered superior to the rest of the genre for its combination of erudition and beauty of sentiment, as well as for its emphasis on virtue, simplicity, reason, naturalness, and admirable conduct. The work was the source of thematic material for pastoral dramas in both England[9] and France.[10] Now, the pastoral drama, in its depiction of a bucolic, moralizing, and sentimental life, can be associated with the philosophy of the later picturesque gardens. And there may be a more specific relationship between this theatrical form and the gardens. For pastoral stage sets were derived from the bucolic

[5] See Reure, *Honoré d'Urfé*, pp. 312-316, and 323-328 for bibliography on attitudes toward *Astrée*.

[6] P. d. Huet, "Lettre à Mademoiselle de Scudery touchant Honoré d'Urfé et Diane de Chasteaumorand," dated 15 December 1699, and included in *Traité de l'origine des romans, révuë et augmentée d'une lettre*, Paris, 1711 (8th ed.), pp. 229-268 (with information on *Astrée*, pp. 225-228). According to Reure, *Honoré d'Urfé*, p. 325, this was probably the original publication of the letter. Other commentators on d'Urfé and *Astrée* were: C. Perrault, *Les Hommes illustres qui ont paru en France pendant ce siècle*, Paris, 1697-1700 (2v.), II (1700), pp. 39-40 (English transl., *Characters Historical and Panegyrical of the Greatest Men that have appear'd in France during the Last Century*, London, 1704); and Abbé Genest, *Dissertations sur la poésie pastorale ou de l'idylle et de l'eglogue*, Paris, 1707, pp. 154-156, 209-210 (discussion of *Astrée*). The *Mercure de France*, July 1729, pp. 1523-1528, contains material on d'Urfé from the "Dissertation touchant Honoré d'Urfé, Auteur du Roman d'Astrée," by Huet, which was also included in *Dissertation sur diverses matières de religion et de philologie, contenants en plusieurs Lettres écrites par des personnes savantes*, Paris, 1712, II, pp. 100-124 (15 December 1699). Huet's letter was mentioned by J. P. Niceron, *Mémoires pour servir à l'histoire des hommes illustres dans la République des lettres*, Paris, 1729-1745 (43v.),

VI, pp. 217-226 (esp. p. 226); and it was still considered important enough to be extensively reviewed in 1752 by A. Gachet d'Artigny, *Nouveaux mémoires de critique et de littérature*, Paris, 1749-1756 (7v.), V, pp. 1-28: "Examen de la Dissertation de M. Huet sur Honoré d'Urfé," with a biography of d'Urfé, correcting Huet.

[7] H. Walpole, *Anecdotes of Painting in England*, Strawberry Hill, 1762-1771 (4v.), IV, pp. 35-36.

[8] G. Rudolph, "La Poésie Pastorale dans le Roman et sur la scène de XVIIe siècle," *Abhandlung zu dem Oster-Program des Herzoglichen Ernst-Reelgymnasiums zu Altenburg*, Altenburg, 1897 (ed. G. Rudolph), who further notes that the native French medieval *pastoretas* and *pastorelles* were lost until modern times, and thus that they cannot be the source of the pastoral drama with which *Astrée* is connected. But a medieval nostalgia did exist: later, Watelet recalled the ancient days of hospitality (see chap. IV, p. 65), a recollection that surely was related to a similar English attitude in which the hospitality of the Tudor manor was recalled (see B. S. Allen, *Tides in English Taste*, I, p. 10).

[9] For *Astrée* and English pastoral dramas, see A. Nicoll, *Restoration Drama: 1600-1700*, London, 1952 (4th ed.), pp. 95-96, 184-185.

[10] For *Astrée* and French pastoral drama, see Rudolph, *Honoré d'Urfé*, pp. 5, 9. See also Atkinson, *Le Sentiment de la nature*, pp. 67-68.

Serlian satiric scene,[11] which developed during the course of the seventeenth and eighteenth centuries to include almost the entire range of expressive possibilities of the later picturesque garden. Already by 1681 the vocabulary of the related *rustique* or *champêtre* scenes of French drama included mountains, valleys, rocks, solitudes, forests, grottos, fields, villages, hamlets, and rustic festivals, as well as the four seasons.[12]

The significance of *Astrée* in the context of this study is indicated by its association in the 1770s with the French picturesque garden. When Walpole again coupled the names of Watteau and d'Urfé, in a reference to "the fantastic scenes of Watteau and Durse (*sic*),"[13] It was in connection with gardening design. Walpole was not the only garden theorist to relate picturesque gardening to this archaic work. The Prince de Ligne mentioned the romance when he cautioned against elaboration and artificiality of garden design in the 1786 edition of his *Coup d'oeil sur Beloeil*.[14] And Lezay-Marnésia would recall the shepherds of d'Urfé in his own work on gardening, published the following year.[15] It is even possible that the pastoral imagery which was associated by these men with *Astrée* and with the paintings of Watteau may have had some relationship to the early development of the English picturesque garden: a view of Richmond (Fig. 1), engraved by Rocque and included in the fourth volume of Campbell's *Vitruvius Britannicus*, published in 1739, contains in the foreground a scene similar to that of Watteau's *Le Pèlerinage à l'isle de Cythère*.

There is no English parallel to *Astrée*, but two other types of French literary sources for gardens are related to English ones. An example of the first, which is characterized by a renewed interest in nature, is an essay by the same Abbé Huet who had written the biography of d'Urfé. In this essay, written sometime before the author's death in 1721, the Abbé stated his views on gardening, and these, according to several later eighteenth-century French gardening critics, preceded the expression of similar views by the English.[16] Admitting that his taste was not in fashion, the Abbé contrasted natural cascades falling at the foot of rocks, grassy

[11] See, for instance, M. Vitruvius Pollo, *Les dix Livres d'architecture*, Paris, 1684 (ed. Perrault) (2nd ed.), p. 178, n. 1: "La Satyrique est ornée de boccages, de cavernes, de montagnes," as opposed to the tragic scene, decorated with columns and other ornaments of a royal palace, or the comic scene, which was composed of private houses.

[12] C. P. Ménestrier, *Des Réprésentations en musique anciennes et modernes*, Paris, 1681, p. 172. In the absence of any study of the relation of the theater and theatrical theory to garden design, it can be pointed out only that a tradition of types of landscape had existed in theater decoration before 1637, when five different types of landscape were suggested and developed for theatrical sets (P. Bjurstrom, *Giacomo Torelli and Baroque Stage Designs*, p. 179): by 1681 an infinite number of types had been established (*ibid.*, p. 199).

[13] H. Walpole, "On Modern Gardening," *Anecdotes*, iv, p. 122.

[14] C. J. de Ligne, *Coup d'oeil sur Beloeil* (all references will be to the Ganay edition of 1922), pp. 159-

160; "Pays d'enchantement! vous êtes fait pour ressusciter dans vos jardins l'Arcadie heureuse. Rendez votre terre digne du séjour de l'Astrée."

[15] C. F. A. Lezay-Marnésia, *Essai sur la nature champêtre*, p. 96: "L'ingénieux d'Urfé dessina ses bergers, / Créa la douce Astrée, et, d'un feu pur et tendre, / Englamma Céladon, Léonide, et Sylvandre, / Les délivra de soins, les couronna de fleurs / Et rappela les jours des Monarques pasteurs."

[16] Mme. Brulart de Genlis, Marchioness de Sillery, *Dictionnaire critique et raisonné des étiquettes de la cour, et des usages du monde*, Paris, 1818, ii, pp. 297-298: "Le célèbre Huet . . . proposa dans ses ouvrages d'imiter la nature dans la composition des jardins. Depuis lui, Addisson (*sic*), dans le *Spectateur*, fit le même proposition . . ."; also A. Laborde, *Description*, pp. 48-49. Dennerlein, *Gartenkunst*, pp. 18-19, has pointed out that no French translation of the *Spectator*, in which Addison stated his views on gardening, or of the *Guardian*, in which Pope's views appeared, existed before 1720 and 1723, respectively.

fields, and the green shade of leafy beeches and great pines, all contained in a beautiful land-scape where "nature displays her riches without disguise," with the fashionable garden, where the water spout was drawn at great expense from some frog pond, the parterre was so artificial that the visitor could not observe natural phenomena such as the changing of the seasons, the *palissades* were arranged with cord and scissors,[17] and where, owing to the lack of shade, it was not possible to walk during the day.[18] In another often cited reference, the Princesse Palatine wrote that she preferred a simple kitchen garden to ornamental gardens with statues and fountains, a stream to sumptuous cascades, and all that was natural to magnificent works of art which inspired only fatigue.[19] Surely these comments are in the spirit of the contemporary writings of Addison and Nourse!

The second type of literary source is that of a renewed interest in antiquity, and in particular in the reconstruction of the ancient country estates of the classical author Pliny. French reconstructions of Pliny's estates were executed by the amateur and official historian of Louis XIV, Jean François Félibien, as early as 1699,[20] almost twenty years before the appearance of Robert Castell's magnificent English folio volume on the subject and fourteen years before Pope endorsed the classical garden of Alcinous in the *Guardian*.[21]

How much classical literary descriptions influenced the designing of early eighteenth-century "Régence" gardens is not now known, but the interest in nature, reflected in the comments of Huet and the Princesse Palatine, is descriptive of a type of garden which already existed at the time these two authors wrote, and which may have originated in the last two decades of the seventeenth century. Its characteristics were described by A. J. Dézallier d'Argenville as early as 1709,[22] and they have been analyzed in a recent study of French gardening of the first half of the eighteenth century.[23] It should be noted that Dézallier's work was translated into English by 1712, where it preceded the gardening books of Switzer and Langley, and that this French work retained its popularity in England during the first half of the century—it appeared in two more English editions in 1728 and 1743.[24]

An outstanding characteristic of the Régence garden was its greater openness to the country-side. This was achieved by means of ditches (or ha-has), which had been introduced into French gardening before 1709 when they were mentioned by Dézallier, and which thus pre-ceded Bridgeman's use of them in England,[25] and by grilles that permitted unobstructed views of the countryside. A system of diagonal allées with radial views replaced the seventeenth-

[17] Huet, *Huetiana*, "Béautez naturelles préférable aux béautez de l'art," pp. 119-121.

[18] *Ibid.*, "Des jardins à la mode," pp. 169-171.

[19] *Correspondence de Mme. la Duchesse d'Orléans*, Paris, 1857 (2v.), ii, p. 66, 16 February 1719. Interest in nature and simplicity are recorded as early as 1665, with the publication of René Rapin's *Hortorum libri quattuor*, which was translated into English by Evelyn in 1673. The interest continued in the 1730s with the publication of N. A. Pluche's *Le Spectacle de la nature*, which achieved seven French editions before 1754. This work also was translated into English by 1736. Both works were available in many French and English editions in the eighteenth century.

[20] For comments on Félibien, see D. Nyberg, "Meissonnier: An Eighteenth-Century Maverick," p. 23 and n. 97.

[21] A. Pope, *Guardian*, 29 September 1713, no. 173.

[22] Dennerlein, *Gartenkunst*, p. 27.

[23] *Idem.*

[24] See *ibid.*, pp. 226-228, for later editions and trans-lations.

[25] A. J. Dézallier d'Argenville, *La Théorie et le pratique du jardinage*, Paris, 1709, p. 77 (all references are to the 1712 English translation, J. James, *The Theory and Practice of Gardening*, unless otherwise cited). See also D. Green, *Gardener to Queen Anne: Henry Wise*, p. 178.

century single vista which had been protracted to infinity. These views were of particular importance for further developments, for they were composed to frame natural scenes as if they were pictures: Dézallier maintained that nothing was more diverting or agreeable in a garden than the aspect of a beautiful countryside where allées would open into "prospects" of villages, woods, rivers, hills, meadows, and other rural aspects which compose beautiful "landskips."[26] Belvederes and seats or benches that took advantage of the views were also recommended by Dézallier in 1709,[27] at the same time that he proclaimed artificiality, such as clipped trees and hedges, out of fashion,[28] and suggested the introduction of simple parterres of grass along with the more formal parterres. Dézallier specifically criticized the unnatural garden composed of high terrace walls, grand stone stairs, arbors, cabinets, trellises, statues, and vases—all of which were later associated with the "architectural" garden deplored by theorists of picturesque gardening. He wished to see such artificiality replaced by a noble simplicity, where stairs, banks, and ramps were composed of grass, where natural arbors and simple hedges were designed without trellises, and where only a limited number of tastefully placed works of sculpture and other ornaments were included.[29] The importance of Dézallier's book for later gardening developments can be estimated by the fact that when the simple style of gardening was revived in the 1750s, Blondel reproduced these remarks almost without alteration.[30]

Around 1730 the simple, natural "Régence" garden was replaced by a new artificial and irrational one.[31] In contrast to its predecessor, intricacy and complexity were now stressed, and the variety, strong contrast, and surprise—all of which were basic components of later picturesque gardens, according to garden theorists of the 1770s—were essential ingredients of the design.[32] In his *Maisons de Plaisance*, published in 1736, Blondel described the effect of such a garden as being due to "the arrangement and variety of all the parts of a garden that cause surprise and amusement." Furthermore, he recommended that "the beauties of a garden should not be perceived at one glance, and that if some of its ornaments are hidden, curiosity will be excited."[33]

The effects of this "rococo" garden were achieved by complete artistic control in the composing of an infinite number of variations on traditional French gardening vocabulary. The design was based on the form of the maze and the labyrinth, where surprise and variety were achieved by means of a series of curved or angled walks.[34] In the new gardens strongly contrasting bosquets replaced the balanced and logical bosquet system of previous gardening design. However, in spite of the variety achieved in the complicated shapes and twisting, curving walks, these French gardens, in contrast to contemporaneous English ones, remained regular. But there is evidence to demonstrate that the French were familiar already in the seventeenth century with the elements characteristic of the eighteenth-century picturesque garden. For instance,

[26] Dézallier d'Argenville, *Gardening*, p. 13. Also see *Mercure*, November 1748, pp. 44-45.

[27] Dézallier d'Argenville, *Gardening*, pp. 77-78.

[28] *Ibid.* (1713 French edition), p. 33.

[29] *Ibid.* (1712 English edition), pp. 18ff.

[30] J. F. Blondel, *Architecture français*, I, p. 46.

[31] Dennerlein, *Gartenkunst*, p. 151.

[32] *Ibid.*, p. 89.

[33] Blondel, *Maisons de Plaisance*, I, pp. 6-7.

[34] For the most comprehensive work on this subject, see Matthews, *Mazes and Labyrinths*. A probable source for later developments of the rococo garden in France and possibly in England is the Labyrinth at Versailles, with its asymmetrical compositions, framed views (taken from a classical and moral fable), and inscriptions identifying the "scenes." See Marie, *Jardins français*, pls. 113, 114; and C. Perrault, *Labyrinte de Versailles*, Paris, 1677.

irregularity had been introduced into French gardens before 1700.[35] Among the early examples are the *Bosquet de la Felicité* at Saint-Cloud (dating from the seventeenth century), *Les Bosquets (côté de Louveciennes)* at Marly (ca. 1700),[36] and the unadorned *Bosquet des Sources* which was designed in the 1680s for the newly erected Grand Trianon before the wing known as the Trianon-sous-Bois.[37] It has been preserved to us in several plans (Fig. 2), and in a description by the Princesse Palatine, who wrote that it was composed of some fifty meandering springs which formed irregular islands, each just large enough to contain a table and a chair.[38] Also, before 1700, garden structures were conceived in exotic or rural styles. But these, too, were designed within the context of the French architectural tradition. Two famous examples from Versailles are Le Vau's "Chinese" Trianon de Porcelain, designed in 1668 (Fig. 3),[39] and Mansart's romantically archeological Colonnade, designed in 1686 (Fig. 4).[40] And two seventeenth-century kiosks at Versailles, with simple wooden Tuscan columns and clipped hedge walls (Figs. 5, 6), may be evidence of pre-eighteenth-century French interest in the basic architectural vocabulary of the primitive hut.[41] In the eighteenth century a related style, the *style champêtre* or rustic style was defined by Blondel as simple, without affectation, a masonry architecture with few openings, as opposed to colonnaded and arcaded structures,[42] and he gave as examples buildings from the seventeenth century: Le Vau's Menagerie at Versailles of 1663,[43] and Mansart's pavilions at Marly. One example of this style was overlooked by Blondel, the simple Trianon-sous-Bois, appended to the elegant Grand Trianon, at Versailles, which was completed by 1689.[44]

The French rococo garden, like the English picturesque garden, may have originated before 1730. The work of the dramatist Charles Dufresny paralleled early English examples.[45] He is said to have preferred to work on unequal and irregular terrain because he needed obstacles to overcome, and to have invented them if they were not at hand. Thus on flat land he would create mounts, which would permit variety and provide areas for views. Indeed, many French

[35] Dennerlein, *Gartenkunst*, p. 95.

[36] Published by Marie, *Jardins français*, pls. 18, 175. See also J. and A. Marie, *Marly*, Paris, 1947, pp. 14-17 and pl. 55. An English equivalent is the "wilderness" in William Temple's contemporaneous garden; see C. Hussey, "Templum Restauratum," *Country Life*, CVI, 25 November 1949, pp. 1578-1581.

[37] Dennerlein, *Gartenkunst*, p. 194, nn. 270, 271. Dennerlein also mentions the groves at Malgrange (1740s) and at Saint-Cloud (1760). See also note 34 above.

[38] From L. Deshairs, *Le Grand Trianon. Architecture—Décoration—Ameublement*, Paris [1908], p. iv, quoting the Princesse Palatine writing in July 1705. See also M. L. Gothein, *History of Garden Art*, II, p. 96; and H. Honour, *Chinoiserie*, p. 165.

[39] For the Trianon de Porcelain, see R. Danis, *La première Maison royale de Trianon: 1670-1687*, Paris, 1927(?).

[40] A. Blunt, "The Hypnerotonmachia Poliphili in Seventeenth-Century France," pp. 126-128.

[41] See Marie, *Naissance de Versailles: le chateau—les*

jardins, Paris, 1968, II, p. 202, and pl. xcix.

[42] Blondel, *Cours d'architecture*, Paris, I, 1771, pp. 417-418.

[43] For the menagerie at Versailles, see G. Mabille, "La Ménagerie de Versailles," *Gazette des beaux-arts*, LXXXIII, January 1974, pp. 5-36.

[44] For the Trianon-sous-Bois at Versailles, see Deshairs, *Grand Trianon*, pp. x-xii, pls. 10, 11, 12.

[45] For a biography of Dufresny, see C. Dufresny, *Oeuvres*, Paris, 1731, I, "Avertissement," pp. 11-17 (and succeeding editions). A contemporaneous biography was published by Titon du Tillet, *Le Parnasse françoise*, Paris, 1732, pp. 595-599. The version published in the *Oeuvres* was taken up by P. J. Grosley, *Londres*, III, pp. 119-121; and by F. de P. Latapie, "Discours préliminaire," in the French translation of Whately's *Observations on Modern Gardening*, pp. v-vj. After these publications, Dufresny was mentioned in almost every major historical account of the French picturesque garden. See also L. A. de Bonafous, Abbé de Fontenay, *Dictionnaire des artistes*, Paris, 1776 (2v.), I, pp. 531-533.

garden theorists considered Dufresny to be the inventor of the picturesque garden, maintaining that he preceded William Kent in the designing of the "new style" of gardening and in the imitating of the Chinese style.[46]

Dufresny was born in 1684; his work as a garden designer was confined to the last ten years of his life, from 1714 to 1724. During this decade he designed mainly small gardens, and he is credited with an irregular plan for the park at Versailles which, according to his biographer, was rejected by the king as too expensive.[47] The dramatist is also credited with the designs for a garden at Migneaux near Poissy, and for two Paris gardens in the Faubourg Saint-Antoine (Le Moulin and Le Chemin creux—titles which suggest a rural ambience), as well as a garden for the Abbé Pajot at Vincennes. This last garden may have been published as the "Folie Pajou" near Vincennes by Le Rouge in the first cahier of his *Nouveaux jardins à la mode*, where it is attributed to Le Nôtre (Fig. 7). The plan of the garden is similar to descriptions of Dufresny's work by his anonymous 1731 biographer. In particular, the many small and varied parts, the changes in level, the ingeniously placed stairs and ramps, and even one irregular section, are similar to the description of Dufresny's style.[48] The designing and decorating of several Parisian houses, the building of a *petite maison* on a small plot of land granted to him by the king, and the remodeling of a windmill that was on the road to Mesnilmontant into a dwelling, complete with a small garden and a terrace,[49] are also attributed to Dufresny. This last design may have preceded the introduction of rural motifs, such as haystacks and woodpiles, into ornamental gardening vocabulary in England by, for instance, Batty Langley in 1728.[50]

There is no doubt that the smallness of scale, ingenuity of invention, variety of form, and artificially contrived rural character place Dufresny's gardens within the rococo style. The spirit of this style was defined by Dufresny's younger theatrical colleague, the dramatist Pierre Carlet Chamblin de Marivaux, who discussed gardening in an allegory on "beauté" and "je ne sçais quoi," published in 1734.[51] Here Marivaux maintained that the formal, beautiful garden was

[46] For the priority of Dufresny over Kent in the inventing of irregular gardens in the Chinese manner, see Dufresny, *Oeuvres*, I, "Avertissement," pp. 15-18; and Latapie, "Discours," p. vji, who also says Dufresny's work predated the first essay of Kent in the bosquets at Esher in the new style which was opposed to that of Le Nôtre. This information was taken up and repeated in all later discussions of Dufresny and Kent. Also see A. N. Duchesne, *Sur la Formation des jardins*, p. 55; and P. F. Rosset, *L'Agriculture*, pt. 2, pp. 95, 118. M. Curten, *Essai sur les jardins*, Paris, 1807, p. 21, noted several designs by Dufresny for gardens in the collection of the architect Antoine, and he verified that they were indeed prototypes for the picturesque garden.

[47] For Dufresny's designs for Versailles, see Dufresny, *Oeuvres*, I, "Avertissement," where the biographer notes that Dufresny made two designs for Versailles, which were good but excessively expensive. Dufresny was credited with a single design for Versailles by Grosley, *Londres*, p. 121; and Latapie, "Discours," p.

viiij. Again, this statement was included and elaborated in later comments on Dufresny. The Versailles plan was described by Rosset, *L'Agriculture*, pt. 2, p. 119, as "à l'imagination singulière & aux contrastes rustiques et du bizarre. . . ." J. M. Morel, *Théorie des jardins*, 1802 (2nd ed.), I, p. 28, n. 1, wrote of the Versailles design: "son projet, d'une grande conception, n'était qu'une aggrégation de tableaux incohérens, un mélange de scènes factices et naturelles, dont l'ensemble présentait des effects plus bizarres qu'agréables, plus singuliers que vraie."

[48] For Dufresny's biography, see note 45 above. For a description of the Pajot garden, see Le Rouge, *Nouveaux jardins à la mode*, cahier i, pp. 24-25, who also mentions that the garden contained a *potager* and a *grande allée* from which it was possible to view all of Paris.

[49] Titon du Tillet, *Parnasse françoise*, pp. 595-599.

[50] Batty Langley, *New Principles of Gardening*, pp. viij-xi, and pl. iii.

[51] P. C. Marivaux, "Le Cabinet du philosophe," from

static and fixed in its perfection and therefore monotonous, and that the "je ne sçais quoi" garden was constantly changing, infinitely variable, composed by chance, irregular, and with a disorder that was in "the best taste in the world." In 1723 Marivaux had founded a French journal, *Le Spectateur françois*, modeled on the English *Spectator*, in which Addison's remarks on gardening, which are considered to be an early indication of the shift in the English attitude toward picturesque garden design, appeared. But Addison's remarks are descriptive of gardening in the period of the simple "natural" garden, before the advent of the rococo style in either England or France. Moreover, there may be a source for Marivaux's description closer at hand: his dramatic works have been compared to the paintings of Watteau.[52] Whatever the connection between these two Frenchmen, surely Marivaux's *je ne sçais quoi* garden was conceived in the same spirit of fantasy and enchantment that the painter conveyed in his works.

Among the French gardens designed in the rococo period, one group is outstanding for its originality and its influence on later gardening developments: the gardens of Stanislaus Leszcynski, exiled king of Poland and father-in-law of Louis XV, who from 1736 ruled the duchys of Lorraine and Bar (interestingly, the site of d'Urfé's *Astrée*). Stanislaus's building activity took place on the estates of Chanteheux, Jolivet, Einville, Malgrange, Commercy, and, above all, Lunéville. The Polish king directed and achieved the designing of his extensive new gardens on these estates in the ten years between 1737 and 1747 when he turned to the planning of Nancy.[53] The fame of his gardens was at least as great as, and may have overreached that of, a contemporary English one—the garden at Stowe, designed by another amateur, Henry Grenville, Lord Cobham.

The designing and siting of the Lorraine estates is based on that of an earlier country estate owned by Stanislaus—Tschifflik, at Zweibrücken, built in 1715-1716, and designed in conscious imitation of the symmetrical arrangement of pavilions at Marly, although the architecture was in the tradition of the simple, wooden buildings of Polish country estates.[54] Thus—and in contrast to the archaeological experimenting associated with contemporaneous English garden structures—Stanislaus's garden structures were a combination of two traditional types: the buildings of the formal French royal gardens and those of his native Poland. The introduction of Polish elements into French garden design gave Stanislaus's gardens much of the exotic appearance that was recorded by visitors; and it was surely a major source for the adopting of new elements of vocabulary into the repertoire of the later French gardens. One other characteristic of these gardens should be noted: the king was interested in originality of effect and economy of means. Thus, fine craftsmanship and permanent materials were often simulated with paint and stucco.[55] Indeed, Stanislaus's estates must have had the appearance of public pleasure gardens.

Among these garden structures are several new types which are of considerable importance for

Marivaux, *Journaux et oeuvres diverses*, Paris, 1969 (ed. F. Deloffre and M. Gillet), pp. 342-351.

[52] H. Rowbotham, *Missionary and Mandarin*, Berkeley, 1942, p. 259.

[53] For Stanislaus and the designing of his estates in Lorraine, see the excellent monographs by P. Boyé, *Les Châteaux du Roi Stanislaus en Lorraine*; and more recently, J. Rau, Gräfin v. d. Schulenberg, *Emmanuel Héré*.

[54] J. Ostrowski, "Tschifflik, Maison de Plaisance Stanislawa Lesczynskiego w Zweibrückewi."

[55] Boyé, *Châteaux du Roi Stanislaus*, p. 92.

later gardening developments. One of Stanislaus's first construction at Lunéville was the Kiosk, which was erected in 1737 (Fig. 8).[56] It was a strange, makeshift structure—its style confounded the French. Voltaire called it "half Turkish and half Chinese."[57] As an attempt at Turkish design, it predates Muntz's design for the fantastic Turkish mosque at Kew (ca. 1750),[58] which has been considered to be a very early design in the Turkish style. As a building in the Chinese style the Kiosk is more successful, for its peaked roof suggests that of a Chinese pagoda. The structure precedes the Chinese houses at Kew (Fig. 10)[59] and at Stowe,[60] both of which were built in the mid-1740s and are again very early designs in this style. But Polish, and even much central European, rural architecture included a system of the constructing of roof trusses that produced a "broken" roof line, similar to that of the curved roof line of a Chinese pagoda. And although the "Turkishness" of the buildings seems to be similar to that of Turkish vernacular architecture which might have been seen by Stanislaus, a derivation from a local Polish tradition cannot be ruled out.

A number of small buildings for entertainment and residence were built along the canal at Lunéville (Fig. 11). They constituted a small village of cottages or "Chartreuses" for the use of Stanislaus's favorite guests.[61] Each cottage-pavilion consisted of a *maisonnette* for dining and cooking, rooms, service pavilions, kitchen gardens, and a small formal garden. This group of buildings was surely inspired by Mansart's pavilions at Marly, and it may be a prototype for the later hamlets of the *jardin anglo-chinois*. Moreover, they predate the better-known hermitages of Mme. de Pompadour (Fig. 32) by almost a decade.[62] The most important building of this group, the Trèfle, a large, squat structure with a scalloped roof and a trefoil plan, was remarkable for its originality and novelty (Fig. 9). It has often been associated with Chinese architecture, and it was the source for the design of several later oriental garden structures, most notably the Japanese Tea House at Sanssouci. But the Trèfle's exotic plan was not derived from China. Its source seems to have been middle European rural trefoil churches or sixteenth-century garden structures in Czechoslovakia, although there is a possibility that it was derived from illustrations or descriptions in travel books to the orient.[63]

In 1742 one other remarkable curiosity was created at Lunéville. It was an animated country village called *Le Rocher*, which was constructed along a steep artificial rock bank on one arm of the canal (Fig. 12).[64] No earlier automated gardens paralleled the complexity or naturalism of this one, which was composed of eighty-two figures, modeled in wood after the inhabitants

[56] *Ibid.*, p. 19. See also F. Baldensperger, "Le Kiosque de Stanislas à Lunéville," and Ostrowski, "Nurt egzotyczny w architekturze Stanisława Lesczynskiego."

[57] Boyé, *Châteaux du Roi Stanislaus*, p. 20.

[58] Published in A. Rowan, *The RIBA Drawings Collection: Garden Buildings*, London, n.d., p. 36.

[59] For a later date and an attribution to Chambers of the Chinese building at Kew, see J. Harris, "Exoticism at Kew," *Apollo*, LXXVIII, August 1963, pp. 103-119.

[60] For the Chinese house at Stowe, see G. Clarke, "The History of Stowe—XV," *The Stoic*, xxv, no. 2, March 1972, p. 67 (ill. p. 66). The house is also illus-

trated in Siren, *China and Gardens of Europe*, p. 30 (from G. Bickham, *The Beauties of Stowe*, London, 1750, opp. p. 35).

[61] Boyé, *Châteaux du Roi Stanislaus*, pp. 26-27.

[62] See Dennerlein, *Gartenkunst*, pp. 102-104, for a discussion of these hermitages.

[63] See Ostrowski, "Nurt egzotyczny," pp. 172-173, for sources of the Trèfle.

[64] For *Le Rocher* and earlier automated gardens, see Boyé, *Châteaux du Roi Stanislaus*, pp. 28-30, and Ostrowski, "Le Rocher, théâtre des automats," and "Rocher, teatr automatow" (Polish version of the same article).

of the area, and arranged in a series of rural vignettes in an informal rural landscape. Included among the elaborate automated scenes were a shepherd playing a tune on his bagpipe while his dog looked after the flock; a peasant carving a piece of wood before his hut; a boy pushing a swing on which a girl was seated; a cat crouching to jump on a rat that bared its teeth; a child stroking a dog that was eating a biscuit; men working at a forge, playing a violin, sharpening knives, smoking pipes, and drinking and singing bacchic airs; women making butter and washing linen; a monkey reaching for an apple; a hermit meditating in a grotto; a cock crowing; a donkey braying; etc.[65] And this was not a silent spectacle: the figures produced the sounds for which they were designed. The mechanics were the work of Stanislaus's clock maker, François Richard, and his son, and the closest prototype is an extraordinary clock, invented by Richard in 1727, and exhibited in 1733 in several European capitals, which contained nearly three hundred figures and in which were included lights, thunder, and the sound of cannon.[66]

Le Rocher represents both a return to, and a development of, mannerist gardening vocabulary of the sixteenth century.[67] But also it has been suggested that *Le Rocher* represents a naive conception of an ideal society, which recorded the image of the sovereign (Stanislaus) working for the welfare of his people.[68] Moreover, the rural subject matter and the irregularity of *Le Rocher* indicate that it may have been one source for the *jardin anglo-chinois*. But whatever its actual influence may be, *Le Rocher* was considered within the picturesque gardening tradition by at least one eighteenth-century critic, James Stuart, who mentioned Stanislaus's automated garden, and sarcastically suggested it to be used as a model for the rural park in the city (*rus in urbe*), a type that would be associated with the *jardin anglo-chinois*.[69]

Others of Stanislaus's estates may have contained elements similar to those found in later picturesque French gardens. The *Bosquets* at Malgrange (Fig. 13), which look back to the *Bosquet des Sources*, also look forward to the tortured paths and streams of the *jardin anglo-chinois*. The combination of working farm and ornamental garden at Chanteheux and Einville suggest such an ornamental garden and experimental farm as the one that was begun in 1783 at Rambouillet. The dovecotes attached to each wing of the château at Chanteheux (Fig. 15) are surely a prototype for a project for a country house by Ledoux (Fig. 16) and for De Ligne's minaret-dovecotes which were attached to his dairy at Beloeil, the latter designed in the form of a mosque.[70] The farm at Jolivet can be interpreted as a link between the traditional menagerie and the later *ferme ornée*.[71] The minuscule monastery that Stanislaus built at Malgrange in 1741 is contemporary with English hermitages, and it may be related to later French ones, although the tradition of the hermitage in France goes back to the sixteenth century—a hermit-

[65] A full description of *Le Rocher* can be found in E. Héré, *Recueil . . . des chateaux . . . que le Roy de Pologne occupe.*

[66] Boyé, *Châteaux du Roi Stanislaus*, pp. 29-30.

[67] See Ostrowski, "Le Rocher," p. 177.

[68] Boyé, *Châteaux du Roi Stanislaus*, pp. 181-182.

[69] James Stuart, *Critical Observations*, pp. 10-12, where he describes *Le Rocher* as "one of the most fla-

grant perversions of taste that was ever exhibited to public view," where "real pastoral objects and rustick images" are degraded by "sticking up clockwork hills, wooden cows, and canvas milk maids all over the grounds."

[70] De Ligne, *Beloeil*, p. 242. The dairy was part of a *village tartare* designed in a *style sauvage*.

[71] For the menagerie at Jolivet, see Rau, *Héré*, p. 143.

age, complete with hermit, was located in the garden at Gaillon.[72] There may have been a mossy hut at Commercy, and a rustic pavilion at Chanteheux,[73] and a cottage and a rustic pavilion with a pointed arcade can be seen in a contemporary painting of Einville (Fig. 14) although they are outside the walls of the château. There were possibly even ruins in these gardens,[74] all contemporary with the development of exotic, rustic, and ruined garden structures in English gardens, and similar in concept to those which appeared later in France. It is to be noted that one wing of the château of Malgrange was designed in a checkerboard "Turkish" pattern similar to that of the later "Turkish" garden structure designed for Kew, referred to above.

One later French garden can be associated with the spirit, style, and possibly even the construction of Stanislaus's work—Monceau, designed by Carmontelle, who surely referred to the earlier work of Stanislaus when he created the Duc de Chartres' Parisian park in the 1770s. It is possible that the complicated series of galleries and pavilions at Monceau recalls Stanislaus's galleries and pavilions at Malgrange, and particularly those at Einville.[75] And the grottolike dining room (Fig. 90) is close in arrangement, if not in form, to the Kiosk at Lunéville (Fig. 8), which also was used for dining and where musicians concealed in the attic space played for the diners.[76]

Stanislaus's court was visited by everyone of any importance. Voltaire wrote poetry[77] and Montesquieu wrote letters[78] about the gardens. If they were not personally inspected, their architecture could be seen in the publication of the work of Stanislaus's architect, Emmanuel Héré, which appeared in 1753 and 1756. It would have been impossible not to know of these extravagant, eccentric creations. Among the many people acquainted with the gardens were several important contributors to later garden theory and design on whom Stanislaus's designs may have had an influence. These include the Comte de Girardin, who designed one of the most important of the new picturesque gardens, Ermenonville, and who was at Stanislaus' court at some time before 1766;[79] Richard Mique, who replaced Héré as Stanislaus's architect in 1758, and who was later the garden designer at Versailles;[80] and the Abbé Laugier, who may have been at Stanislaus's court, or who may have received his information about it from Héré's *Recueil*.[81] In Laugier's treatise, *Essai sur l'architecture*, published in 1753, at the end of the section concerned with gardens, the author described a thrifty prince, recognized by contemporaries to be Stanislaus,[82] who, with economy, had created much that was novel, different, and

[72] For Gaillon, see Gothein, *History of Garden Art*, I, p. 417.

[73] Boyé, *Châteaux du Roi Stanislaus*, p. 46; Rau, *Héré*, p. 166.

[74] Boyé, *Châteaux du Roi Stanislaus*, p. 96.

[75] See Rau, *Héré*, p. 136, for the development of the orangerie-dining hall garden building.

[76] Boyé, *Châteaux du Roi Stanislaus*, pp. 19-20.

[77] *Ibid.*, p. 20. See also chapter II, n. 1.

[78] *Ibid.*, p. 97.

[79] J. H. Volbertal, *Aux Environs de Paris*, p. 8; and Ganay, "Les Jardins d'Ermenonville," p. 3. Girardin

was married at Lunéville on 20 April 1761; his travels to Italy, Germany, and England took place shortly thereafter (Martin-Decaen, *Girardin*, p. 7).

[80] Boyé, *Châteaux du Roi Stanislaus*, p. 100.

[81] For alternate opinions on Laugier's presence at Stanislaus's court, see R. de Nolhac, *Le Trianon de Marie Antoinette*, p. 51; and W. Herrmann, *Laugier*, p. 110, n. 34.

[82] See, for instance, E. C. Fréron, review of Laugier's *Essai sur l'architecture* in *Année littéraire*, 1755, II, p. 352.

always delightful and gracious. The gardens of this prince were beautiful and infinitely diversified; the water was designed in all possible variations from columns to cascades, and even formed into illuminated rooms. And in these gardens the buildings were of all shapes: they pleased less by the richness of the materials than by novelty of design and elegance of form. Laugier advised artists to go to the "school" of the prince, where they would learn a thousand new ways to surprise, to please, and to enchant.[83]

Of all the critics of French garden design of the 1750s, the Abbé Laugier may have been the most optimistic about the direction the art was taking. Other contemporary critics were less happy with the state of gardening. One, in 1756, praised the traditional formal French,[84] another, in 1755, the informal English garden.[85] Both types were considered to be more natural than the "ridiculous taste" of the new French gardens that were in the *petit goût* of the rococo style. But even Laugier complained that self-conscious affectations were too much in evidence in contemporary gardens. Like Huet, he felt that in order to enjoy nature it was necessary to leave these gardens and to go to the country.[86] Indeed, Laugier's remarks on what was delightful in garden design—he called for green grass, murmuring brooks, shade, picturesque views, and an air of neglect from which all signs of affectation were removed—are also similar to Huet's comments on gardens and to the general philosophy of the natural garden of the early eighteenth century, and they are far removed from the theatrical effects of Lunéville.

Laugier's position can be interpreted as an anticipation of the attempt during the second half of the eighteenth century to synthesize the intimacy, intricacy, and delight of the rococo garden with the simplicity, naturalness, and grandeur of its "Régence" predecessor. His remarks on gardening were preceded by those of at least one critic, Jean-François Blondel, whose *Architecture française*, published in 1752, indicates the beginning of the revival of the earlier "natural" French garden,[87] as his *Maisons de plaisance* had marked the high point of the rococo style sixteen years earlier. Blondel's four desiderata for gardens were traditional: regularity, vista, shade, and variety. His criticism of Versailles, similar to that of Laugier, was that the park was too artificial and "sad." Blondel felt that a garden should be a tranquil place in which to walk, and a retreat for philosophical meditation.[88] To obtain these qualities, he recommended (as had Dézallier) the use of only those elements of traditional garden art that reflected natural simplicity, and where labor, artifact, and expense—such as arbors, hedges, and turfed ramps—were not apparent.[89]

Blondel's 1752 point of view may have anticipated developments in garden theory of the

[83] Laugier, *Essai sur l'architecture*, pp. 291-293. A garden similar to that of Laugier's description was discussed by J. F. de Bastide in "La Petite Maison," in Bastide's *Contes*, Paris, 1763 (4v.), II, pt. I, pp. 47-48. An earlier version of "La Petite Maison" was published in the *Nouveau Spectateur* in 1758 (8v.), II, pp. 361-412; but the work may have first appeared in 1754 (contemporaneously with Laugier's description), according to P. L. Jacob, in the preface to the reprint of *La Petite Maison*, Paris, 1897, pp. ix-x, although it is not located in the *Journal Oeconomique* of that year, as the writer suggests.

[84] C. N. Cochin, article in *Mercure*, August 1758, pp. 182-188, reprinted in *Recueil des quelques pieces concernant les arts*, Paris, 1757, pp. 62-69.

[85] Fréron, review of Laugier's *Essai* in *Année littéraire*, 1755, II, pp. 322-339. Also see Herrmann, *Laugier*, p. 145, n. 21.

[86] Laugier, *Essai*, p. 280.

[87] J. F. Blondel, *Architecture française*, I (1752), pp. 45-46. See also Dennerlein, *Gartenkunst*, p. 159.

[88] Blondel, *Architecture française*, p. 46.

[89] *Idem.*

1770s. The several types of gardening he distinguishes—the garden, the park, the forest and the woods—are similar in concept to the divisions of garden types of Whately, Girardin, and Walpole. His description of the "promenade," where there are "broad, interesting, and varied points of view," where one finds in nature the means of satisfying the view by the juxtaposition of opposing objects which range from formal regularity to "that beautiful disorder that produces valleys, hills, mountains . . . ," suggests Whately's riding. Finally, the contrast of the formally arranged garden near the main architectural group, symbolizing modern civilization and "the tumultuous life," to the irregular, natural, and infinitely variable spectacle of "the tranquil life" of the outlying park is already within the spirit of Watelet's 1774 *Essai sur les jardins*.

In 1754, within two years of the publication of Blondel's remarks on gardening, a philosophically oriented garden similar to that recommended by Blondel was begun by the distinguished amateur and writer Claude-Henri Watelet.[90] The garden was considered by contemporaries to be one of the most important of the picturesque gardens, and it was included in all major accounts of them. For this reason, and because it has languished in undeserved obscurity, it and its owner will be discussed in some detail here.

Watelet was born in 1718, the son of the wealthy minister of finances of Orléans.[91] He was sent to Italy by his father in his early twenties, and he would later note that this voyage inspired him with a taste for Italian literature, in particular for the Italian pastoral drama, on which he modeled a short pastoral drama of his own, *Silvie*.[92] Through this source he would have been acquainted with the idealized natural settings for these theatrical pieces. Watelet was also concerned with the simple and rustic nature of his immediate environment. Along with many contemporary amateurs, collectors, and artists, he acquired prints and drawings of Dutch and Flemish rural scenes, and he executed drawings and etchings in this genre (Figs. 17, 18).[93] His attempt to synthesize both idealized Italian and specific northern attitudes toward nature is reflected in his work on the theory of painting, *L'Art de peindre*, which he published in 1760, and in his design of his garden.

In 1754, while on a sketching expedition, Watelet discovered his future estate, just outside of Paris near Bezons. It consisted of three islands in the Seine and a section of the mainland (Figs. 22, 23). Its original condition is recorded in a series of etchings made by the artist Le Prince,[94] after drawings by Saint-Non (Figs. 19, 20, 21, 28, 30) and from a description in a chapter of Watelet's book on gardening.[95] Watelet was attracted to the spot by the naturalness of the site,

[90] For Watelet and Moulin-Joli, see Bibliography: Individual Gardens.

[91] R. Portalis, *Les Dessinateurs d'illustrations*, pp. 628-639.

[92] Watelet, *Recueil de quelques ouvrages de M. Watelet*, Paris, 1784, "Note sur Silvie," pp. 11-52; and Henriot, "Un Amateur d'art au XVIIIe siècle, l'académicien Watelet," p. 176.

[93] Watelet wrote his friend the artist Desfriches on 19 December 1760: "J'ai fait . . . un voyage pittoresque et phisique dans les Vosges; j'en ai rapporté une soixantaine des dessins coloriés . . ." (quoted in P. Ratois de Limay, *Un Amateur orléanais au XVIIIe siècle: Aignan-*

Thomas Desfriches [1715-1800], Paris, 1907, p. 171; see also M. J. Dumesnil, *Histoire des plus célèbres amateurs*, Paris, 1856-1858 [3v.], III, pp. 182-199 [Watelet correspondence with Desfriches]). A study of the theory of landscape painting in the eighteenth century is much needed. For the sixteenth-century background to the concepts of *paysage idéal* and *paysage réaliste*, see E. Gombrich, "Renaissance Artistic Theory and the Development of Landscape Painting," *Gazette des beaux-arts*, XLI, 1953, pp. 336-360.

[94] For Le Prince, see J. Hédon, *Jean Le Prince et son oeuvre*, Paris, 1879.

[95] Watelet, *Essai*, pp. 125-137.

by the variety and diversity of the terrain, by the number of picturesque views that could be obtained, and by the distance of the property from the "sterility" of society (located in the city), where, according to Watelet, men searched in vain for happiness rather than tasted in peace the delights of study and the beauties of nature.[96] He also saw many possibilities for developing this self-contained and long-abandoned estate. According to Watelet, the site already contained water, considerable planting, including a neglected orchard and an allée of lime trees, and charming views. From the Le Prince illustrations, the estate also appears originally to have contained at least three abandoned structures, one of which, the mill, on a bridge connecting the islands with the mainland, gave Watelet's garden its name: Moulin-Joli.

The land was acquired on a ninety-nine-year lease from a Benedictine monastery[97] by Le Comte, Watelet's business manager and the accommodating husband of Watelet's mistress, and the development of it began immediately. Watelet confined his major effort to the largest of the three islands, known locally as the Ile Marante. His design for it was in the tradition of French formal gardens (Watelet referred to it as a *jardin françois*), with straight allées opening on to picturesque views of the countryside, a *boulingrin*, and a *rond-point*. Only the northern-most tip of the island was irregular. It may have been designed in this manner to conform to the irregularity of the point, but the design also recalls the irregularity that may have been introduced into garden design early in the eighteenth century by the dramatist Dufresny. This island-garden seems to have contained no garden structures, although Watelet added paths, belvederes, sheep, considerable planting (including groves, "rooms," and trellises), and two bridges, one of which, in the "Dutch" style, spanned all three of the small, low islands to the height of the tree branches, which formed a covered passage above it (Fig. 24). Occasionally space between the branches would permit framed picturesque views, or the bridge would widen to include seats, or stairs would descend from it to one of the islands. The other bridge, a *pont volant* or "Chinese bridge," was bordered with flowers in urns (Fig. 25).[98] The garden also contained many poetic inscriptions of a moral and sentimental character, generally carved into the bark of trees. One source for Watelet's inscriptions and for the philosophical character of the garden may have been Shenstone's Leasowes, which was begun ten years before Moulin-Joli was purchased. But Watelet would not have seen the English pastoral farm, and a French source, as yet unknown, for Moulin-Joli is more likely.

The island-garden was designed within a sophisticated rococo tradition with allées intersecting at oblique angles, and many viewpoints. But the mainland garden was designed in a modest fashion that recalled rural gardens before the period of Louis XIV. Watelet added a garden composed of simple squares (possibly a kitchen garden) to the already existing allée of lime trees and the orchard, and he probably remodeled and added to the existing structures which were indicated in Le Prince's etchings. Along the allée Watelet designed a cow barn which was

---

[96] *Ibid.*, p. 140.

[97] Document DQ 414. doss. 10763, deposited in the Archives de la Seine. However, Quénéhen, *Histoire de Colombes*, p. 378, n. 1, and p. 380, n. 4, notes from documents in the communal archives at Colombes that the site was bought by Le Comte in 1750.

[98] For the bridges at Moulin-Joli, see De Ligne, *Beloeil*, p. 188. A third bridge, constructed of boats, and noted by Mme. Vigée Lebrun, *Souvenirs*, 1, letter ix, pp. 150-151, may have been added after Watelet wrote his *Essai*.

combined with a dairy (*laiterie d'agrément*) (Fig. 26).[99] It was simply articulated, with the exception of a strongly rusticated frame for a niche containing a statue, and it is reminiscent of such pre-Louis XIV examples of country estate agriculture as, for instance, the entrance to the Château of Saint-Sépulchre, designed by Le Vau before 1664 (Fig. 27). The famous mill was retained and restored, as we can see in a comparison of one of Le Prince's etchings (Fig. 28) with an illustration of the completed structure (Fig. 29), and a menagery mentioned by Watelet may have been contained in the wing appended to the mill.

Opposite the mill was Watelet's house, which was probably remodeled from another of the existing buildings (Fig. 30). The "restoration," surely the correct term for its eventual appearance, was recorded in an etching by Watelet and Marguerite Le Comte (Fig. 31). The wing shown appended to the house on the plan probably contained the Salon de Café which Watelet mentioned in his description of his estate.[100] The house was designed by Watelet's painter friend, François Boucher, whom Watelet titled "architecte par amitié." Of all the early eighteenth-century French artists who collected illustrations of northern landscapes, Boucher surely comes first to mind. His own work from the 1730s on includes illustrations of idealized timeless and placeless landscapes containing towers, mills, dovecotes, bridges, silos, and thatched rustic huts which were designed in a purely anonymous style common to both the Italian and the northern countrysides (Figs. 33, 56, 71). Occasionally Boucher included elements of classical architecture in his landscapes, such as simple colonnaded porches, altars, and even circular monopteral temples. It is within this context that we must see Boucher's "restoration" of Watelet's house, which, according to its owner, resembled in its simplicity the presbytery of a curate.[101] The building was indeed without academic or classical pretensions: it was a simple *maison bourgeois*. The style was in complete accord with Watelet's philosophy of a life without affectation or display, as he would later describe it in his *Essai*, which will be discussed in chapter IV. The house also was surely inspired by such garden structures as Madame de Pompadour's hermitages, which were designed from 1748 in the *style champêtre* (Fig. 32).[102] The spirit as well as the style of the hermitages were similar to those of Watelet's house: the Hermitage at Versailles was described by one visitor as "small, unshowy, much in the manner of a farmhouse. . . . Everything for use or ornament of the inside, expressed neatness and a noble sweetness. . . . Everything breathed a country-air."[103]

Although Moulin-Joli was seen by many visitors during its forty-some years of existence, it was designed in too personal a taste to be universally popular. Horace Walpole, who saw the garden in 1775, noted that it was "pierced and divided into straight narrow walks (*en berceau*) and surrounded by a rude path quite round," where "to give this étoile the *air champêtre*, a plenary indulgence has been granted to every nettle, thistle and bramble . . . in one word, [Watelet's] *island* differs in nothing from a French garden into which no mortal has set foot for the last century." But even Walpole was affected by the charm of the surrounding country-

---

[99] Watelet, *Essai*, p. 147.

[100] According to A. N. Dézallier d'Argenville, *Voyage pittoresque des environs de Paris*, Paris, 1779, pp. 9-12, the café was intended to appear to have been built of ancient elms.

[101] Watelet, *Essai*, p. 141.

[102] See note 62 above.

[103] Mlle. de Fauques, *The History of the Marchioness de Pompadour*, London, 1759(?) (2v.), II, pp. 19ff. (quoted by Dennerlein, *Gartenkunst*, pp. 115-116).

side, the prospects to which were—in a considerable development of Dézallier's views at the ends of allées—"peepholes . . . so small that you seem to look through the diminishing end of a spying-glass" out to "a château, a *clocher*, a village, a convent, a villa and a hermitage."[104]

Many Frenchmen also felt that Watelet's design for Moulin-Joli was too extreme. The Prince de Ligne, in 1775, noted that the French "déterminés" criticized the wildness of the island, which they felt contained too much grass, woods, and even irregularity. But De Ligne himself was enthusiastic about the estate, and he commended the site for its privacy, and for the contrast of the water with the verdure, which he said should inspire all Anglomaniacs. He recommended that all those whose hearts were not hardened go to Moulin-Joli, where reading, gazing, and weeping were the effects not of sadness, but of a delicate sensibility. He assured the reader that regrets, joys, and memories would pass before the spectator, who should meditate on the inscriptions, sigh with the lovers, and bless M. Watelet.[105] And the Abbé de Lille wrote about this spot:

> *Tel est le simple style où, suspendant son cours,*
> *Pure comme tes moeurs, libre comme tes jours,*
> *En canaux ombragés la Seine se partage,*
> *Et visite en secret la retraite d'un sage.*
> *Ton art la seconda; non cet art imposteur,*
> *Des lieux qu'il croit orner hardi profaneur.*
> *Digne de voir, d'aimer, de sentir la nature,*
> *Tu traitas sa beauté comme une vierge pure*
> *Qui rougit d'être nue, & craint les ornements.*[106]

As a hospitable amateur and collector, Watelet befriended many artists. He knew not only Boucher, who designed his house, but also the painter Hubert Robert, who was his guide in Rome during his second trip to Italy in 1763.[107] And he knew Saint-Non, who introduced him to Jean-Jacques Rousseau, with whom he may have been in correspondence by 1759.[108] Watelet's garden was high on the list of those visited by fashionable society: Marie-Antoinette visited it when she was formulating the design of her *jardin anglais* at the Trianon.[109] And through the medium of these artists and people of fashion who visited the amateur at his estate, the philosophy and style of Moulin-Joli were disseminated.

In spite of the fact that the garden was formal, it was considered, as we have noted, by later

[104] H. Walpole, *Letters*, IX, pp. 241-242, 6 September 1775, Walpole to W. Mason.

[105] De Ligne, *Beloeil*, pp. 186-188.

[106] J. De Lille, *Les Jardins*, pp. 71-72: "Such is the simple style where, suspending its course, the Seine, pure as your morals, free as your days, separates itself into shady canals, and secretly visits the retreat of a sage. Your art supports it; not the false art which profanes the places it pretends to adorn. Worthy to see, to love, to feel nature, you treat its beauty as a pure virgin, who blushes at her nudity, and fears adornment."

[107] P. Hofer, "Venuta in Roma," and "A Visit to ROME in 1764."

[108] J. J. Rousseau, *Oeuvres complètes*, Paris, 1959-1964 (ed. B. Gagnehin and M. Raymond) (3v.), I, "Confessions," p. 511, mentions Watelet. L. Guimbaud, *Saint-Non et Fragonard*, Paris, 1928, p. 140, notes that Watelet was introduced by Saint-Non to Rousseau at Montmorency in 1759.

[109] F. Grimm, *Correspondance*, X, p. 522, December 1774.

critics and guides to be among the most outstanding of the picturesque gardens, and it was included in all major accounts of French gardens of this type, although Métra described it as "in the English taste."[110] The Prince de Croÿ, in 1772, noted that "Moulin-Joli . . . is the freshest and most agreeable site to be seen, for its flowing water and beautiful fields. These qualities are united with a taste for the best Roman architecture and the best picturesque tone."[111] As the mania for the *jardin anglo-chinois* diminished after the mid-1770s, Moulin-Joli would take on a new and national significance. In 1779 Hirschfeld noted that this representative of the *style françoise* was "a true model for the [French] nation,"[112] and the poet J. A. Roucher recommended it as an example of taste in the embellishing of a landscape.[113]

Unfortunately, the garden was as fragile as many of the later picturesque ones. After Watelet's death in 1786 it passed briefly to Marguerite Le Comte, who sold the estate to a man named Gaudron. This owner was not sympathetic to the property: he may have been responsible for the proliferation of buildings on the estate which are recorded in a drawing at the Bibliothèque Nationale. After the Revolution the estate fell into the hands of a copper smith, who leveled the trees and divided the property. The destruction was total.[114] One of the chief mourners was Mme. Vigée Lebrun, who at one time had hoped to save the estate from its fate.[115]

Moulin-Joli can be considered as an attempt to revive the spirit of garden design of the first two decades of the eighteenth century. The emphasis on nature and the revival of elements of the pre-Louis XIV style of gardening, and the *air champêtre* of the architecture, all are indications of the pre-rococo style. An *Epitre* addressed to Watelet as a "partisan of beautiful nature" in 1750 by the critic Elie Fréron must be read with the foregoing in mind. Fréron opened his poem with a description of the type of nature to which Watelet was committed: it was both cold and sad (terms which, interestingly, were used by Laugier and Blondel for formal, artificial gardens). Watelet was described as a "headstrong philosopher":

> *De la simple et froide* NATURE,
> *Cette triste divinité,*
> *Qui n'ose, dans sa marche obscure,*
> *De son éternelle parure*
> *Varier l'uniformité.*

This point of view is opposed to that of:

> *Art charmant, Dieu de ma patrie,*
> *Le merveilleux naît sous tes pas;*
> *Enrichis toujours ces climats*
> *Des trésors de ton industrie;*

---

[110] F. Métra, *Correspondance secrète*, I, p. 147, 2 January 1775.

[111] E. de Croÿ, *Journal*, III, pp. 21-22, 30 April 1772.

[112] C. C. L. Hirschfeld, *Theorie der Gartenkunst*, I, p. 45.

[113] J. Roucher, *Les Mois*, chant iii, pp. 151ff.

[114] Henriot, "Watelet," p. 93.

[115] L. E. Vigée Lebrun, *Souvenirs*, I, pp. 150-153.

Laisse gronder les partisans
De ta rivale désolée;
De nos villes et de nos champs
Pour jamais elle est exilée.

The "art" that Fréron praised was not that of the formal and elaborate French rococo garden, but the exotic, unnatural "art" of China:

Qui suit la Nature a la piste,
Ne sera jamais qu'un copiste,
Qu'un malheureux imitateur;
Le Chinois seul est créateur;
Il donne un nouvel ordre aux choses.
Fertile en prodiges divers,
Ses riantes métamorphoses
Font éclore un autre universe.

The Chinese style did indeed give a "new order" to nature, as Fréron described it:

Fleuves, coulez sur les montagnes;
Détachez-vous du firmament,
Etoiles, parez les campagnes;
Poissons, quittez votre élément;
Vous, oiseaux, rampez sur la terre;
Cerfs, rhinocéros, éléphants,
Volez au séjour du tonnerre;
Et vous, mortels impertinents,
Venez sous diverses figures,
Par mille grotesques postures,
Ne divertir à vos dépens.[116]

116 . . . Of simple and cold NATURE, that sad divinity, who dares not, in its sombre march, with its unchanging adornment, to vary its uniformity.

Charming Art, god of my native land, the marvelous is born where you walk; always enrich this climate with the treasures of your industry; let the partisans of your dreary rival grumble; she is exiled for ever from our cities and our fields.

He who follows in the steps of Nature will never be more than a copyist and a bad imitator; the Chinese alone are creators; they give a new order to things. [With] fertile and prodigiously diverse [imagination], their happy metamorphoses bring forth another universe.

Rivers, run under the mountains; stars, detach yourselves from the firmament and adorn the fields; fish, leave your elements; you, birds, creep on the earth; stags, rhinoceri, elephants, fly to the source of thunder; and [all] assume diverse faces with a thousand grotesque attitudes to entertain you, impertinent mortals, at your expense."

The poem was first published in *Lettres sur quelques ecrits de ce temps*, 1752ff., III, pp. 40-43, 12 January 1750, with the title "Epitre de M. Fréron à M. V+++, receveur-général des finances." Cited in *Les Confessions de Fréron, 1719-1778*, Paris, 1876 (ed. C. Barthélemy), pp. 342-345: "Apologie de l'art 'Epitre adressé le premier jour de l'an à un Amateur de la belle Nature, en lui envoyant des magots, des papiers de la Chine et d'autres colifichets.'" In a later publication of the "Epitre" (*Année littéraire*, 1771, I, p. 66), Fréron would explain that the "Apologie de l'art" was ironic.

What Fréron described is, indeed, the rococo garden, but now fantastically conceived, and related not to the French tradition, but to the exotic art of China. Interest in China was surely the result of the contemporaneous fad for chinoiserie: in a section of Fréron's *Epitre* the "riens . . . de la Chine" with which interiors were to be decorated are discussed. But the introduction into gardening repertoire of a foreign style, as opposed to the integration of foreign vocabulary into the French style, is new. The extent and implication of this attitude before 1750 can only be surmised at present. Its roots are located in early reports on China by Jesuit missionaries and travelers' accounts of Chinese gardens, from which we learn that they contained rare beasts and birds, serpentine paths, artificial rocks, grottos, and labyrinths, and that they were irregular.[117] It is doubtful that these descriptions ever actually were duplicated in early eighteenth century gardens, but the legend of the Chinese garden to which these accounts gave rise was perpetuated in garden literature. It is, for instance, from this background that the accounts of Chinese gardens mentioned by the English writers Sir William Temple and Robert Castell were surely derived.[118]

The French retained the initiative in the production of accounts of such gardens throughout the first half of the century. The most extensive description of Chinese gardens before 1750, and one which was continually referred to in both France and England throughout the eighteenth century, was a product of France. It is contained in a letter from the Jesuit missionary and artist, Jean-Denis Attiret, written on 1 November 1743, and published in 1749, and describes the Chinese emperor's gardens in Peking.[119] These constituted an oriental microcosm of pavilions, streams, rivers, and other bodies of water, small islands, hills, valleys, exotic planting disposed in infinite variations, as well as menageries, and a miniature town and farm. Attiret's description achieved considerable attention not only in France (where the obvious parallel with Stanislaus's gardens—for instance, both were built quickly, Stanislaus's in ten, the Chinese in twenty, years—was surely noted) but also in England, where in 1752 it appeared in several periodicals and a pamphlet.[120] It would later be recalled in both French and English literature on the picturesque garden.

Illustrated scientific and travel literature of the seventeenth century are one outgrowth of the earlier accounts by visitors to China.[121] These, too, and in particular the prolific, often erroneous, and very popular work of A. Kircher, are another source for picturesque garden literature. However, although Chinese scenes of nature did appear in European minor arts before 1700, the only major artistic medium in which the Chinese garden made a physical appearance be-

[117] For early descriptions of Chinese gardens, see J. Gonzales de Mendoza, *Historia de las coses mas notables, rites y costombres, del gran Reyne de la China . . .* , Rome, 1585; N. Trigault, *De Christiana expeditione apud sina suscepta ab societate jesu,* n.p., 1610; A. Semonedo, *Imperio de la Chine,* Madrid, 1642 (all prior to the French Jesuit accounts); and, in particular, L. Le Comte, *Nouveaux mémoires sur l'état présent de la Chine,* Paris, 1696 (2v.).

[118] N. Pevsner and S. Lang, "Sir William Temple and Sharawaggi."

[119] J. D. Attiret, letter of 1 November 1743, from *Lettres édifiantes,* XXVII, 1749, pp. 7-43.

[120] E. Harris, "*Designs of Chinese Buildings* and the *Dissertation on Oriental Gardening,*" in J. Harris, *Sir William Chambers,* London, 1970, p. 150, n. 33.

[121] Illustrations of Chinese gardens and landscapes began to appear in A. Kircher, *China Monumentis qua sacris qua profanis illustrata,* Amsterdam, 1667 (French translation, 1670); and J. Nieuhoff, *Het Gezantschap der Neërlandtsche Oost-Indische compagnie,* Amsterdam, 1665, which was the source for illustrations by J. B. Fischer von Erlach for his *Entwurff einer historischen Architectur.*

fore the eighteenth century was the theater. The first example of an imaginative essay on the Chinese garden may have been in the stage directions for the one in the final act of Henry Purcell's *Fairy Queen*, first produced in 1692. These called for "a transparent prospect of a Chinese garden, the architecture, the trees, the plants, the fruit, the birds, the beasts quite different to what we have in this part of the world." To be included were arches, arbors, and a hanging garden.[122] A French counterpart to Purcell's Chinese garden has yet to be discovered. But it is fitting that this first known description should be a theatrical one, for the *jardin anglo-chinois* would be associated with theater design.

By mid-century the interest in gardens in the Chinese style had fused with the concept of the rococo garden. Fréron's *Epitre* is the earliest instance, to date, of such a fusion, but in his poem the "Chinese" and the "natural" gardens are still distinct. The *Epitre* was followed in 1753 by Laugier's *Essai*, in which, while also supporting Blondel's philosophical, "natural" garden, the Abbé had praised Stanislaus's estates. This account may be the first attempt at a synthesis of the natural and artificial styles. It may also mark the first time that a European equivalent for the Chinese garden was suggested. For, in connection with his praise of Stanislaus's designs, the Abbé recommended a consideration of the Chinese garden, about which he may have been informed wholly through Attiret's letter. However, the Chinese garden was to Laugier a product not of literary description, but of theatrical devices: it was composed of fantasy, caprice, and imagination, and it was a place where "the fairies display their enchantments," but where all appears to be natural and composed without resort to artifice.[123] It was, indeed, a garden modeled on Stanislaus' creations.

[122] For Purcell's description of the Chinese garden, see R. E. Moore, *Henry Purcell and the Restoration Theatre*, London, 1961, pp. 127-128.

[123] Laugier, *Essai*, p. 281. For Laugier and the Chinese garden, see also Herrmann, *Laugier*, pp. 140-147.

CHAPTER II

French Opinion on the English Picturesque Garden

Among the Frenchmen to see the first English attempts by Pope, Bridgeman, and Kent to create a picturesque garden were the Baron de Montesquieu and Voltaire, who visited England in 1729-1730 and 1726-1729, respectively. Both men later developed country estates in which they maintained that they had imitated the English style of gardening. But Voltaire's estates at Délices and Ferney (Fig. 34) were developed with formal gardens. As Hirschfeld noted, at Ferney the trees were even cut into spheres and cones.[1] And Montesquieu's estate at Labrède also was probably based on French rather than English models. What little information we possess about this park comes from the botanist F. P. Latapie, who had been educated by Montesquieu at Labrède.[2] From his description, the estate would seem to have been designed well within the style of the traditional French formal garden, in spite of the fact that Montesquieu would praise the free, varied, and natural prospect of the English countryside when writing his "Essay on Taste" for the *Encyclopédie*.[3] What seems to have interested both Mon-

[1] C. C. L. Hirschfeld, *Theorie der Gartenkunst* (all references are to the French translation, *Théorie de l'art des jardins*), v, p. 295. For Voltaire's "English" gardens, see C. Thacker, "Voltaire and Rousseau." In 1761 Voltaire wrote to his friend George Keate: "J'ose me flatter que Milord Burlington en aurait été content; mes jardins ne sont point à la française, je les ai faits les plus irréguliers, et les plus champêtres que j'ai pû; j'ose les (?)oire tout à fait à l'anglaise, car j'aime la Liberté je hais la simétrie." He added: "Je suive(?) les leçons de Mr. Thull, en fait d'agriculture; et je finis ma carrière comme Virgile le avait commencé la Sienne, en cultivent la terre." (British Museum, MS. 30.991, p. 19 *r*, *v*; Voltaire to Keate, 4 April 1761). It is possible that Voltaire's English influence is related to the philosophical writings of Shaftesbury. Shaftesbury's famous lines on the "formal Mockery of Princely Gardens" as opposed to "the rude Rocks, the mossy *Caverns*, the irregular unwrought Grottos, and broken *Falls* of Waters, with all the horrid graces of the Wilderness . . ." ("The Moralists," pp. 393-394) is close to Voltaire's "Epitre au Roi de Prusse" (dedicated to Stanislaus, and written in 1738) where Voltaire wrote: "J'aime mieux ces vastes forêts; / La nature libre et hardie, / Irrégulière dans ses traits, / S'accorde avec ma fantaisie." For a development of Voltaire's relationship with Shaftesbury, see N. L. Torrey, *Voltaire and the English Deists*, New Haven, 1930. For an alternate interpretation of Voltaire's "Epitre" see Herrmann, *Laugier*, p. 144, n. 54.

[2] Latapie's information is included in J. Baurein, *Variétés bordelaises*, v, pp. 40-41. Professor F. G. Pariset has communicated to me that the Château de Labrède is illustrated in its surroundings only in some "more or less fantastic" drawings, and Madame la Comtesse de Chabannes, now owner of Labrède, and M. J. P. Avisseau, Curator of the Municipal Archives of Bordeaux have communicated that there is no contemporary information on Montesquieu's "English" park in the archives either at Labrède or in Bordeaux. We do, however, know that there were Latin inscriptions on pyramids at Labrède (see P. F. Barrière, *Un grand provincial . . . Montesquieu*, pp. 107-108, and Montesquieu, *Oeuvres complètes*, Paris, 1950-1955 (ed. Nagel), II, p. 409 [1386 (64)], pp. 446-447 [1545 (62)]).

[3] Translated and published by A. Gerard, *Essay on Taste*, London, 1759, pp. 260-261. For further references to gardening see also the two other *Encyclopédie* articles on taste by Voltaire and D'Alembert published with Gerard's *Essay*.

tesquieu and Voltaire were not the physical characteristics of the English garden, but its under-lying philosophy, as it was reflected in literature, of the relation of the estate to the open countryside and to agriculture, although even here evidence indicates that Montesquieu's concept of an estate both useful and agreeable took shape in the early 1720s before his trip to England.[4]

The first French traveler to notice the physical appearance of the picturesque gardens in England may have been the Abbé Le Blanc, who spent a part of 1737 and 1738 there. Le Blanc's correspondence on his English visit, published in 1745,[5] and in particular his letters to G. L. L. Buffon, gardener to the king,[6] are informative concerning the attitude of a cultured Frenchman of progressive taste on English gardening. The Abbé would play an important role in the forming of French neoclassical taste when, along with Soufflot and Cochin, he would accompany the Marquis de Vandières (later, the Marquis de Marigny) on his famous taste-setting trip to Italy in 1749,[7] and it is possible, then, that he also might have had a part in the establishing of French mid-century views on picturesque gardening.

The Abbé disliked the unvaried expanses of nature in the English country estates. He noted that "the immensely large bowling-greens of this country . . . are too naked and uniform: nature must be diversify'd to please,"[8] for as "somebody has remark'd, *tiresomeness is the daughter of uniformity*. An extensive meadow, strikes you in a very agreeable manner, at first sight; but if it is not terminated by some rising ground, and divided by a rivulet and some trees; you soon grow weary, of what you at first so much admir'd."[9] Indeed, his criticism was similar to that which would be made by Chambers and Carmontelle of the gardening designs of Brown. But he also disliked the unnatural appearance of English topiary gardens, then still in fashion, in which the English gardeners "cut all sorts of trees into the most monstrous and ridiculous shapes."[10] And he noted that "Many English endeavour to give [their gardens], what they call in their own language a romantic air; that is to say, almost *Picturesque*;[11] but fail in it, for want of taste. The places, where they propose to imitate the venerable ruins of Antiquity, present to your eyes nothing but the pitiful remains of a ruinous house; objects, which in great, are noble and majestic; when represented in miniature, become childish and ridiculous."[12] As an example of this type he cited the garden—possibly Stowe (Fig. 36)[13]—of "a nobleman of this Kingdom," who spent immense sums on its embellishment. But, according to Le Blanc, the Englishman made his park more surprising than agreeable by constructing, in a few acres,

[4] Barrière, *Montesquieu*, pp. 102-104.

[5] Abbé J. B. Le Blanc, *Lettres d'un François* (all references are from the English translation, *Letters on the French and English Nations*). See H. Monod-Cassidy, *Un Voyageur philosophique au XVIIIe siècle, l'abbé Jean-Bernard le Blanc*, Cambridge, Mass., 1941, p. 56, for information about later editions of the *Lettres*. See L. C. Fougeret de Monbrun, *Préservatif contre l'Anglomanie*, Minorque, 1757, for opposition to Le Blanc's point of view.

[6] Le Blanc, *Letters*, i, letters xli, pp. 316-323; xlvii, pp. 368-373; ii, letter lii, pp. 13-21; see also letter to Comte de Caylus, i, letter xxxvi, pp. 279-287. For Buffon, see W. F. Falls, *Buffon et l'agrandissement du Jardin du Roi à Paris*, Philadelphia, 1933 (with bibliography).

[7] For the Abbé Le Blanc's trip to Italy, see S. F. Kimball, *The Creation of the Rococo*, pp. 187-188, 211.

[8] Le Blanc, *Letters*, i, p. 369 (letter xlvii).

[9] *Ibid.*, i, pp. 368-369 (letter xlvii).

[10] *Ibid.*, i, pp. 369-370 (letter xlvii).

[11] For the terms "romantic" and "picturesque" see J. J. Rousseau, *Oeuvres complètes*, Paris, 1959- (ed. B. Gagnehin and N. Raymond), i, pp. 1793-1795, with bibliography.

[12] Le Blanc, *Letters*, ii, pp. 13-14 (letter lii).

[13] For the extreme popularity of Stowe, see below, p. 34; it had achieved considerable fame in France already by 1750 (*Mercure*, February 1750, p. 140).

several small temples modeled after those of ancient Rome. Le Blanc noted that although one or two temples would have produced the effect of enchantment the owner desired, too many destroyed the effect.[14] The only garden Le Blanc referred to by name was Richmond, where he felt that the neighboring area had less the air of the countryside than of an immense garden, and he compared it to Milton's *Paradise Lost*.[15] But he criticized one garden structure in the park as in "childish taste"—Merlin's cave (Fig. 35)—noting that "So far from finding any thing in this building that savours of enchantment and the magician's power, it is impossible to conceive of any thing of worse taste."[16]

In contrast to what he interpreted as the artificial imitation of nature in English gardens, Le Blanc preferred nature to be primitive, uncultivated, and on a grand scale, as it existed, for instance, in the forest of Fontainebleau (Fig. 37), where "the rude and ill-shaped rocks, the venerable trees . . . present our sight with a more majestick and grander aspect, than all the laboured neatness of the best kept gardens."[17] But Le Blanc also suggested that nature should be combined with art. That is, nature should be imitated with vegetation of different greens, and of different shapes, for variety, as it had been depicted in the paintings of Claude.[18] There was only one element of the English estate that Le Blanc acknowledged to be superior to that of the French, and that was agriculture, for "the care with which the country is cultivated with [the English], is a consequence of the plenty in which the farmer lives."[19]

Le Blanc was so committed to the rural life that his ideas anticipate even those of Rousseau and Watelet. He wrote that "The iron age is only felt in towns; because they are the center of distraction, envy, ambition and perfidy. They are unknown in the country, unless they are brought there. But how many people are followed thither by a train of all vices. They live there as in town, possessed with the same cares, intoxicated with the same follies, or devoured by the same passions. These will never know the happy days of the golden age. The iron age will pursue them every where."[20]

By 1750 Mme. du Boccage, who had translated Milton's *Paradise Lost* in 1748, only two years before her journey to England,[21] would be more enthusiastic about the English garden. In comments in a letter to her sister, she compared contemporary garden design in the two countries:

---

[14] Le Blanc, *Letters*, II, p. 14 (letter lii).

[15] *Ibid.*, p. 26. Milton's *Paradise Lost* will be cited by several Frenchmen as a source of the *jardin anglo-chinois*; see, for example, De Lille, *Les Jardins*, pp. 29, 127-134 (4th ed., Paris and Rheims, 1782, cited here); Latapie, "Discours préliminaire," from the French translation of Whately's *Observations*, pp. xlj-lii. The architect Bélanger would mention Milton's work as the equivalent of descriptions of the Chinese garden (J. Stern, *A l'Ombre de Sophie Arnould: François-Joseph Bélanger, Architecte des Menus-Plaisirs*, Paris, 1930 (2v.), I, pp. 29-30, letter to Mme. Joly, c. 1790s, original on deposit in the Bibliothèque de l'Histoire de la Ville de Paris, N.A. MS. 182, fol. 271-272).

[16] Le Blanc, *Letters*, I, pp. 282-283 (letter xxxvi).

[17] *Ibid.*, II, p. 15 (letter lii). For the forest of Fontainebleau, see C. Michel, *La Forêt de Fontainebleau dans la nature, dans l'histoire, dans la littérature et dans*

l'art, Paris, 1909, with bibliography.

[18] Le Blanc, *Letters*, II, pp. 17-18 (letter lii).

[19] *Ibid.*, I, p. 297 (letter xxxvii), and p. 177 (letter xxv): ". . . whoever has eyes, must be struck with the beauties of the country, the care taken to improve lands, the richness of the pastures, the numerous flocks that cover them, and the air of plenty and cleanliness which reigns in the smallest villages. Those who do not look on England as a very fruitful country, are vastly mistaken." And, pp. 178-179: "The vast tract of land seen from the top of Richmond-hill, has more the air of an immense garden than of a country prospect. It presents the eye in some sort with an image of terrestrial paradise."

[20] *Ibid.*, I, p. 177 (letter xxvi).

[21] M. A. Fiquet du Boccage, *Le Paradis Terrestre, poème imité de Milton*, London, 1748. For Milton's *Paradise Lost*, see note 15 above.

"There are some thickets here laid out in our modern taste, in which the *English* think there is too much symmetry. They prefer to [our] spouting waters those which have a level surface, as more natural; and winding walks to straight alleys, the extremity of which is immediately taken in by the eye. They even make canals run in a serpentine form, that they may appear the more natural, and cast unequal shades upon the banks, which are covered with green turf and trees, in the form in which they are produced by nature."[22]

Mme. du Boccage mentioned visits to eight English parks including Saint James's Park in London, Kensington, Syon, Hampton Court, Chiswick, and Greencastle near Oxford (owned by the Baron Schutz, keeper of the king's wardrobe), and she commented extensively on Richmond and Stowe. Richmond contained "A vast terrass covered with a grass-plot, which runs along the river side, [and] constitutes its principal ornaments: the numerous and pleasant thickets present to the view a place of considerable extent, called the Forest; where, the better to imitate nature, art has, without any order, planted great trees, some of them erect, some of them crooked, one half withered away, another surrounded with shrubs. The Park, which is filled with deer and all sorts of game, would have been nothing but meadows, if taste had not varied and divided them into cultivated lands, or raised them into eminences surrounded with canals, which have a communication with the *Thames*. These canals lead to a Grotto, the stones of which, unpolished without-side, form within a vault adorned with sculptures." Her opinion of Merlin's "grotto" was more favorable than Le Blanc's had been: "The famous MERLIN, Counsellor to King ARTHUR, who was believed to be begot by an incubus, has there likewise his cave, made in imitation of that which he occupied in Wales, the place of his nativity. The late Queen, who was a lover of subterranean caverns, caused one to be constructed in the form of a labyrinth, in which narrow, dark and winding alleys conduct the steps of the curious. We there meet with the figures of travelers, who seem to walk trembling towards the entrance of the cavern. A low and gothic door, filled with hieroglyphics, leads to this awful place, to which you descend by a walk covered with pebbles over-grown with moss."[23] The element of surprise and contrast is as much related to Edmund Burke's description of the Sublime, which would be published some seven years later, as it is a continuation of the rococo interest in surprise and contrast.

Stowe was so extensive that Mme. du Boccage walked there three hours accompanied by a guide but she did not see the whole of the grounds. She wrote an extensive description of them, in which her attention was concentrated not on the landscape setting, but on the many inscriptions and garden structures, such as the monument to friendship, the column, the pyramid, the hermitage, etc.[24] She also commented on the "few marble statues" in England, where (in an early indication of French interest in memorials to famous men) she noted that "They do not, like us, multiply the images of the Pagan gods, which christianity should consign to oblivion: instead of this, they immortalize their great men: the statues erected to their honour are,

---

[22] Du Boccage, *Recueil de Oeuvres* (all references are from the 1770 English translation, *Letters concerning . . . France*), II, pp. 51-52, letter to her sister, 16 May 1750.

[23] *Ibid.*, pp. 49-50, 16 May 1750. Mme. du Boccage mistook Merlin's "cave" for the Hermitage, also known as the "grotto"; see Judith Colton, "Kent's Hermitage for Queen Caroline at Richmond," *Architectura*, 1974, no. 2, pp. 181-191.

[24] *Ibid.*, pp. 62-66, 4 June 1750.

like seed, capable of producing others to all eternity." But she criticized the expense, number, and exoticism of the monuments, which "often do much more honour to the genius of the nobleman to whom they belong than the execution to the artists; and which surprize as well by their multiplicity as by the immense sums that have been spent on them."[25]

Like her discussion of Merlin's grotto at Richmond, some of Mme. du Boccage's descriptions of Stowe suggest an awareness of the emotional aspects of nature, which also would be developed by Burke in his essay on the sublime (and which had been suggested in Le Blanc's use of the term "Romantic," a term which would be associated by Chambers with the emotional effects of the sublime). Thus, at Stowe she describes an artificial mount of pines and shrubs, "which the rocks produce, and three springs, which dart through crevices, after many turnings and windings, [to] form a lake, and lose themselves in subterraneous caverns lined by pebbles; where, after their fall, they form baths. The roaring of the water, which pleases at the same time that it terrifies, constitutes the whole charm of this lake."[26]

In these descriptions the English gardens are surely seen with French rococo eyes, as exotic curiosities. A definite attitude toward such gardens has developed. Thus such an observation as "they presented us at the end of each alley . . . sometimes a turret, sometimes an obelisk, mills, a circus, elysian fields, colonnades, a pretty temple dedicated to the God of Love . . ." is as directly related to Dézallier's even earlier descriptions of French gardens as it is to the actual English ones. And, like Le Blanc, Mme. du Boccage's acknowledgement of the superiority of England is restricted to agriculture; her praise of English agricultural wealth and the open estates suggests by comparison the poor condition of the French farmers: ". . . we visited even the cottages of shepherds and the houses of farmers. People of this class have their houses well furnished, are well dressed, and eat well . . . their cattle lies (*sic*) under the open air without being afraid of wolves, which were long since destroyed in this country, and corn is kept a whole winter at the mill without being spoiled. In *France* our farms ruin us by the number of buildings we erect upon them: but it would be a difficult matter to reconcile our country peasants to this economy."[27]

After the Peace of 1763, according to the Prince de Croÿ, English gardens began to be imitated in France,[28] and the French began to look to the English garden for possible applications of its style to their own gardens. One unique visual illustration of the French concept of the ideal English garden is a sketch of an imaginary English garden attributed to the prince and published by Le Rouge in 1776 in the first cahier of his *Nouveaux jardins à la mode* (Fig. 38). Many of the elements that make up the "English" garden in this sketch either stem from a common eighteenth-century tradition (including a menagerie, enclosed court, grassy slope, tufts of flowers, a large copse, and an Italian villa), or recall the best remembered features from the most often visited English gardens—a "wild cascade" (Richmond), a Chinese house (Stowe and Kew), an antique column (Stowe), a natural woods (Painshill), a pagoda (Kew), a

[25] *Ibid.*, p. 64. Interest in memorials to famous men began contemporaneously in France. See Titon du Tillet, work cited in chapter I, n. 45.

[26] *Idem.* Illustrated in Bickham, *Beauties of Stowe*, p. 4.

[27] *Ibid.*, p. 61, 4 June 1750.

[28] E. de Croÿ, *Journal*, III, p. 140, entry dated 27 April 1774, where de Croÿ mentions that the taste for Chinese gardens also had appeared thirty years previously in Holland.

colonnade or circular monopteral temple on a mount (Stowe). The result is a combination of elements from the earliest and most artificial stage in the development of the English garden, and Croÿ's garden is as artificial and cramped as its English prototypes. Indeed, it has even more of the excessive attention to detail and ostentatious display for which the English parks had been criticized by the French. One garden accessory here, the *vat-et-vient*—surely a *va-et-viens* or ferry such as "Le Bac" at Ermenonville—seems to be purely French.

Although there must have been many French visitors to English gardens at this time, we know little at present about who they were, the dates of their visits, or what gardens they saw. But impressions of French visits after 1763 tend to codify earlier French opinions about English gardens. Of these, the most frequent observation concerned the number of buildings. By 1782, even the Prince de Ligne, one of the most enthusiastic connoisseurs of the *jardin anglo-chinois*, who mentioned among the English gardens that he had visited Wimbolton, Twickenham, Chiswick, Blenheim, Wilton, Richmond, and Kew,[29] complained of "templomanie" in English gardens.[30] In particular, "Staw" was considered by the prince to contain too many buildings.[31]

Also during the 1760s a concept of the English garden, implicit in earlier observations, emerged. In 1765, the Baron von Holbach, in an interesting development of Le Blanc's notion of the "romantic," criticized the melancholy, sentimental, associational character of the English gardens, which he noted were designed to permit visitors who wished to be alone to retire. He commented on the taste of one rich estate owner who had planted many cypresses and had dispersed among the trees busts of philosophers, sepulchral urns, and antique marbles; he called the garden a Roman cemetery, although he said that the owner referred to it as the Elysium.[32] The baron may have been referring to Stowe, although a view of the exedra at Chiswick could fit his description (Fig. 39). The Baron de Tschoudy, writing in the *Encyclopédie* in 1776 on "Bosquets," criticized "perspective ruins" and tombs and urns mingled with cypresses which he considered to be an element of English gardens, and which he felt produced an effect not unlike a landscape by Salvator Rosa. He asked, "Is a promenade created so that it will evoke melancholy?" He preferred a type of garden where verses would be inscribed that were dictated by "a delicate taste," where he could meditate, book in hand, and be interrupted only by the voice of love or the complaint of humanity, where he might shed several tears, and in which the contrasts were due both to the variability of nature and the charm of art.[33] He was surely thinking of Moulin-Joli.

It is in the light of the preference for the French meditative "natural" gardens as opposed to the English melancholy one shown in the baron's remarks that we must consider two French descriptions of "natural" gardens of the early 1760s. The first is by Denis Diderot, a friend of Von Holbach. It has been suggested that Diderot, in a letter to Sophie Volland (dated 1762), described La Briche, the estate of Rousseau's close friend Mme. d'Epinay, as a garden showing

[29] The last two gardens were "les plus belles que j'aie vue," De Ligne, *Beloeil*, p. 107.

[30] *Ibid.*, p. 105.

[31] *Ibid.*, p. 106.

[32] D. Diderot, *Oeuvres complètes*, Paris, 1776 (ed. J. Assézat and M. Tourneaux), XIX, pp. 182-183, Diderot to Sophie Volland, 6 October 1765.

[33] Baron de Tschoudy, "Bosquets," *Encyclopédie*, Supplément II, 1776, p. 23. For a similar description of Moulin-Joli, possibly the source for the Baron's remarks, see chapter I, p. 18.

English influence. Diderot wrote that the garden and the park had a "wild air," and that he was pleased by the "large bodies of water, whose banks are covered with rushes and swamp herbs, and are connected by an old bridge, ruined and covered with moss; bowers that have never been touched by a gardener, trees planted without symmetry; fountains flowing from a natural source; a space which is not large, but which is unfamiliar."[34] Indeed, his observations could constitute the first description of an irregular garden in France. But it is more likely that they were related to the concept of idealized, uncultivated nature which is both proto-Rousseauian and a part of the literary tradition of pastoral imagery associated with d'Urfé's *Astrée*. That concept already had been expressed in such a formal garden as Moulin-Joli.

The second description is by Rousseau and appeared in *Julie: ou la Nouvelle Héloïse*, published in 1761. Rousseau was critical of the formal garden for its unnaturalness (like Huet and Laugier he thought that the garden would be abandoned for a walk in the country), and for the "false taste of grandeur" in which the owner was "lost like a poor worm." And he was also critical of the gardens of the "petty virtuosi," citing in this category the Dutch tulip gardens, but referring perhaps also to the small fashionable French gardens of the 1750s. These he saw as examples of a taste "that has something idle and precious in it, which renders it puerile and ridiculously expensive." He felt that the man of taste would make everything in his garden commodious and agreeable, simple and natural; and that he would consider symmetry the enemy of nature and of variety. This point of view is consistent with French gardening theory as it developed during the first half of the eighteenth century, as well as with English gardening trends.[35] The argument for a French source for Rousseau's views on gardening is strengthened by the fact that the philosopher equated the Chinese and English gardens, and that he was opposed to both of them for the unnaturalness with which they imitated nature. In this connection he specifically mentioned Stowe.[36] Indeed, if we are to believe the anonymous author of *Le Jardin de Julie*, written in 1763 (prior to Rousseau's visit to England), Rousseau did not think highly of the English garden, and he would not have suggested imitating it.[37]

It has been proposed that Rousseau was influenced by Addison in his theories on landscape and gardens.[38] Admittedly, the Alpine wilderness described in Letter xxiii of *Héloïse* is perhaps related to an Addison essay in the *Tatler*,[39] and Julie's orchard in Letter cxxx may be related to Addison's description of his own garden in the *Spectator*.[40] But there is no doubt that Rousseau's description of an ideal garden, like his theory, reflects the French tradition. Rousseau's friendship with the amateur Watelet has already been noted. Julie's garden, in its natural-

---

[34] Diderot, *Oeuvres*, XIX, p. 122, Diderot to Sophie Volland, 5 September 1762.

[35] Rousseau also recommended that his ideal garden be completely enclosed (in the manner of the rococo garden), since "The taste for perspective and distant views proceeds from the disposition of men who are never satisfied with the place where they are" (Rousseau, *Eloisa*, III, p. 116—all references are from this English edition, fully cited in the Bibliography).

[36] *Ibid.*, III, p. 118; and see P. Willis, "Rousseau, Stowe and *Le Jardin anglais*: speculations on visual sources for *La Nouvelle Héloïse*," *Studies on Voltaire*

and the Eighteenth Century, xc, 1972, pp. 1791-1798.

[37] Rousseau, *Oeuvres complètes* (1788-1793 ed.), IV, p. 465. Also see E. Neumeyer, "The Landscape Garden as a Symbol with Rousseau, Goethe, and Flaubert," *Journal of the History of Ideas*, April 1947, p. 196, n. 30.

[38] Kimball, "Les Influences anglaises dans la formation du style Louis XVI," p. 32.

[39] Addison, *Tatler*, no. 81, Thursday, October 13, to Saturday, October 15, 1709.

[40] Rousseau mentioned reading the *Spectator*: see *Oeuvres* (1959-1964 ed.), I, p. 110, and p. 1282, n. 4.

ness, simplicity, and adaptation to the existing conditions of the site, is similar to Watelet's Moulin-Joli, and Rousseau's philosophy of gardening resembles that expressed in greater detail by Watelet in his *Essai sur les jardins*. Rather than describing the real English garden Rousseau added to the French legend about it: for when he was in England in 1766-1767, he was quoted as saying that he wished that the numerous temples of the English gardens "were changed into cottages, and other dwellings, which (under the tenure of keeping up the picturesque circumstances required by the owner) might be made the reward of industry, and the consolation of distress."[41] The opinion is in the spirit of French theoretical works on gardening of the 1770s by Watelet and Girardin.

Rousseau's ideas were taken up by later writers on England. In 1777 when Lacombe's guide to London appeared, the author remarked, at the end of an extensive description of Stowe, that the English, in their concern for their extravagant gardens, had forgotten to immortalize themselves by establishing farms and villages which would enrich their country and make the names of the benefactors dear to their nation.[42] Finally, in 1786 La Coste closed a long description of Stowe with the comment that its beauties were the product of art submitted to opulence,[43] rather than (it is implied) to usefulness and practical benefit.

By 1770 F. J. Grosley in his guide to London provided the most objective and comprehensive French description of the new English style of garden yet to appear.[44] But although Grosley's guide appeared in the same year as Whately's *Observations on Modern Gardening*, he was surely not influenced by it, for his observations are a purely French interpretation of the English garden. He notes in particular that the English had abandoned symmetry completely. In all the gardens he had seen, he had not found a single allée trimmed and shaped in the French manner; indeed, he said, the French style was conserved in England only as a sample of bad taste. English taste, he observed, had also moved away from the French concept of trimmed "rooms." Instead, the English sought their models in natural forests. The main allées of their parks were designed as if they were forest routes which had been formed by chance, and they were bordered with all types and sizes of trees, while the allées designed for walking imitated forest paths—they never ran for more than two yards in a straight line. Grosley further commented on the English art of composing the plantings which separated and marked the paths. The basic design generally included a border for the paths of forest flowers which were planted in a random fashion; behind the flowers were small bushes, and behind these, taller trees, with then a final planting of the tallest and best-formed trees. Thus the planting was arranged in a pyramid, a form which, incidentally, was a primary one in French aesthetic theory.

Grosley cited Chiswick as an example of this style of garden design (Fig. 40). Here, he noted, land that was originally flat had been altered to make terraces and hills, each of which was crowned with an antique temple; and a "wide river" with a winding course divided the prin-

[41] D. Malthus, "Introduction," R. L. Girardin, *Essay on Landscape*, London, 1783, pp. liii-liv.

[42] F. Lacombe, *Observations sur Londre (sic)*, pp. 143-148. Except for this passage, however, the guide follows Grosley's *Londres* in his comments on garden-

ing.

[43] La Coste, *Voyage philosophique d'Angleterre*, I, p. 90.

[44] P. J. Grosley, *Londres*, III, pp. 105-129.

cipal parts of the park and multiplied the points of view from the "château." But, in a criticism which was an elaboration of Von Holbach's observations, Grosley noted that the main allée, which provided the major view and was planted with cypresses and arranged with urns and funerary monuments in the antique style, had the air of a cemetery and suggested an approach to a temple of melancholy (Fig. 39).[45]

Of the four other English gardens discussed by Grosley, the least space was devoted to Stowe,[46] more to Oatlands (described here for the first time)[47] and to a garden in Chelsea owned by the Chevalier Glym,[48] and by far the most space was given to Kew, which had just been redesigned by Chambers and was considered by the Frenchman to unite the richest and the most varied elements of English taste (Figs. 41, 42, 43). Here, Grosley explained, the extensive groves were disposed so that each one was complete in itself, and the visitor passed from each one without being aware that anything existed beyond it. These groves contained a gothic chapel, a circular temple dedicated to Victory which was situated on top of an artificial hill, and the famous Chinese pagoda. Grosley did not mention the mosque, or the other garden structures there.[49] According to him, the groves were distributed around the center of the park, which formed an immense esplanade of unequal proportions and was watered by an artificial stream. The guide described without comment the most artificial element of the park, a large wooden bridge, situated in the middle of the field and with no other function than to add to the variety of the view.[50] He noted that this center space, or pasture, was given over to a herd of cows, ewes, and goats.[51] Farther on in his guide, Grosley, like Le Blanc and Mme. du Boccage, commented favorably on the state of farming in England, a nation in which he observed that even the animals enjoyed liberty, because they were permitted to graze in open pastures.[52]

Although Grosley's work is the result of first-hand observation, it summarizes previous French views on the English garden, and it suggests means of transposing the style into the French one. His guide also had some influence on later, better known, French works on the English garden: in 1776, when Le Rouge published the first cahier of his *Nouveaux jardins à la mode*, he cited extensively from Grosley.[53] And Grosley was the first writer to revive the legend that Dufresny had priority over the English in the designing of picturesque gardens,[54] a statement to be elaborated on within the following year by Latapie in his translation of Whately's *Obser-*

[45] *Ibid.*, pp. 108-109.
[46] *Ibid.*, p. 116.
[47] *Ibid.*, pp. 116-118.
[48] *Ibid.*, pp. 120-122.
[49] For the garden ornaments, see Chambers, *Gardens and Buildings at Kew*.
[50] According to Chambers, *Kew*, p. 6, the bridge spanned an artificial river and led to an island. The design was taken from one of Palladio's wooden bridges; it was remarkable for the fact that it was erected in one night.
[51] Grosley, *Londres*, pp. 110-114.
[52] *Ibid.*, pp. 127-128. For a further extension of the concept of liberty associated by the French with the picturesque garden, see L. P. Ségur, *Mémoires ou souvenirs et recollections*, Paris, 1824-1826 (3v.), here quoting from *Memoires and Recollections of Count Segur*, London, 1825-1827 (3v.), i, pp. 130-131: "It has always . . . been a subject of surprize to me, that our government and statesmen, instead of reproaching as frivolous and foreign to the national spirit, that rage for English fashions, which suddenly sprung up throughout France, did not perceive in it the desire of another species of imitation, and the germs of a mighty revolution in the public mind. They were not in the least aware that, while we were destroying in our pleasure grounds, the straight walks and alleys, the symmetrical squares, the trees cut in circles and the uniform hedges, in order to transform them into English gardens, we were indicating our wishes to resemble that nation, in other and more essential points of nature and of reason."
[53] Le Rouge, *Nouveaux jardins*, cahier i, p. 26.
[54] Grosley, *Londres*, pp. 119-121.

vations on Modern Gardening[55] and by Blondel in the first volume of his *Cours d'architecture.*[56]

French knowledge of the English picturesque garden was not wholly restricted to literary accounts and to preconceptions. At the same time that French attitudes toward the English gardens were crystallizing, during the 1770s, the number of illustrated examples of the English garden which the French gardening enthusiast might use increased considerably. Chief among the disseminators of these examples was Le Rouge, who included among the illustrations in his long series of cahiers on the *jardin anglo-chinois*, plans of Richmond, Stowe, Esher, Wanstead, and Syon; views and details from many English gardens; and materials from English pattern books, especially the publications of Halfpenny and Langley. His work should, however, be viewed less as a source for the development of the French picturesque garden than as documentation of a taste that had already been achieved, and that took from the English style elements similar to its own.

One exception to the French legend of the English garden is the accurate visual record made by the architect Bélanger of his visits to English country estates, probably in 1777-1778 on a second trip to England.[57] Among the contents of the architect's English sketchbook (which included drawings of gardens and parks, country and city houses, garden buildings and even agricultural equipment), were illustrations of the grounds of Stowe, Bowood, Oatlands, Ilam, Stourhead, Wanstead, Wilton, the Leasowes, Fonthill, Claremont, Hagley, Painshill, two unidentified parks, and the rocky formations at Dovedale and the cascades of Matlock Baths (Figs. 44-51). These last two natural landscapes and many of the parks were already known from descriptions by Whately in his *Observations on Modern Gardening*. Bélanger was also in Sussex. Not only did he include Oatlands among his sketches, but he also drew the rotating bridge at Weybridge. And thus he must have seen the earlier essays on the English picturesque garden at Painshill and the *ferme ornée* at Woburn, which were both in this area. It should be noted that the gardens which Bélanger saw and from which Le Rouge took material are gardens which were designed before 1750, that is, the more ornamental, artificial, "rococo" ones, so that French taste seems to be consistently oriented toward these examples.

And, in spite of the new material available after 1763, the old attitudes toward the English

[55] Latapie, "Discours," pp. vj-vij.
[56] Blondel, *Cours d'architecture*, IV (1774), pp. 7-8.
[57] J. F. Bélanger, "Croquis d'un voyage en Angleterre," deposited at the Bibliothèque de l'Ecole Nationale Supérieure des Beaux-Arts in Paris, cat. no. 1762. J. Stern, *Bélanger*, I, p. 5, discusses the book, but dates it from Bélanger's trip to England in 1766-1767. He does suggest the possibility of a second trip to England. D. Stillmann, "Gallery for Lansdowne House: International Neoclassical Architecture and Decoration in Microcosm," *Art Bulletin*, LII, March 1970, p. 78 and n. 36, accepts the possibility, and dates the book from a later assumed trip in 1778, on the evidence of buildings indicated in the sketches which did not exist in 1767. Kenneth Woodbridge has formed the same conclusion, based on the fact that buildings constructed after 1767 are included in the sketchbook and that one estate was not acquired by the owner mentioned by Bélanger until 1768. There is the additional possibility

that the book contains material from both a 1767 and a 1777 trip to England.

There is lamentably little specific information on visits by French architects to England. We do know that Legeay was in England in 1766 (J. M. Pérouse de Montclos, *Etienne-Louis Boullée*, p. 41, who further suggests that Legeay was influenced by the English gardens, p. 43); Pierre Patte was in England in 1768, but only to examine Saint Paul's; Gondoin visited England around 1765 (J. Adhémar, "L'Ecole de Médicine," *L'Architecture*, XLVII, no. 3, 15 May 1934, p. 106). M. Mosser, "Projets . . . pour Menars," p. 282, suggests that De Wailly was in England at the same time. And S. Eriksen, *Early Neo-classicism in France*, London, 1974, p. 143, speculates that Ledoux visited England during 1763-1765. On Ledoux in England, see also M. Gallet, "Palladio et l'architecture française dans la seconde moitié du XVIIIe siècle," *Les Monuments historiques de la France*, 1975, no. 2, pp. 48-49.

garden continued. Blondel included them in his comprehensive discussion on gardening in the first volume of his *Cours*.[58] Blondel considered that this type of garden fell into two distinct categories. The first was that of the Chinese garden, for which Blondel's information seems to have come mainly from the work of his famous English student, William Chambers. Chambers's essay, "The Art of Laying out Gardens according to the Chinese," had been in circulation in France since its publication in 1757.[59] Using this source, Blondel added one new element to the French image of the English garden which had only been hinted at previously by Mme de Boccage: that was that these gardens were composed of "scenes," in which the most delightful and the most terrible objects were imitated, with the greatest possible contrast. Also, like Chambers, Blondel commented on the great amount of water in the Chinese garden, and he mentioned the arrangement of trees, which was studied, as if for a painting, to provide variety. This arrangement was imitated by the English and most of the German nations, according to Blondel.

Blondel surely was not impressed favorably by these English essays, for he concluded his description of this category with the remark that "Nations [which are] otherwise very enlightened regard symmetry as a fetter to genius, and a servile subjection to the rules of Art." And in the introduction to the first volume of his *Cours d'architecture* he also discussed the designing, on the pretext of variety, of "small, enclosed areas, hillocks, winding roads, zig-zag paths, irregular ponds, caverns, cliffs, unrelated groves of trees of many different species, mingled with kiosques, pavilions, obelisks, colonnades and tombs scattered here and there," all of which Blondel felt could only produce a confusion very unlike the orderly symmetrical composition of French gardens.[60] It may be that Blondel was thinking of the French *jardin anglo-chinois*, for his description is similar to that given by the reviewer of Watelet's *Essai sur les jardins* in the September 1775 *Journal des sçavans*. In the review, such a design was considered to be a product of French "Anglomanie"—a style which was, according to the reviewer, disowned by the English.[61]

The second category of English garden discussed by Blondel was one based not on adherence to garden vocabulary and design but on literary associations. Blondel described, with some inaccuracies, one example; the garden of "Denbigh" near Dorking in Surrey, owned by Jonathan Tyers, manager of the Vauxhall gardens in London.[62] According to Blondel, Tyres's garden was situated on the slope of a "mountain" and was subdivided by allées designed to represent the vicissitudes of human error. Those rising up the hill were well maintained, those descending were rough and obstructed. In the garden were moral inscriptions and a temple dedicated to death. At the extremity of this "funereal solitude" was a valley planted with pines and cypresses, where at the entry were posted two human skeletons (male and female), who seemed

[58] Blondel, *Cours*, I (1771), pp. 144-157; also see *ibid.*, IV, pp. 6-9.

[59] See chapter III, notes 14, 15.

[60] Blondel, *Cours*, I, p. 150.

[61] *Journal des Sçavans*, September 1775, pp. 598-599.

[62] Blondel, *Cours*, I, pp. 151-153. For Denbies in Surrey near Dorking, see E. W. Brayley, *A Topographical History of Surrey*, London, 1841-1842 (5v.), v,

pp. 90-92. Tyers purchased the estate in 1734; it was sold and the garden destroyed soon after his death in 1767. Blondel was not well informed; the two "skeletons" were "male" and "female" skulls on a shelf at the termination of one of the walks. See also *Scots Magazine*, XXIX, 1767, p. 456 (from S. H. Monk, *The Sublime*, New York, 1935, p. 165).

by their poses to warn those who passed of the end of man. The most frightful spectacle in this "sombre valley," according to Blondel, was a grotto which was divided into two parts: in one was depicted Disbelief, expiring in despair, and surrounded with all the sinister attributes that had served to mislead him; in the other was a Believer in eternal life, calm and serene at the moment even of death, and with symbols around him of all that had contributed to his perseverance in the path of hope and virtue.[63]

Blondel suggested that his Chinese and moral gardens should be models for, respectively, the the gardens of "men of the world," and of religious meditation.[64] Indeed, the two types seem to have been consciously contrasted, at least in several instances, both in England and in France. Tyers surely designed his own garden as a complement to his public Vauxhall gardens. And the French financier Beaujon would build his monastic and utilitarian Chartreuse in a deliberate contrast to the extroverted charm of his other Parisian estate, the Hotel d'Evreux.[65]

Blondel may have been thinking of Stowe, the best known of all the English gardens, as the counterpart to Tyres's singular garden. In the introduction to the first volume of the *Cours* he described the immense sums that had been spent by "several English Lords, in their imitation of modern Gardens, to judge by those at *Stowe*. . . ."[66] Blondel's knowledge of the garden may have been based on the description of Stowe which he cited: a "new work" translated from the English by a man of taste,[67] that is, Latapie, who had added to Whately's already extensive description of Stowe in his *Observations on Modern Gardening* a description of his own, based on his visit to this garden in 1770.[68] As the English garden, represented by Stowe, began to be equated with the Chinese one, as it was described by Attiret and by Chambers, the French became outspokenly critical of Lord Cobham's estate. Thus by 1775, A. N. Duchesne noted that such an attempt to imitate nature would result only in a debased copy, or worse, and would be capricious; he related the Chinese emperor's garden, based on Attiret's description, to that of Stowe,[69] as an artificial and costly reproduction of nature.

The association of this type of English garden with that of the Chinese may be based entirely on literary parallels rather than on the imitation by the English of an actual Chinese source. Indeed, in all the early eighteenth-century experimenting with garden design, only one possible connection of either French or English garden design with that of China has been documented to date. It has been suggested that engravings of Chinese gardens in the possession of Lord Burlington after 1724 influenced William Kent's experiments in picturesque garden design.[70] But although Kent's mounts and clumps are similar to those in the engravings, there are alter-

[63] Blondel, *Cours*, I, pp. 151-153. There are several other "moral gardens" recorded in literature before 1750: Joseph Spence described one in *Polymetis*, London, 1747, pp. 1-3; and Aaron Hill described one in 1734 (see D. Watkin, *Thomas Hope, 1769-1831, and the Neoclassical Idea*, London, 1968, pp. 148-151). At least one "moral garden" was created in France (A. Laborde, *Description*, pp. 127-130): the Ermitage du Mont-d'Or near Lyons.

[64] Blondel, *Cours*, I, p. 153.

[65] For Beaujon's Chartreuse, see chapter VI, p. 112.

[66] Blondel, *Cours*, IV, pp. 6-7.

[67] *Idem.*

[68] Latapie, "Description détaillé des jardins," from the French translation of Whately, *Observations*, pp. 348-401. A map of Stowe is included.

[69] A. N. Duchesne, *Sur la Formation des jardins*, pp. 84-86.

[70] R. Wittkower, "English Neo-Palladianism, the Landscape Garden, China, and the Enlightenment." Wittkower's source is B. Gray, "Lord Burlington and Father Ripa's Chinese Engravings," *British Museum Quarterly*, XXII, 1960, pp. 40-43.

native sources within the European gardening tradition for this gardening vocabulary. More-over, the Chinese influences on Kent, real or assumed, have little significance for the place assigned him by eighteenth-century English writers in the development of the English pictur-esque garden. Kent was considered by the English from the 1750s to be the man responsible for the invention of the picturesque garden, a purely English creation.[71] However, he was con-sidered by the French from the 1770s to be responsible for introducing into England the Euro-pean equivalent of the Chinese garden, an achievement in which Dufresny was often consid-ered to have preceded him. Continually in French descriptions of the *jardin anglo-chinois* Kent is mentioned as a forerunner of the new French garden and as having received his inspi-ration from the Chinese.[72] Thus Kent alone of all the English garden designers was acknowl-edged by the French to be associated with the French development of the picturesque garden. This should be kept in mind when we find him discussed in French garden literature—with the exception of occasional references to Pope, he is the only English garden designer singled out by the French. His work is included, for instance, in the first cahier of Le Rouge's *Nou-veaux Jardins à la mode*, where there is a plan of Burlington's estate at Chiswick, the garden of which had in part been designed by Kent; and there are illustrations of the Chiswick garden architecture in the form of marginal vignettes to the Le Rouge plate of Boutin's Tivoli (Fig. 87).

The interest of the French in Kent, as a Chinese-inspired garden designer, may be explained by the fact that by the end of the 1770s, when the popularity of the *jardin anglo-chinois* had reached its peak, the characteristics of the "Chinese" garden had come to be accepted by some French garden theorists and designers as French, while those of the moral gardens were con-sidered to be English. Foremost among those holding these views was Louis Carrogis, called Carmontelle, the designer of Monceau. Carmontelle's theory will be discussed in chapter IV, but it can be mentioned that in his explanation of illustrations of his design for the park, pub-lished in 1779, he stated that the object of the French garden should be to embellish the coun-tryside with taste and talent. The atmosphere the designer wished to create was one appropriate for the enjoyment of society, where "all becomes festive."[73] The "sombre and wild" appearance and melancholy associations Carmontelle related to the English garden were by all means to be avoided. Instead, the designer wished to please and interest with the widest possible variety. It should be noted that Stowe was directly associated with Monceau in at least one pamphlet, written by a Frenchman, C. F. de Lubersac, in 1775.[74]

An anonymous English author also differentiated between the French and English gardens, in an *Essay on the Different Natural Situations of Gardens*, published in 1774. The "situations"

[71] See chapter III, pp. 60-61, in particular, Walpole, "On Modern Gardening," *Anecdotes*, IV, pp. 55-69.

[72] Blondel, *Cours*, IV, pp. 7-8; Duc d'Harcourt, *Traité de la decoration des dehors*, pp. 78-79; and De Lille, *Les Jardins*, pp. 26-27, 116 (where Kent is contrasted with Le Nôtre). Later, L. F. Baltard, *Athenaeum*, December 1808, p. 3, n. 12, still equated Kent with the *jardin chinois*. More generally, the English were con-sidered to have received their inspiration from China

—De Ligne, *Beloeil*, p. 102: "Il est pourtant sûr que c'est à eux les Chinois [que] les Anglois doivent leur réputation."

[73] L. Carmontelle, *Jardin de Monceau*, pp. 3-6.

[74] C. F. Lubersac de Livron, "Monuments qui se trouve dans les Jardins de Plaisance du BARON DE COBHAM, près de Londres, & ceux de Mr. le DUC DE CHARTRES, à la Barrière de Monceau, près de Paris," in *Discours sur les monumens publics*, pp. liv-lx.

with which the author was concerned were those of the terrain: high land, sunken valley, unequal land, and flat land. For the fourth situation (flat land) he suggested the admission of "all the magnificence of Versailles" and the "artificial mounts of the flat Dutch gardens" in order to "give as much pleasure to the senses as possible." He recommended that, in order to create greater variety, "buildings of all species under the sun . . . should here find place. In short, every agreeable object, that creates surprise, and that exhibits a view of magnificent art, should enter into the composition of such a garden." He further commented that these effects were "more proper, when in the neighborhood of a great city, and thrown open to all the world, than when in a remote province." And he not only related this type of garden to France but also to Stowe, saying, "for that reason some of the French gardens have an excuse, which those at Stowe have not." He also equated gardens with the theater: "[A] garden like this," he wrote, "is a kind of fairy land. It is in comparison of other Gardens, what an Opera is in comparison of a Tragedy: neither of them should be judged by the ordinary rules of experience or taste, but by the capricious ones of variety and fancy."[75]

The most detailed contemporary comparison of French and English gardens was made by C. C. L. Hirschfeld. This author not only differentiated between the styles of the picturesque garden in England and in France but he also considerably developed the French stereotyped view of English gardens. He maintained that the French garden was ornamental, the English one uncultivated (*négligé*); the English sought the country for their rural pleasures, while the French took the city with them to the country; the Englishman was a practical and economical gardener, the Frenchman was rarely other than a decorator; the French designed to produce admiration and surprise, the English designed to achieve a variety of ideas and sentiments; the French were concerned with proportions, the English with scenes and pictures; the English displayed the landscape, the French displayed the owner; and the goal of the English designer was a profound melancholy, shocking transitions, and great contrasts which resulted in a "sublime tone," the goal of the French designer was to produce only agreeable sensations.[76]

By 1785 the French began to reverse their previous views and to see English gardens not as products of a taste for the artificial, either melancholic or ornamental, but for the natural. In that year Mme. Roland wrote that Kew was "the most interesting [garden] that I have ever seen; the most skilful art cannot be better disguised; every thing breathes nature and freedom; every thing is grand, noble and graceful. . . . How aukwardly (*sic*) and ridiculously have we imitated the English gardens, with our little divisions, our ruins, which have the appearance of children's baby houses, our affectation of gloominess, that assemblage of contradictions and monuments only fit to be laughed at!" She cited Ermenonville as an example of French taste. In a comparison similar to that of Hirschfeld, she wrote, "The beauty of [the English] gardens is allied to a profound sentiment of the beautiful and the sublime; the beauty of ours, more allied to wit, to its agreeable sallies; we are pretty, delicate, regular or pleasing in this kind of decoration; the English are proud and fascinating."[77] And in 1788 the Baron von Wimpfen published

---

[75] *Essays on the Different Natural Situations of Gardens*, London, 1774, pp. 24-25 (and included in the 1801 edition of Whately's *Observations*).

[76] Hirschfeld, *Art des jardins*, v, pp. 308-309.

[77] M. J. Phlipon Roland de la Platière, *Oeuvres* (all references are from the English translation, *Works*, 1800), pp. 206-209, 1 July 1784, Mme. Roland to her daughter.

a description of the English garden, based on Chambers's 1757 description, but he no longer considered it as an artificial imitation of nature: here now nature rather than man was "the first architect."[78]

There is one other thematic motif which was associated with the English country estate from the time of Le Blanc's comments, and which also underwent a considerable development during the 1770s—agriculture, which now was associated by the French garden designer with the ornamental garden. Le Rouge in 1776 added to the material he extracted from Grosley, a definition of the English *ferme ornée*. The concept of the *ferme ornée* had been developed by the French before this date, but Le Rouge's account is the first by a French author of the English one, and it differs from that of both previous French and English authors. Le Rouge described a countryside formed of undulating land which was shaped into amphitheaters, where projecting hills provided variety and were inhabited by beautiful horses, sheep, ewes, etc., which were always at liberty and were separated from the park by a ha-ha; and he added, "It is this that the English call a *ferme ornée*."[79] By 1785 Von Hartig appended to a description of the English garden, again modeled on the description in Chambers's "Art of Laying out Gardens according to the Chinese," a section on English farms (*métairies*). These, he said, contained everything necessary to agriculture, and he compared them to a garden near Paris, possibly Boutin's Tivoli, where the owner only imitated the English style and designed a "farm" without either field or pasture to feed the cows.[80]

But although the French showed considerable interest in both agriculture and the *ferme ornée* after 1775, the early eighteenth-century English *ferme ornée* is seldom described. From the written comments, there are only a few indications that the French knew of gardens other than the purely ornamental ones of Chiswick, Stowe, Richmond, and Kew, although surely the many other estates which were developed in the vicinity of London during the 1720s and 1730s were also visited: Grosley and Lacombe did include the garden of Oatlands in their descriptions. No other account of the gardens in this area seems to have been published except that of J. de Cambry, who, in 1788, described Woburn Farm, Oatlands, Painshill, and "Twitenham."[81] The writer noted that Woburn Farm was the farm of a "grand seigneur" who preferred pictures of nature and of its useful fecundity to vain and capricious ornaments and ruinous fashionable follies.[82] This contrasts strongly with Whately's earlier description of Woburn Farm as a *ferme ornée*, and an early attempt to "blend the useful with the agreeable,"[83] an attempt still far from the desirable degree of simplicity which he maintained had been achieved by the time of his writing.[84] Whateley censured the garden for defects which would be characteristic of later French *jardins anglo-chinois*: a "profusion of ornament" and "elegant decorations."[85] Only in 1807 would a French writer, M. Curten, devote a long and sympathetic description to the place, although he still noted that "it can be said that

---

[78] A. S. de Wimpfen, *Lettres d'un voyageur*, pp. 54-57.

[79] Le Rouge, *Nouveaux jardins à la mode*, cahier i, p. 26.

[80] F. de P. von Hartig, *Lettres sur la France*, pp. 112-118. For the *ferme ornée* see chapter v, pp. 98ff.

[81] J. de Cambry, *Promenades d'automne en Angleterre*, pp. 128-145.

[82] *Ibid.*, p. 130.

[83] Whately, *Observations*, p. 181.

[84] *Ibid.*, p. 161.

[85] *Idem.*

Woburn Farm is perhaps too rich in its divers decorations, which are related to those of the *Jardins ornées.*"[86]

After the Revolution the French pre-Revolutionary attitude toward the English garden lingered on for a time. J. M. Morel, author of the major French treatises on the picturesque garden, never saw an English garden until after the first edition of his work had appeared. He did not, after visiting England, consider that it was necessary to alter the second (1802) edition of his work. In the introduction to this edition he did mention Woburn Farm, Stowe, and Brown's work at Blenheim, and he cited Kew, Stourhead, Wilton, Oatlands, Hagley, and the Leasowes. He criticized the English gardens for artificial expanse and the lack of regard in their design for a specific character (or *genre*).[87]

But with the new century French authors began to see the English gardens with English eyes. A new garden and a new type of gardening design were now recognised. In 1803, G. L. Ferri de San-Constante, with the same critical eye as Morel, would discuss, along with the ornamental garden-park, Stowe, the pastoral farm, the Leasowes, for the first time. Of the Leasowes he noted that "it is designed for the shepherds of Guarini and of Fontenelle. There are no pastures here, no closures, no animals, nor any of the farm buildings which are included in the *genre pastorale. . . .*"[88] (However, Painshill, Kew, Richmond, and Oatlands, among others, were cited by the author as being too ostentatious.) This may be the first admission by the French that the English also designed in the French manner of Moulin-Joli. The French had withdrawn their claims to the creating of their own style of picturesque garden. A few years later Mme. de Genlis, in her memoires, would recall from distant memory the Leasowes and Stowe as two outstanding English gardens, which still had not been equaled in France.[89]

[86] M. Curten, *Essai sur les jardins*, Lyon, 1807, pp. 50-51.

[87] J. M. Morel, *Théorie des jardins* (2nd ed.), pp. cxv-cxxviij.

[88] G. L. Ferri de San-Constante, *Londres et les Anglois*, III, p. 189.

[89] Mme. Brulart de Genlis (Marchionesse de Sillery), *Mémoires*, 1825-1826 (8v.), I, p. 167.

PART II   THE THEORY

CHAPTER III

Gardening Theory: England

One of the earliest and most important of the sources of picturesque gardening theory originated in France. It evolved from the voyages to the East undertaken by French Jesuit missionaries. Attiret's description of the emperor of China's garden, published in 1749, had its roots in this long tradition of Jesuit accounts of travels in China. However, other voyages to the East in the 1740s marked the commencement of a more secular interest in China. Among those undertaking such travels was P. Poivre, who journeyed extensively to the East between 1740 and 1756; material from his reports on China would be incorporated in the 1760s into a system of social and fiscal reform for France. There was P. Osbeck, who returned from China and the East Indies to Stockholm, where in 1758 he delivered a paper on his experiences. There were the voyages to China and the East Indies in 1747 and 1748, possibly undertaken by C. Noble;[1] and the travels of William Chambers to the East—in particular, his latest voyage of 1748-1749, which may have been the inspiration for the first attempt at formulating a theory of the picturesque garden.

Chambers maintained that his *Designs of Chinese Buildings*, published in 1757, was based on his China journey.[2] The main purpose of the work appears to have been to correct the prevailing English taste for chinoiserie: the author stated in his preface that the book was undertaken so that it "might be of use in putting a stop to the extravagencies that daily appear under the name of Chinese, though most of them are inventions, the rest copies. . . ."[3] The major emphasis was on the "authentic" illustrations of Chinese buildings: appended to the discussion were examples of "some of their furniture, utensils, machines, and dresses." It is only at the end of the preface that Chambers says, "The Chinese excell in the art of laying out gardens. Their taste [is] . . . what we have for sometime past been aiming at in England, though not always with success. I . . . hope [my account] may be of some service to our gardeners."[4] This statement is in the tradition of earlier suggestions (by, for instance, Addison

[1] P. Poivre, *Voyage d'un philosophe, ou Observations sur les moeurs et les arts des peuples de l'Afrique, de l'Asie, et de l'Amérique*, Iverdun, 1768; P. Osbeck, "Anledninger til nyttig Uperksamhet under Chinesiska Resor," paper delivered in Stockholm in 1758 (from *Intradestal i Vetenskaps Academien*, II, Stockholm 1756-1758); [C. F. Noble], *A Voyage to the East Indies in 1747-1748*, London, 1762.

[2] For Chambers's two Chinese publications, see R. C. Bald, "Sir William Chambers and the Chinese Gar-

den;" and E. Harris, "*Designs of Chinese Buildings* and the *Dissertation on Oriental Gardening*."

[3] Chambers, *Designs of Chinese Buildings*. See works by E. Edwards and M. Darby, P. Decker, W. and J. Halfpenny, B. Langley, C. Over, T. Wright of Derby, and W. Wrighte cited in the Bibliography and published for the most part in the 1750s, illustrating the proliferation of mid-century English pattern books on garden chinoiserie.

[4] Chambers, *Designs*, pp. b r, v.

and Switzer) that the Chinese garden might be considered as a model for the English garden,[5] but Chambers now granted Chinese design superiority over English practice, which he here implied was defective.

Chambers's famous account "Of the Art of Laying out Gardens among the Chinese," appended to the *Designs*, is brief, only six pages in length.[6] It contains a general description of the art of Chinese garden design. This, according to Chambers, was based on a variety of scenes which could be classified as pleasing, horrid, or enchanted.[7] These categories have their origin not in Chinese gardening theory but in Addison's earlier divisions into the beautiful, the great, and the uncommon. However, where Addison merely suggested that there were parallels in unimproved nature to his categories, Chambers maintained that, although "nature is their pattern," the Chinese artificially heightened natural effects to produce their "scenes." For instance, a rapid underground stream could be utilized to produce a turbulent noise of undetermined origin; the judicious arrangement of buildings and rocks would permit the wind to "cause strange and uncommon sounds"; the Chinese might introduce into their gardens "extraordinary trees, plants, and flowers," and "different sorts of monstrous birds and animals," "impending rocks, dark caverns, and impetuous cataracts," trees which "look as if shattered and blasted by lightening," "buildings in ruins or half-consumed by fire," and "miserable huts."

If the variety and the quality of the experience was heightened artificially by the Chinese, according to Chambers, so was the degree of contrast in the types of scenes presented. The author noted that, among the Chinese, artifices of surprise were included: "dark caverns and gloomy passages, at the issue of which you are, on a sudden, struck with the view of a delicious landscape, enriched with every thing that luxuriant nature affords most beautiful. At other times you are conducted through avenues and walks, that gradually diminish and grow rugged, till the passage is at length entirely intercepted, and rendered impracticable, by bushes, briars, and stones: when unexpectedly a rich and extensive prospect opens to view. . . ." Chambers then briefly discussed scenes for different times of day: the effects produced by water; the optical effects which could be produced by a variation in the size and color of the vegetation—an observation made previously by Laugier in his discussion on gardening;[8] and finally he

---

[5] J. Addison, "Pleasures of the Imagination," no. 414, 25 June 1712 (Bond ed., III, p. 552); S. Switzer, *Ichnographia Rustica*, I, p. xxxviii.

[6] Chambers, *Designs*, pp. 14-19.

[7] However, the "scenes" could be infinitely variable. There were "scenes" even for different times of day, and they could be viewed from different locations, where the effects of the same object might be completely unrelated. Chambers further noted (*ibid.*, p. 18) that "the Chinese gardeners . . . consider a plantation as painters do a picture, and group their trees in the same manner, as these do their figures. . . ."

A second source for Chambers's "scenes" may be N. A. Pluche's *Le Spectacle de la nature*, especially volume II, Dialogue II: "The Parterre" (all references cited are from the 1736-1739 English edition), pp. 85-86. Here Pluche says, "We may diversify the Prospect as much as possible, by passing from one Division of the Gardens to another: New Tastes and new Characters may rise before us. One part presents us with an Air of Grandeur, another has a more sprightly appearance. . . . Another Portion of the Garden, glooms with a solitary savage Air, and qualifies the Mind for the Sedateness of Contemplation. . . . An unfertile Spot, that resounds with the Northern Blasts, may be converted into a Grotto. . . . When we thus can regulate all Plots and Situations in a judicious manner, and are able to compleat each Object by Nature's Model; we may diversify her Aspects and multiply her Beauties."

[8] Laugier, *Essai*, p. 281: "Il faudroit qu'un jardinier fût un excellent peintre, ou du moins qu'il possédât éminemment cette partie de la peinture, qui consiste à bien connoître la sympathie des couleurs différentes & les différents tons de la même couleur; alors il assortiroit la verdure de maniere à causer des surprises, & à nous faire goûter des plaisirs extraordinaires."

noted that the Chinese were not always opposed to straight lines, a method of design that calls to mind French formal gardening.

The essay initiates several new developments in gardening literature. First, the description of the Chinese garden went beyond that of any previous account. Second, the "authentic" account of the Chinese garden was no longer a mere literary curiosity but a potential guide to the realization of an actual garden type. Finally, this was the first essay devoted solely to gardening in which the designing of a garden was considered as purely aesthetic and unequivocally divorced from previous association with the technical aspects of horticulture.

The theories underlying Chambers's description are not unique. Edmund Burke, then editor of the *Annual Register*, included material in the first issues which would supplement his *Enquiry into the Origins of Our Ideas of the Sublime and the Beautiful* (published in the same year as the *Designs*). Montesquieu's essay on taste, written for the *Encyclopédie*, which included comments on natural gardens, was published in an English translation (slightly abridged) in the first (1758) issue of the *Register*.[9] Burke also caused the whole of Chambers's essay to be printed in that issue.[10]

The ties between the theories of Burke and Chambers may be the result of a comprehensive, international outlook and respect for tradition reflected in the work of both men. Burke's attitude was based on a belief (in which the statesman was, interestingly, influenced by Montesquieu) that history was a process in continual evolution, related to custom, habit, and tradition. Thus, at the end of his life, Burke would be strongly opposed to the French Revolution, as a solution based on abstract issues rather than on a historical continuum.[11] Chambers, too, was committed to an international point of view. He was in France shortly after his return in 1749 from his last voyage to the East. During his stay in Paris, if not before, his China journey may well have taken on for him some of the philosophical and social color that was attached by the French to accounts of China.[12] We know that Chambers established and maintained lifelong connections with his French associates. It is even possible that he would have found it difficult not to maintain sympathy with the French after the outbreak of the war in 1756. Indeed, his work must have been sympathetic to the French, for although war had broken out the year before the publication of the *Designs*, the work appeared in French as well as in English,[13] and it was immediately distributed in France, read at the Academy of Architecture,[14]

[9] *Annual Register*, I, 1758, pp. 311-315. For a contemporaneous translation of Montesquieu's *Essay* into English, see chapter II, note 3. Burke's abridged version stresses Montesquieu's rococo emphasis on the necessity for surprise, a quality that is, as was noted in chapter II, close to the quality of contrast in the Sublime.

[10] *Annual Register*, I, 1758, pp. 319-323. See D. Wiebenson, " 'L'Architecture terrible' and the 'jardin anglo-chinois,' " for the relationship of Chambers and Burke.

[11] E. Burke, *Reflections on the Revolution in France*, London, 1790. For Burke's approach to the French Revolution, see C. P. Courtney, *Montesquieu and Burke*, Oxford, 1963, pp. xiii-xiv. In this connection, it is interesting to note that Burke also devoted a large part

of the first volumes of the *Register* to a study of the history of the Seven Years' War. The statesman did not turn seriously to politics until after 1765, when he became secretary to the Marquess of Rockingham, but his concern with history dates from his knowledge of the work of Montesquieu in the mid-1750s (*ibid.*, p. 30). Burke was influenced by the writings of the French philosopher in his own unfinished work, the *Abridgement of Natural History*, written in 1757 (*ibid.*, pp. 46-57).

[12] See chapter V, pp. 101-102. For the dates of Chambers's stay in Paris (1749-1750, 1751-1752) and in Rome, see Eriksen, *Neo-classicism*, p. 141.

[13] See note 16 below.

[14] *Procès-verbaux de l'Académie Royale d'Architec-*

and well received by the French press.[15] Moreover, Chambers's essay on the Chinese garden was considered by the French to be one of the most significant, indeed, probably the most significant, source of the *jardin anglo-chinois*. It was frequently cited, quoted, and reproduced.[16] Hirschfeld later would say that Chambers's *Designs* was "the common fount from which all other descriptions . . . were created."[17] And, finally, Chambers seems to have been associated, at least by one Englishman, with French gardens.[18] Later, when the picturesque garden was considered by many Englishmen as a purely English contribution to the mainstream of European art, Chambers would publish his *Dissertation on Oriental Gardening*, a work devoted solely to the Chinese garden, in which he asked for the blending of what were English and French garden design systems—that is, of the incorporation of both art and nature into a single work.[19] Chambers would face considerable opposition to his new work from some of his countrymen, but Burke would remain a supporter of his ideas.[20]

There is no doubt that Chambers's book is within the tradition of rococo chinoiserie. In the preface to the *Designs* the author stated, "I look upon [the buildings of the Chinese] as toys in architecture: and as toys are sometimes, on account of their oddity, prettyness, or neatness of workmanship, admitted into the cabinets of the curious, so may Chinese buildings be sometimes allowed a place among compositions of a nobler kind."[21] But in the essay, Chambers went beyond the frivolity of the rococo to consider the emotional content which was implied in this style, and which could be achieved by means of associations based on the powers of

---

ture, Paris, 1911-1929 (ed. H. Lemonnier), VII, p. 20, 30 July 1759. See also *ibid.*, VIII, p. 136, 16 November 1772, where J. D. LeRoy read Chambers's later work, the *Dissertation on Oriental Gardening*, to the Academy.

[15] For reviews, see D. Mornet, *Le Sentiment de la nature en France*, p. 227, who notes that immediately after publication of the *Designs* reviews appeared from *Bibliothèque impartiale*, 1757, p. 343, from *Journal étranger*, September 1757, p. 96, and from *Journal encyclopédique*, June 1757, p. 103. Mornet also cites later reviews.

[16] By G. L. Le Rouge, who reprinted the entire work as the fifth volume of his series *Nouveaux jardins à la mode*; by Hirschfeld, *Art des jardins*, I, pp. 94-113, with extensive commentary, and pp. 113-118, although it was his object to prove that the gardens Chambers described did not exist in China; and also by Latapie, in his French translation of Whately's *Observations*, pp. ix-xxiij, where a large section of the *Designs* is printed; by De Lille, *Le Jardin*, pp. 116-126; by Blondel, *Cours*, I, 1771, pp. 149ff., who borrows from the *Designs* for the description of the Chinese garden; and by A. N. Duchesne, *Sur la Formation des jardins*, Paris, 1775, pp. 61-62: "Les idées Chinoises sur la distribution des Jardins, exposées en 1757, par m Chambers . . . on fait en Angleterre & en France un tel progrès, qu'on veut, comme les Chinois, rassembler dans le même Jardin, des scènes riantes, horribles & enchantées, ou Romanesques; les varier, les contraster, & surtout les présenter

comme des accidents naturels heureusement recontrés." And Chambers's description seems to have become a common conception of the Chinese garden by 1788, when A. S. de Wimpfen, *Lettres d'un voyageur*, Amsterdam, 1788, I, p. 55, wrote: "En Chine, un jardin est un amas désordonné de roches, suspendues, d'affreuses cavernes, de cataractes impétueuses, d'arbres et d'édifices brisés et mutilés par la fondre, le tout entremêlé de plantes extraordinaires et d'animaux monstreux."

[17] Hirschfeld, *Art des jardins*, I, p. 82 (all references are to the French text).

[18] A. Young, *Travels in France during the Years 1787, 1788, and 1789*, Bury St. Edmunds, 1792-1794, p. 69, 23 October 1787 (on the *jardin anglo-chinois* at the Trianon): "It contains about 100 acres, disposed in the taste of what we read of in books of Chinese gardening, whence it is supposed that the English style was taken. There is more of Sir William Chambers here than of Mr. Brown—more effort than nature—and more expence than taste. . . . The only fault is too much crouding: which has led to another, that of cutting the lawn by too many gravel walks, an error to be seen in almost every garden I have met with in France."

[19] See below, pp. 50-58.

[20] For Burke's support of Chambers, see Chambers's correspondence on deposit at the British Museum, MS. Add. 41.134, pp. 21b *v.*, 21c.

[21] Chambers, *Designs*, Preface, p. a *v.*

the imagination stimulated by the effects of art. A year before Chambers published his *Designs*, Isaac Ware brought out the first edition of his *Complete Body of Architecture*. Here Ware specified what surely was Chambers's intent in the *Designs*:

> The Chinese, whom we follow as we do the French in follies, may set us glorious examples. While we imitate their bells and lathwork lattices; while every carpenter is employed to erect the painted pavilion in their manner, . . . we do not observe the boldness of their genius, or the happy extravagance of their fancy in the indisposition of their gardens; as much superior to ours, as different from it. . . . The Chinese method, extreamly [*sic*] worthy to be introduced among us, gives every thing, though laboured, the air of native beauty; they value themselves upon breaking in on symmetry and order; and, by the wildness of their fancy, dispose their tufts of thickets in so whimsical a manner, that nature seems outdone in her own freedom . . . .
>
> We read accounts of them with a peculiar pleasure; and wish to tread in our own richer and more pleasant country those fairy rounds and walks of sylvan deities. All appears at the first thought enchantment; we recollect the castles and the forests wherein knights-errants of old time were bred by their magicians; but when we examine the accounts more coolly, there is nothing extravagant, improbable, or impracticable: nature is carried up into extreams, but it is in her own way, by steps we see her every day pursue in her free scenes; and as there is nothing but what we may readily comprehend, so is there no part that we may not imitate.
>
> The materials are in our hands, and the work is easy. Our country is as much above that of the Chinese in its natural aspect, as the genius of our people: we have been misled, but when once set right there is no difficulty in excelling them.[22]

Ware's work suggests the spirit of Chambers's *Dissertation on Oriental Gardening*, which would not be published until 1772. Ware's comments also may be influenced by French sources. The Abbé Laugier, in his *Essai sur l'architecture* published in 1753, like Ware, had called for an infinite variety of effects in gardening, which he maintained would result in the fantasy, caprice, and enchantment of the Chinese garden.

But although there were commitments to picturesque gardening design reflected in Ware's and in other mid-century architectural publications, Chambers's "Art of Laying out Gardens" was almost a solitary contribution to the field of the theory of picturesque gardening literature until the 1770s when the bulk of the work on the new picturesque garden began to appear. However, there are indications, as we shall see below, that Chambers's early work is not an isolated phenomenon but rather an external manifestation of contemporaneous efforts to formulate gardening theory in England (similar to efforts that were taking place at the same time in France), a manifestation which had resulted by the 1750s in several opposing policies toward gardening.

[22] I. Ware, *Complete Body of Architecture*, pp. 645-646.

It is possible that by 1765 a fully developed theoretical approach to the new style of gardening had been achieved, when it is believed that Thomas Whately's *Observations on Modern Gardening*, published in 1770, may have been completed.[23] Whately's thesis was that gardening was entitled to recognition as a liberal rather than as an applied art.[24] His purpose in writing his book was to organize the pragmatically acquired knowledge of picturesque gardening into a comprehensive and systematic body of gardening methodology, typology, and vocabulary. Indeed, so meticulous was Whately's attention to all the aspects of the new style of garden design, that Walpole would later say that Whately "rather exceeds than omits any directions."[25] The work would become the standard treatise on gardens in the new style: no later author could ignore its contribution.[26] In view of its importance, its contents will be discussed in some detail here.

The first section of Whately's work is concerned with the materials—the vocabulary—of gardening. They are divided into the three traditional and natural elements of ground, plants, and water. The division had been made in previous garden literature only in terms of specific functions—hills, fruit trees, lawns, fountains, etc.—and not in terms of categories of elements. Now there was introduced a fourth element, rocks, and one artificial element, buildings. Whately was concerned, not with the practical horticulture which had figured prominently in the majority of gardening books of the seventeenth and eighteenth centuries, but with the picturesque and expressive properties of these basic materials. Thus, ground formations had an original and intrinsic character, which could be modified but not changed;[27] planting could be varied according to "botanical distinctions";[28] water could be adapted to any desired emotional content, from the terror of a torrent to the melancholy of a secluded pool;[29] rocks could express dignity, terror, or fancy, although their principle expression was "wild";[30] and buildings were the most flexible of all the gardening materials—according to Whately, "The peculiar excellence of buildings is, that their effects are instantaneous," that is, that their character could be comprehended immediately.[31] They could be used to distinguish, break, or adorn the scenes to which they were applied, for they would raise and enforce the natural character of the site.[32]

Whately next elaborated on the effects of the use of this vocabulary in garden design. He began by warning that "art was carried to excess, when from accessory it became principle."[33] Such was the case in the formal garden, where ground, wood, and water were "reduced to mathematical figures," similar to those of architecture.[34] The new style of gardening, on the

[23] I. W. U. Chase, *Horace Walpole*, p. 155.

[24] Whately, *Observations*, pp. 1-2.

[25] H. Walpole, "On Modern Gardening," p. 144.

[26] See S. Felton, *On the Portraits of English Authors on Gardening*, London, 1830 (1st ed. 1828), p. 72.

[27] Whately, *Observations*, p. 13.

[28] *Ibid.*, p. 25.

[29] *Ibid.*, pp. 61-62.

[30] *Ibid.*, p. 99.

[31] *Ibid.*, p. 126.

[32] *Ibid.*, p. 118. See also G. L. Hersey, "Associationism and Sensibility in Eighteenth-Century Architecture," *Eighteenth-Century Studies*, IV, pt. i, Fall 1970, pp. 71-89.

[33] Whately, *Observations*, p. 136.

[34] *Idem*. Burke, *Enquiry*, pp. 100-101, previously criticized the formal garden for the same reasons: ". . . there is in mankind an unfortunate propensity to make themselves, their views, and their works, the measure of excellence in everything what soever. Therefore having observed, that their dwellings were most commodious and firm when they were thrown into regular figures, with parts answerable to each other; they transferred these ideas into their gardens; they turned their trees into pillars, pyramids, and obelisks; they formed their hedges into so many green walls, and fashioned

contrary, was a result not of decorative patterns, but of picturesque beauty and character. But picturesque beauty was not achieved by imitating paintings. Indeed, Whately recommended that landscape painting should be referred to only as a model,[35] for he had specific qualifications for the term picturesque, which he felt was "applicable only to such objects in nature as, after allowing for the differences between the arts of painting and gardening, are fit to be formed into groupes [*sic*], or to enter into a composition, where the several parts have a relation to each other; and in opposition to those which may be spread abroad in detail, and have no merit but as individuals."[36] In other words, picturesque meant to Whately an arrangement of several elements in a composition.

Whately then proceeded to discuss character, which for him was composed of different methods of expression, both traditional and modern. He divided character into three categories: emblematic, imitative, and original.[37] Of these, the emblematic was the least susceptible to immediate comprehension, for it involved literary allusions and associations which "must be examined, compared, perhaps explained, before the whole design of them is well understood."[38] Here Whately may have been thinking of the group of "moral gardens" developed in the 1730s.[39] According to him, emblematic character was achieved with "statues, inscriptions, and even paintings, history and mythology, and a variety of devices."[40] He recommended that "though an allusion to a favourite or well-known subject of history, poetry, or of tradition, may now and then animate or dignify a scene, yet the subject does not naturally belong to a garden, the allusion should not be principal; it should seem to have been suggested by the scene: a transitory image, which irresistibly occurred; not sought for, not laboured; and have the force of a metaphor, free from the detail of an allegory."[41]

Imitative character was created "when a scene, or an object, which has been celebrated in description, or is familiar in idea, is represented in a garden."[42] Whately concluded that with this form of character the "affectation of resemblance destroys the supposition of a reality," and the "consciousness of imitation checks the train of thought."[43]

For Whately, original character was the most satisfactory for use in a garden, for here free rein could be given to the imagination: "Certain properties, and certain dispositions of the objects of nature, are adapted to excite particular ideas and sensations; . . . they . . . are obvious at a glance, and instantaneously distinguished by our feelings. Beauty alone is not as engaging as this species of character . . . it aims only at delighting the eye, but the other affects our sensibility."[44] Whately maintained that "the mind is elevated, depressed, or composed, as gaiety,

---

the walks into squares, triangles, and other mathematical figures, with exactness and symmetry, and they thought that if they were not imitating, they were at least improving nature, and teaching her to know her own business. But nature has at last escaped from this discipline and their fetters; and our gardens, if nothing else, declare we begin to feel that mathematical ideas are not the true measure of beauty."

[35] Whately, *Observations*, p. 147. For Whately's full discussion of the relation of painting to gardening, see *ibid.*, pp. 146-150.

[36] *Ibid.*, p. 150.
[37] *Ibid.*, pp. 150-156.
[38] *Ibid.*, p. 151. See also J. D. Hunt, "Emblem and Expression in the Eighteenth-Century Landscape Garden."
[39] For the moral gardens, see chapter II, note 63.
[40] Whately, *Observations*, p. 150.
[41] *Ibid.*, p. 151.
[42] *Idem.*
[43] *Ibid.*, p. 152.
[44] *Ibid.*, pp. 153-154.

gloom, or tranquility, prevail the scene; . . . quitting the inanimate objects which first gave [our passions] their spring, we may be led by thought above thought, widely differing in degree, but still corresponding in character, till we rise from familiar subjects up to the sublimest conceptions, and are rapt in the contemplation of whatsoever is great or beautiful, which we see in Nature, feel in Man, or attribute to divinity."[45] Surely Whately was influenced by Burke, who had written, "we are bound by the condition of our nature to ascend to these pure and intelligent ideas, through the medium of sensible images."[46] Indeed, Whately's work can be seen as a further and more comprehensive carrying-out of the principles stated by Burke in his *Enquiry*, which were first experimentally related to gardening by Chambers in 1757.

There is no doubt that Burke's *Enquiry* was a major contribution to the evolution of picturesque garden theory in the second half of the eighteenth century. Whately and all later theorists are indebted to Burke's emphasis on immediate emotional response, on the importance of the imagination in the abstracting of a general emotional "conception" from a specific object.[47] There is little description of gardening in Burke's work, although Burke did criticize the formal garden for its architectural character,[48] a criticism echoed by Whately; but his description of "the noise of vast cataracts, raging storms, thunder, or artillery, [which] awaked a great and aweful sensation in the mind . . ."[49] may well be the inspiration for Whately's description of the New Weir on the Wye.[50] This description would in turn be elaborated by both Chambers and Watelet.[51] Burke's influence on gardening literature was widespread. It was absorbed into not only Chambers's "Art of Laying out Gardens" and Whately's *Observations*, but also

[45] *Ibid.*, pp. 155-156.

[46] Burke, *Enquiry*, p. 68.

[47] For an alternate interpretation of the origin of "original" or "expressive" character, see Hunt, "Emblem and Expression."

[48] See note 34 above.

[49] Burke, *Enquiry*, p. 82.

[50] Whately, *Observations*, pp. 108-109:

Mines are frequent in rocky places; and they are full of ideas suited to such occasions. To these may sometimes be added the operations of the engines; for machinery, especially when its powers are stupendous, or its effects formidable, is an effort of art, which may be accommodated to the extravagencies of nature.

A scene at the New Weir on the Wye, which in itself is truly great and awful, so far from being disturbed, becomes more interesting and important, by the business to which it is destined. It is a chasm between two high ranges of hill, which rise almost perpendicularly from the water; the rocks on the sides are mostly heavy masses; and their colour is generally brown; but here and there a pale and craggy shape starts up to a vast height above the rest, unconnected, broken, and bare: large trees frequently force out their way amongst them; and many of them stand far back in the covert, where their natural dusky hue is deepened by the shadow which overhangs them. The river

too, as it retires, loses itself in woods which close immediately above, then rise thick and high, and darken the water. In the midst of all this gloom is an iron forge, covered with a black cloud of smoak [*sic*], and surrounded with half burned ore, with coal, and with cinders; the fuel for it is brought down a path, worn into steps narrow and steep, and winding among precipices; and near it is an open space of barren moor, about which are scattered the huts of the workmen. It stands close to the cascade of the Weir, where the agitation of the current is increased by large fragments of rocks, which have been swept down by floods from the banks, or shivered by tempests from the brow; and the sullen sound, at stated intervals, from the strokes of the great hammers in the forge, deadens the roar of the waterfall. Just below it, while the rapidity of the stream still continues, a ferry is carried across it; and lower down the fishermen use little round boats, called truckles, the remains perhaps of the ancient British navigations, which the least motion will overset, and the slightest may destroy. All the employments of the people seem to require either exertion or caution; and the ideas of force or of danger which attend them, give to the scene an animation unknown to a solitary, though perfectly compatible with the wildest romantic situations.

[51] See note 116 below and chapter IV, note 37.

into the anonymously published *Rise and Progress of the Present Taste in Planting*,[52] and even into the section on gardens in Kames's *Elements of Criticism*.[53]

Whately next considered categories of types of picturesque gardens. Previously, the codification of garden types was based on categories of the imagination, as they had been described by Addison in the *Spectator*, and adapted to gardens by Chambers in his 1757 essay.[54] But Whately categorized them according to the practical qualities of size and use: farm, garden, park, and riding. However, his classifications were still related to the earlier ones. The "distinguishing properties" of his first three types—simplicity, elegance, and greatness[55]—are identical to those of Addison's uncommon, beautiful, and great: simplicity, for example, is a quality of original, or unique, which is uncommon. The new category of the riding, pleasantness[56] (variation of scene), is composed of the properties of the other three types.[57]

The park and the garden are traditional garden types. A distinction between them was still made by Switzer and Langley,[58] and Whately, following this convention, discussed them separately. However, by the time Whately's *Observations* appeared, Walpole had proposed a new composite type of garden which is connected with a park,[59] a type descriptive of the actual picturesque garden. Whately continued to recognize, however, the merging of the two types when he described them as, for instance, a park bordering a garden, and a park blended with a garden. What was new in Whately's description of the two types was that it was based on a detailed study of the available vocabulary and of the ways in which it was applied in order to bring out and enhance the character of the particular site. Whately instructed the reader that "the business of the gardener is to select and to apply whatever is great, elegant, or characteristic . . . ; to discover and to shew all the advantages of the place upon which he is em-

---

[52] The *Rise and Progress* has passages which, in turn, seem to have influenced Chambers's *Dissertation*. For instance:

[*Dissertation* (1st ed.), pp. 36-37]: Their scenes of terror are composed of gloomy woods, deep valleys inaccessible to the sun, impending barren rocks, dark caverns, and impetuous cataracts rushing down the mountains from all parts. The trees are ill formed, forced out of their natural directions, and seemingly torn to pieces by the violence of tempests: some are thrown down, and intercept the course of the torrents; others look as if blasted and shattered by the power of lightening. . . . [*Rise and Progress*, p. 25]: Here blasted Pines and ragged Cedars stand, / And desolation covers all the land.

[*Dissertation*, p. 37]: Bats, owls, vultures, and every bird of prey flutter in the grooves. . . . [*Rise and Progress*, p. 26]; Here screech-owls, bats, voracious birds of night, / In solemn stillness sleep secure from sight.

[*Dissertation*, p. 39]: . . . the earth trembles . . . by the power of confined air. [*Rise and Progress*, p. 26]: Dubious we stand what winding wald to

take, / As trembling waves the earth beneath us shake.

[*Dissertation*, p. 40]: His road then lies through lofty woods, where . . . innumerable monkies, cats and parrots clamber upon the trees. . . . [*Rise and Progress*, p. 28]: While Citron, Orange, Rose and Myrtle shades, / Wave pensile o'er the cool pellucid glades; / There Pheasants, Parrots, and Maccaws unfold, / Their many-coloured plumes suffus'd with gold. . . .

[53] A. Home, Lord Kames, "Gardening and Architecture," pp. 302-306.

[54] See p. 40 above.

[55] Whately, *Observations*, p. 157.

[56] *Ibid.*, p. 159.

[57] Whately may have been influenced in his divisions by similar, though not identical, Serlian categories of tragic, comic, and satiric "scenes" for theatrical productions. See chapter 1, note 11.

[58] B. Langley, *Principles of Modern Gardening*, pp. ix-xvi; S. Switzer, *Nobleman, Gentleman, and Gardener's Recreation*, pp. xiii-xiv, xxvi-xxvii; *Ichnographia rustica*, I, pp. xxiv-xxxv.

[59] Walpole, "On Modern Gardening," pp. 117-151.

ployed; to supply its defects, to correct its faults, and to improve its beauties. For all these operations, the objects of nature are still his only materials."[60]

Whately's types of farm and riding are more original. Neither the farm, which was utilitarian, nor the riding, which lay beyond the immediate area of the estate, had been previously considered in gardening theory, although elements of rural vocabulary were included by Langley in one of his designs for ornamental gardens.[61] The farm is the first of the four types to be discussed. Whately subdivided the type "farm" into four separate categories: ornamental, simple, ancient, and pastoral. He was also concerned with historical developments, and he considered the useful/agreeable garden, or the *ferme ornée*, exemplified by Woburn Farm, to be the earliest stage, and the pastoral farm, exemplified by the Leasowes, to be the most recent development of the type "farm."[62] In this latest stage, "the ideas of *pastoral poetry* seem now to be the standard of that simplicity; and a place conformable to them is deemed a farm in its utmost purity."[63] For Whately this "highest" development of the farm was reached when the farm retained only its rural aspect (the Leasowes was "literally a grazing farm lying round the house"),[64] and no longer had any practical function. Literary and emotional associations were substituted for utility. These associations were achieved by means of what may be the ultimate expression of the emblematic character, the use of inscriptions which directed thought toward the particular emotion intended to be evoked at a particular location. However, Whately admitted that "in general, inscriptions please no more than once; the utmost they can pretend to, except when their allusions are emblematical, is to point out the beauties, or describe the effects, of the spots they belong to; but those beauties and those effects must be very faint, which stand in need of this assistance."[65]

According to Hussey, the riding had been developed during the seventeenth century as a wide allée cut through the outlying wooded area of an estate, to facilitate hunting and for carriage rides.[66] In adopting this form for his fourth garden type, Whately considered the property of a riding "to extend the idea of a seat, and appropriate a whole country to a mansion."[67] The riding thus was neither self-contained nor private: it "depends on objects without for its pleasantness,"[68] and even villages might be included within its design.[69] The idea seems novel. It is, however, a variation on the opening-up of the garden to the country which was first suggested by Addison, and was similar to ideas being developed at the same time by, for instance, Chambers and Walpole, which extended the concept of gardening to include public as well as private, and even urban as well as rural, space.[70]

Whately concluded his work with a separate chapter on the seasons. He may be the first theorist on gardening to consider the effects of light, times of day, and the seasons on landscape. His thesis is that every place or building has an appropriate hour, climatic condition, or

---

[60] Whately, *Observations*, pp. 1-2.

[61] Langley, *Principles*, pp. viij-xi, and plate iii ("Design of a Rural Garden"), which includes haystacks and woodpiles.

[62] See chapter v for a discussion of the *ferme ornée* and pastoral farm, as they develop into the two major types of French picturesque gardens.

[63] Whately, *Observations*, p. 162.

[64] *Idem.*

[65] *Ibid.*, p. 170.

[66] C. Hussey, *English Gardens and Landscapes*, p. 15.

[67] Whately, *Observations*, p. 227.

[68] *Ibid.*, p. 159.

[69] *Ibid.*, pp. 230-232.

[70] See pp. 54-55 below, and chapter vi, pp. 114-115.

season in which it is seen to best advantage. His description of the effect of the setting sun on the Temple of Concord and Victory at Stowe suggests the extent of the emotional effect to be achieved by the proper application of his method and vocabulary:

> . . . there is a moment when [the Temple] appears in singular beauty; the setting sun shines on the long colonnade which faces west: all the lower parts of the buildings are darkened by neighboring wood; the pillars rise at distant heights out of the obscurity; some of them are nearly overspread with it; some are chequered with a variety of tints; and others are illumined almost down to their bases. The light is gently softened off by the rotundity of the columns; but it spreads in broad gleams upon the wall within them; and pours full and without interruption on all the entablature, distinctly marking every detail: on the statues which adorn the several points of the pediment, a deep shade is contrasted to splendor; the rays of the sun linger on the side of the temple long after the front is over-cast with the sober hue of evening; and they tip the upper branches of the trees, or glow in the openings between them, while the shadows lengthen across the Grecian Valley.[71]

Whately's examples are based on English gardens for which the designs were begun before 1750 (Moor Park, Ilam, Claremont, Esher, Blenheim, Wilton, Leasowes, Woburn, Painshill, Hagley Park, Stowe, and Persfield), and his work represents a codification of the theory that had developed from experiments with their designs. His examples thus belong to the pre-Brown phase of the evolution of the picturesque garden when the emphasis was on "imitating" nature rather than on "correcting" her. They conform less to contemporary English than to French principles of garden design, and this fact may indicate one reason why Whately's work would become an important source of French gardening theory.[72] Even J. F. Blondel, who was opposed to the new style of garden, placed Thomas Whately in the "first rank, in spite of his taste for the new style."[73] The work was translated into French by F. de P. Latapie in 1771, one year after its English publication, as *L'Art de former les jardins modernes. . . .*[74] In this translation the *Observations* took on a new character. Latapie appended a long "Discours préliminaire" in which he included a letter from Whately describing the kind of French criticism that the *Observations* had already received, and clarified some of his own opinions.[75] The "Discours" also contained a brief history of the background of the picturesque garden, in which Latapie stressed the role of Dufresny in the invention of the type,[76] and quoted extensively

---

[71] Whately, *Observations*, pp. 243-244.

[72] Moreover, Whately, like the French, was not opposed to formal gardens in public spaces; see his letter to Latapie in the French translation of *Observations*, p. liv.

[73] Blondel, *Cours*, IV, p. 14; further praise of Whately's book, *ibid.*, pp. 8-9.

[74] For Latapie, see *Biographie universelle*, XXIII, p. 315. Latapie was educated by Montesquieu at Labrède. He was the companion of the philosopher's son on his trip to Italy, and he visited England in 1770. He completed his career with the occupying of the chair of

the botanical Jardin des Plantes at Bordeaux.

[75] See Bibliography for complete reference. Latapie's and later French criticism of Whately centered around the philosophical, and sometimes obscure, method by which Whately presented his argument, the lack of illustrations to clarify his theory, and the disregard for symmetry. In his letter (pp. lij-lviij), Whately clarified his position on symmetry, which he felt was proper in situations where it conformed to use, such as in public gardens, while his system was designed only for private gardens.

[76] *Ibid.*, pp. vj-viij.

from the one English treatise most sympathetic to French gardening, Chambers's *Designs*.[77] He also included Attiret's long description of the emperor of China's garden,[78] and he followed his translation of Whately's work with his own description of the English garden closest in spirit to that of the French, Stowe.[79] Moreover, throughout the text Latapie added his own notes and observations, providing a French context in which to read the English work.

In Latapie's version, Whately's work became the standard authority on the picturesque garden for the French. Even as the translation appeared in 1771, Walpole wrote; "They have translated Mr. Whately's book and the Lord knows what barbarism is to be laid at our door."[80] And in the same year F. M. Grimm noted that "It is impossible that the English system [of gardening] will not be adopted before long by all nations of taste and sensibility: French symmetry will always be boring, but there is an inexhaustible charm in the system of the English gardens. What will hasten this desirable revolution in France will be the attentive reading of *L'Art de former les jardins modernes*."[81]

One other major English theoretical work on gardening was considered by later French theorists as a seminal work for the development of the irregular French picturesque garden—Chambers's second book on the Chinese garden, *Dissertation on Oriental Gardening*, which was published in 1772 in both English and French.[82] Here Chambers wrote with one major objective in mind. He stated that the book was brought out in reaction to the direction of the recent development of the picturesque garden in England.[83] It was intended, he said, to promote a "judicious mixture" of both the "artful" and the "simple" styles of gardening,[84] as exemplified in a "new system" of gardening achieved in China,[85] where "the usual method of distributing Gardens . . . is to contrive a great variety of scenes, to be seen from certain points of view."[86] This was a principle fundamental, of course, to all theories on the picturesque style. But Chambers was less certain of the natural effects he associated with the "simple" style than were other theorists. In his introduction, he declared that "Chinese Gardeners take Nature for their pattern."[87] However, he continued, "nature . . . affords . . . but few materials to work with. Plants, ground and water, are her only productions . . .";[88] and he concluded that "Art must therefore supply the scantiness of nature."[89]

Chambers's emphasis on art is strengthened by the fact that he opened his discussion of

---

[77] *Ibid.*, pp. ix-xxiij.

[78] *Ibid.*, pp. xxiij-xxxvij.

[79] *Ibid.*, pp. 348-401: "Description détaillée des jardins."

[80] Walpole, *Letters*, VIII, p. 65, 5 August 1771, Walpole to J. Chute.

[81] F. M. Grimm, *Correspondance littéraire*, IX, pp. 348-349, 1 July 1771.

[82] Hautecoeur, *Histoire de l'architecture classique*, V, p. 20, credits a M. de Chaulnes with the French translation of the *Dissertation*. But Chambers (Correspondence on deposit at British Museum, Add. ms. 41.133, p. 101 *v*, Chambers to Le Roy, 4 May 1773), states that the translator was "sieur de la Rochette," and that he was responsible for the "Avertissement du

Traducteur," in the second edition of the *Dissertation*, where he had written in admiration of Chambers's work: "Les jardins de l'Orient tels que M. de Chambers les décrit méritent certainement le nom de Jardins épiques." It is interesting that Morel (*Théorie des jardins*, p. 236), referred to the "pays," such as Ermenonville, as similar to a "poème épique."

[83] Chambers, *Dissertation* (all references are to the first edition, unless otherwise noted), pp. iii-vii.

[84] *Ibid.*, p. vii.

[85] *Ibid.*, p. viii.

[86] *Ibid.*, p. 19.

[87] *Ibid.*, p. 12.

[88] *Ibid.*, p. 14.

[89] *Idem.*

gardens not with natural, but with artificial elements. These were: buildings; grounds "laid out with great regularity, and kept with great care"; sculpture such as statues, busts, bas-reliefs, which "are not only ornamental, but which by commemorating past events, and celebrated personnages, awaken the mind to pleasing contemplation"; and "antient inscriptions, verses, and moral sentences," which are placed on "large ruinated stones, and columns of marble, or engraved on trees and rocks; such situations being always chosen for them, as correspond with the sense of the inscriptions; which thereby acquire additional force in themselves, and likewise give a stronger expression to the scene."[90] Chambers's description is equally applicable to the Leasowes, Moulin-Joli, or to Ermenonville, which was just being developed, and will be discussed in chapter v.

On the other hand, Chambers's opposition to pure nature is strongly brought out in the "Discourse" to the second edition, where he expanded his criticism of the contemporary English style of gardening, whose "excessive simplicity can only please the ignorant or weak, whose comprehensions are slow, and whose powers of combination are confined."[91] In this edition, purity was equated with insipidity:[92] "artists and connoisseurs seem to lay too much stress on nature and simplicity . . . too much nature is often as bad as too little. . . . Whatever is familiar, is by no means calculated to excite the strongest feelings; and though a close resemblance to familiar objects may delight the ignorant, yet to the skilful, it has but few charms, never any of the most elevated sort and is sometimes even disgusting. . . ."[93]

In the "Discourse" he then turned to attack the supporters of the simple style when he stated that his work was not aimed at one person—"yon stately gentleman in the black perriwig" (that is, Capability Brown),[94] but rather at "All connoisseurs . . . [who] agree in despising our enchanted, or supernatural scenery; which, they say, is trifling, absurd, extravagant, abounding in conceits and boyish tricks; that operating chiefly by surprize, it has little or no effect, after a first or second inspection, and consequently can afford no pleasure to the owner: yet our best Artists . . . often introduce it; either where the plan is extensive, and admits of many changes; or, where the ground is barren of natural varieties."[95] And Chambers added in a note: "In China they have an innumerable multitude of connoisseurs and criticks; who, with a very superficial knowledge, a few general maxims, and some hard words, boldly decide on subjects they do not understand; hence the whole fraternity is fallen into disrepute."[96]

There is no doubt that Chambers had written his work in opposition to the empirically trained amateurs, and in support of the trained, internationally oriented professionals. Indeed, he concluded the "Discourse" with a plea for the practice of gardening as a purely professional art. Here he called for "a system much more complicated and dependent on genius, on skill, and on nice judgement, than that which has hither to been pursued." As opposed to William Temple, who, in his 1685 comments on the imitation of the Chinese method of gardening in Europe, had warned gardeners that "there may be more honour if they succeed well, yet there

[90] *Ibid.*, p. 17. For a similar description in the *Encyclopédie* in 1776, see chapter II, p. 28.
[91] *Ibid.* (2nd ed.), p. 147.
[92] *Ibid.* (2nd ed.), p. 148.
[93] *Ibid.* (2nd ed.), pp. 145-146.
[94] *Ibid.* (2nd ed.), p. 157.
[95] *Ibid.* (2nd ed.), p. 155.
[96] *Idem.* (2nd ed.).

is more dishonour if they fail, and it is twenty to one they will,"[97] Chambers declared: ". . . it is at least as glorious to hazard arduous attempts; and more honorable even to fail in manly pursuits, than to succeed in trifling, childish enterprizes. Let the timid or the feeble meanly creep upon the earth, with uniform, sluggard pace; but the towering spirit must attempt a nobler flight, and climb the paths that lead to fame."[98]

Chambers's work must be seen also as a further development of the ideas he first introduced in 1757. For, in the first edition of the *Dissertation*, he enlarged considerably on the sketchy outline of gardening supplied earlier in his "Art of Laying out Gardens." He continued to maintain a basic structure to his method of gardening derived from Addison's characteristics, described as pleasant,[99] terrible,[100] and surprising or supernatural.[101] But at the same time he considered garden types within the two broad areas of natural and "heightened" or artificial gardening. For Chambers, natural gardening was composed of "common scenery."[102] By this he meant a great variety of scenes to be seen from different points of view; and in large gardens, scenes for different times of day and seasons, all chiefly of the "pleasing kind" or falling within Addison's characteristic of "pleasant" or beautiful. The seasons, which had been discussed in detail by Whately separately from his treatment of the characteristics of scenes,[103] were for Chambers the source or inspiration of these scenes. According to him, even these natural scenes were composed of seasonal types of architecture and other artifices with which he was as much concerned as with planting. For winter there were conservatories; for spring, menageries, aviaries, and dairies, and buildings for sports; for summer, ballrooms, banqueting rooms, concert rooms, and pleasure pavilions—here Chambers included Attiret's description of the imitation of a city in the emperor of China's garden;[104] and for autumn there were hermitages, almshouses, ruins, half-buried triumphal arches, mausoleums, and sepulchers, designed to "fill the mind with melancholy, and incline it to serious reflection."[105]

Chambers's discussion of the elements making up "common" scenery is similar in approach to Whately's discussion of gardening vocabulary, although Chambers's does not follow Whately's clear-cut divisions. Indeed, the first topic discussed by Chambers, walks and roads,[106] was not mentioned by Whately. Here, Chambers was opposed to cul-de-sacs and "belts" on the grounds that the first were disappointing termini, and the second, repetitious, although he approved both straight roads and those with natural curves.[107] Furthermore, Chambers considered only three of Whateley's five materials: water,[108] buildings (and bridges),[109] and plants (where, with his botanical recommendations, he was the only writer on the picturesque garden to continue the earlier horticultural tradition of gardening literature).[110] He may have been thinking of Whately's reservations on artifice when he insisted that the many embellish-

[97] W. Temple, "Upon the Gardens of Epicurus; or, of Gardening, in the Year 1685" (ed. S. H. Monk), p. 30.

[98] Chambers, *Dissertation* (2nd ed.), pp. 159-160.

[99] *Ibid.* (1st ed.), p. 35.

[100] *Ibid.*, pp. 36-37.

[101] *Ibid.*, pp. 38-43.

[102] *Ibid.*, p. 35.

[103] *Ibid.*, pp. 22-35.

[104] *Ibid.*, pp. 32-33, and Attiret, letter from *Lettres*

édifiantes, pp. 23-32. See Bibliography for complete reference.

[105] Chambers, *Dissertation* (1st ed.), p. 35.

[106] *Ibid.*, pp. 44-63.

[107] *Ibid.*, pp. 51-52. Even Whately, *Observations*, p. 254, advocates straight walks (for winter walking).

[108] Chambers, *Dissertation* (1st ed.), pp. 63-71, 73-76.

[109] *Ibid.*, pp. 71-73.

[110] *Ibid.*, pp. 77-91.

ments (bridges, pavilions, temples, palaces, and other structures) he recommended would not deprive gardens of "rural character, and give them rather the appearance of splendid cities, than scenes of cultivated vegetation."[111] He maintained that they would be arranged "with art" to "enrich and beautify particular prospects, without any detriment to the general aspect of the whole composition, in which Nature almost always appears predominant...."[112] But the common source for both these writers is Burke's *Enquiry*. This common source would explain the fact that in several instances Chambers appears to have borrowed from Whately's descriptions to illustrate his points. Thus, the introduction of statues and inscriptions and even paintings into gardens[113] is similar to Whately's description of emblematic character; both authors discuss bridges,[114] buildings,[115] and both even mention mines and forges—part of Chambers's vocabulary, in the second edition, for scenes of terror.[116]

However, Chambers's main interest was not in the natural but in the artificial type of gardening. The pleasing scenes in the artificial category were only briefly described. They included all the range, variety, and perfection of nature and art which would "exhilerate the mind, gratify the senses, or give a spur to the imagination."[117] But in his discussion of terrible and surprising scenes, he surpassed even his 1757 descriptions of the fantastic. Some of the more extraordinary effects were "repeated shocks of electrical impulse," "showers of artificial rain," "instantaneous explosions of fire," "cries of men in torment," and "howls of ferocious animals,"[118] which recall Burke's comment that "The angry tones of wild beasts are . . . capable of causing a great and aweful sensation."[119] Among others were air, water, and optical deceptions such as the use of air to "form artificial and complicated echoes,"[120] and an oriental fantasy of "beauteous Tartarean damsels, in loose transparent robes, that flutter in the air, [who] present [the traveller] with rich wines . . . [and] crown him with garlands of flowers. . . ."[121] Later, in the "Discourse" appended to the second edition, Chambers would develop "supernatural Gardening" even further to include "a display of many surprising

[111] *Ibid.*, p. 72.

[112] *Idem.*

[113] *Ibid.*, p. 36, 41-42; Whately, *Observations*, p. 150.

[114] *Dissertation* (1st ed.), pp. 71-73; Whately, *Observations*, pp. 72-77.

[115] *Dissertation* (1st ed.), pp. 23-25; Whately, *Observations*, pp. 116-134.

[116] *Dissertation* (2nd ed.), p. 131; (1st ed.), pp. 36-37:

> . . . the buildings are in ruins; or half consumed by fire, or swept away by the fury of the waters: nothing remaining entire but a few miserable huts dispersed in the mountains, which serve at once to indicate the existence and the wretchedness of the inhabitants. Bats, owls, vultures, and every bird of prey flutter in the grooves; wolves, tigers and jackalls howl in the forests; half-famished animals wander upon the plains; gibbets, crosses, wheels, and the whole apparatus of torture, are seen from the roads; and in the most dismal recesses of the woods, where the ways are rugged and overgrown with weeds, and where every object bears the marks of depopulation, are temples dedicated to the king of vengeance, deep caverns in the rocks, and descents to subterraneous habitations, overgrown with brushwood and brambles; near which are placed pillars of stone, with pathetic descriptions of tragical events, and many horrid acts of cruelty, perpetrated there by outlaws and robbers of former times: and to add to both the horror and sublimity of these scenes, they sometimes conceal in cavities, on the summits of the highest mountains, foundries, lime-kilns, and glass-works; which send forth large volumes of flame, and continued columns of thick smoke, that give to these mountains the appearance of volcanoes.

See A. Kircher, *Mundus subterraneus*, Amsterdam, 1665, especially the section on volcanoes in part i, for a possible source for Chambers's description.

[117] *Dissertation* (1st ed.), p. 36.

[118] *Ibid.*, p. 39.

[119] Burke, *Enquiry*, p. 84.

[120] *Dissertation* (1st ed.), p. 41.

[121] *Ibid.*, p. 40.

phoenomena, and extraordinary effects, produced by air, fire, water, motion, light, and gravitation, they may be considered as a collection of philosophical experiments, exhibited in a better manner, upon a larger scale, and more forcibly than is common."[122] Although these "effects" seem to be an extraordinary product of Chambers's fantasy, many of them are a standard part of the repertoire of theatrical techniques as they were developed in the eighteenth century.[123] Moreover, electricity and artificial thunder were phenomena that had captured the imagination of the contemporary Frenchman.[124] A machine that produced artificial lightning was exhibited in Paris in 1771.[125] It is interesting to note that Chambers's "philosophical experiments" also anticipate nineteenth-century technological expositions.

Chambers defended his recommendation of excessive artificial effects in a letter, written to an unknown gentleman (probably in 1772, following the publication of the first edition of the *Dissertation*),[126] on the grounds that they "make only a small part of my general plan, in which Great Nature, in various forms & under various modifications, always appears triumphant." But it was a Nature closely allied to Art, for Chambers further stated that simplicity "may easily be carried to a blameable excess, & though in general, a close adherence to selected nature, should be recommended, yet there are many occasions [such as, to relieve monotony, to adorn rude and ungrateful tracts of land, and to enliven gardens] where Art, and even whim, may be admitted with propriety and success, if the contriver be a man of taste and judgement."[127]

In the letter, Chambers mentioned one further purpose of his work. He declared that his system was intended "to decorate kingdoms, even the World, & far from attending merely to the narrow views of selfish individuals, I would diffuse the comforts of cultivation to all mankind."[128] He was advocating a universal garden, and an agricultural one! However, the proposition was not novel. Addison in 1712 had suggested the opening-up of the estates to unite with the countryside.[129] By 1771 the prospect had become a common element of the English picturesque garden: it was strongly advocated by Walpole.[130] Chambers was continuing what was by then a well-practiced tradition in both England and France when he declared in the first edition of the *Dissertation* that the Chinese hide "boundaries of their own grounds; and [endeavour] to make an apparent union between them and the distant wood,

[122] *Ibid.* (2nd ed.), p. 157.

[123] Extraordinary and supernatural effects were initiated from the installation by Torelli in 1678 of the Salle des Machines in the Tuilleries. They were developed considerably by Servandoni, who was with the theater in 1724, and took charge of it in 1728. Chambers may have seen, and surely knew, his works. Boucher's activities for the theater are verified for 1744 to 1748 and 1760 to 1766 (see Bjurström, *Torelli*, p. 210).

[124] See, for instance, Rosset, *L'Agriculture*, pt. i, pp. 22-23, 41-42, where the studies of the American, M. Franklin, are mentioned, as well as those of the Frenchman, M. Dalibart, who experimented with creating artificial thunder and lightning at Marli-le-ville.

[125] L. Petit de Bachaumont, *Mémoires secrets*, v, pp. 333-334, 21 July 1771, where the promoting of a machine that generated electricity was undertaken by M.

le Duc de Pecquigny. Bachaumont commented, "il en résulte des éclairs, des foudres artificiels très-curieux."

[126] Chambers's "Letter of Sir William Chambers to a Gentleman who had objected to certain parts of his *Treatise on Oriental Gardening*," is deposited with the Library of the College of Architecture, Cornell University, bound with a copy of the second edition of the *Dissertation*. It is published in R. C. Bald, "Sir William Chambers and the Chinese Garden," pp. 308-310; and J. Harris, *Sir William Chambers*, London, 1970, pp. 192-193.

[127] *Idem.*

[128] *Idem.*

[129] Addison, "The Pleasures of the Imagination," *Spectator*, number 412, 23 June 1712 (Oxford ed., III, pp. 540-542).

[130] Walpole, "On Modern Gardening," p. 146.

fields and rivers."¹³¹ Whately's inclusion of the riding among his garden types is another manifestation of the desire to extend the garden beyond the boundaries of the private country estate. And in 1771, even Walpole had predicted: "If no relapse to barbarism, formality and seclusion is made, what landscape will dignify every quarter of our island, when the daily plantations that are making have attained venerable maturity!"¹³² The union of private with public space was not restricted to a consideration only of the rural countryside; urban spaces were also considered. Chambers's discussion of the inclusion of the village in the emperor of China's garden¹³³ parallels Whately's description of carrying the riding through a village, although Chambers considered his village as more a theatrical than a pictorial device.

But Chambers's vision went beyond the opening-up of the English private estate to the countryside. In the second edition of the *Dissertation*, he wrote that he saw the "whole kingdom" transformed into "one magnificent vast Garden, bounded only by the sea; the many noble seats and villas with which it abounds, would give uncommon consequence to the scenery; and [he continued] it might still be rendered more splendid, if instead of disfiguring ... churches with monuments, [the] Chinese manner of erecting mausoleums by the sides of the roads was introduced ... and if all ... public bridges were adorned with triumphal arches, rostral pillars, bas-reliefs, statues, and other indications of victory, and glorious achievements in war; an empire transformed into a splendid Garden, with the imperial mansion towering on an eminence in the center, and the palaces of the nobles scattered like pleasure-pavilions amongst the plantations."¹³⁴ The description recalls both such imaginary views of ancient Rome as Piranesi's imaginary reconstruction of the Via Appia (Fig. 156),¹³⁵ and such an extensive French royal estate as Marly.

When the second edition of the *Dissertation* was brought out in 1773, Chambers made only a few, but significant, revisions and elaborations of the original text. He heightened his unfavorable description of contemporary English gardening by introducing a critical account of the fashionable serpentine river;¹³⁶ he elaborated in an even more fantastic manner (in spite of his awareness of the reaction to the first edition) on his original description of "scenes" with the descriptions of the Kiao-king (or water palaces),¹³⁷ which may have had a prototype in the "floating islands" of Italian and Dutch gardens,¹³⁸ and the Hoie-ta (or submerged habitations);¹³⁹ and he added new sections on cascades,¹⁴⁰ and the willow.¹⁴¹

But the main addition to the second edition was "An Explanatory Discourse," which Chambers alleged to have been written by a Chinese named Tan Chet-qua, where the "Principles"

¹³¹ *Dissertation* (1st ed.), p. 20.
¹³² Walpole, "On Modern Gardening," p. 148.
¹³³ See note 104 above.
¹³⁴ *Dissertation* (2nd ed.), pp. 133-134. Pluche, *Spectacle*, III, p. 34, also describes a landscape extended into a city in his description of a river which runs through rural scenes and towns where "Rows of lofty structures and costly Palaces on each side grace its Banks." The description is contemporaneous with Meissonnier's similar, brilliant design for the Place Dauphine (see J. Garms, "Projects for the Pont Neuf . . ."). See also chapter VI, notes 10 and 16.
¹³⁵ See chapter VI, pp. 117-118 and note 72.

¹³⁶ *Dissertation* (2nd ed.), p. vii.
¹³⁷ *Ibid.* (2nd ed.), p. 45.
¹³⁸ Duchesne, *Sur la formation des jardins*, p. 79: 'si l'eau trouve un lieu bas, où elle puisse former un petit Etang, on saura y fabriquer une Ile flottant, établie d'abord sur des tonneaux liés en vannerie grossière, pour contenir la terre . . . qui suivant qu'on l'a observé, sont celles qui contribuent la plus à la solidité des grandes Iles flottantes de Flandres & d'Italie."
¹³⁹ *Dissertation* (2nd ed.), p. 73.
¹⁴⁰ *Ibid.* (2nd ed.), p. 85.
¹⁴¹ *Ibid.* (2nd ed.), p. 90.

of the *Dissertation* were "illustrated and applied to Practice." The "Discourse" is, as its title suggests, a further explanation, clarification, and attempt to make practicable the ideas of the *Dissertation*. In it, Chambers made two new, major points. First, he shifted his emphasis away from the artificial and toward the "natural" style of gardening,[142] when he suggested that "wherever there is room to expand, when propriety be introduced," natural gardening would be proper,[143] and he restricted the "richer and more artificial manner" to the proximity of great cities or elegant structures.[144]

Perhaps Chambers's shift in the second edition of the *Dissertation* from exotic artificial effects to equally fantastic but less costly natural effects is a result of criticism of the extravagance of his system. Where he had noted in his first edition that "nothing is too great for Eastern magnificence to attempt: and there can be few impossibilities, where treasures are inexhaustible, where power is unlimited, and where magnificence has no bounds,"[145] he amended the statement in the "Discourse" to read: "That our artificial stile of Gardening is expensive, is doubtless true, yet certainly not ruinously so. In my former voyage, I knew an unfortunate prince, who, on a very moderate allowance from his relations, supported a court in splendour; and with the surplus, formed one of the most extraordinary, as well as magnificent artificial Gardens I ever saw."[146] Surely, when Chambers wrote these lines, he was thinking of Laugier's description of Stanislaus's designs for his estates, with which the Abbé concluded his discussion of gardening in the *Essai*.[147] It may be that Chambers had seen these gardens when he was in France.[148]

The second new point Chambers made in the second edition of the *Dissertation* was to recommend French gardening design to English designers. He had already suggested that many traits of the formal garden be included in the natural garden: for example, the use of straight lines, which were supposed to produce grandeur,[149] and of regular, geometrical figures which are "beautiful in themselves."[150] He had proposed also that the hedges bordering walls be clipped, in a manner "common in most countries in Europe," although he did urge that "the

---

[142] *Ibid.* (2nd ed.). However, when discussing the transformation of the landscape by natural means, Chambers's fantasies were as great as they had been for the artificial style (*ibid.*, pp. 130-132): among the more extraordinary devices that he suggested was the treatment of "commons and wilds, dreary, barren and serving only to give an uncultivated appearance to the country, particularly near the metropolis" which could be formed into scenes of terror, composed of "gibbets, with wretches hanging . . . upon them; [or] . . . forges, colleries, mines . . . and different objects of the horrid kind. . . . The cottagers, with the huts in which they dwell, want no additional touches, to indicate their misery: a few uncouth straggling trees, some ruins, caverns, rocks, torrents, abandoned villages, in part consumed by fire, solitary hermitages, and other similar objects, artfully introduced and blended with gloomy plantations . . . stone quarries, chalk pits, mines . . . [which] might be converted into the most romantic scenery imaginable, by the addition of some planting, intermixed with ruins, fragments of sculpture, inscrip-

tions, or any other little embellishments; and, in short, there would be no deviation, however trifling, from the usual march of nature, but what would suggest, to a fruitful imagination, some extraordinary arrangement, something to disguise her vulgarity, to rouse the attention of the spectator, and to excite in his mind a succession of strong and opposite sensations."

[143] *Ibid.* (2nd ed.), p. 161.

[144] *Ibid.* (2nd ed.), p. 142.

[145] *Ibid.* (1st ed.), p. 93.

[146] *Ibid.* (2nd ed.), p. 149.

[147] Laugier, *Essai*, pp. 291-293; and see chapter 1, pp. 13-14.

[148] Chambers, *Designs*, p. 16, had mentioned Chinese interest in hydraulics (an interest also shared by Stanislaus): "They frequently erect mills, and other hydraulic machines, the motions of which enliven the scene."

[149] *Dissertation* (1st ed.), p. 15.

[150] *Ibid.*, pp. 15-16.

shears be used sparingly."[151] Chambers even referred specifically to French gardening when he commented, "I have often seen, in China, *berceaus* and arbours, not of lattice-work, as in France, but of bamboo, hazel, and elm."[152] But now in the "Discourse" he included a long description of the French garden, close to Ware's description of the Chinese garden, quoted above. He noted that "every recess is the retreat of a God, every prospect a scene of enchantment; . . . in their best works there is such a mysterious, pleasing intricacy in the disposition, such variety in the objects, so much splendour and animation in the execution of every part, that the attention of the spectator never flags; the succession is so rapid, that he is hurried on from one exhibition to another, with his mind constantly upon the stretch: he has only time to be pleased; there is no leisure to reflect, none to be disgusted with the extravagence of what he sees; . . . there are many things to be borrowed from them, which might be adopted . . . with considerable advantage."[153] He also recommended the Italian and even the unfavored Dutch manner of gardening: "There should be meats for every palate . . . that all may find something to their liking, and none go away disappointed or dissatisfied. . . ."[154]

The work was surely not in the spirit of contemporary taste. Chambers was well aware of this, for he wrote to his friend, the French architect J. D. Le Roy, "With regard to my book on Gardening, you will find many Singular Ideas in it and in general a System that resembles so little those that are adopted in Europe that I have not dared to own the work. It is better that Criticism falls on the Chinese than on me."[155] It has been suggested that the French turned to Chambers's publications, and especially to the illustrations of his one actual garden at Kew as a source for their own garden designs.[156] Not only was his published work readily available; it was also the most in sympathy with the concepts of the French, even though Chambers alone of all English garden theorists was singled out in France for criticism because of the theatrical and imitative devices he suggested for gardening, and this despite the fact that it was precisely these devices which would be developed for the *jardin anglo-chinois*. Perhaps Chambers was influenced by the rococo gardens he saw in France when he visited there in 1749-1750 and 1751-1752, or perhaps he acquired a knowledge of them from French visitors to London. The closest equivalent to Chambers in France was Carmontelle, the designer of Monceau, who wrote in the prospectus to his book on this garden that he wished to make Monceau "a garden . . . based on fantasy, . . . the extraordinary, and the amusing, and not on the desire to imitate a Nation which, in designing natural Gardens, spoiled nature by composing gardens without imagination." Carmontelle cited Chambers's *Dissertation* as the source and support for his argument,[157] and his opposition to the English garden was in part an opposition, like Chambers's, to gardens in the style of Capability Brown.

But Chambers's work may have been far more than a source for French interpretations of the picturesque garden. The projected works of the architect E. L. Boullée are also related

---

[151] *Ibid.*, p. 50.

[152] *Idem.*

[153] *Ibid.* (2nd ed.), pp. 150-151. Compare Ware's description, p. 43 above.

[154] *Ibid.* (2nd ed.), p. 156.

[155] Chambers, Correspondence deposited in the British Museum, MS. Add. 41.113, p. 85 *r*, Chambers to Le Roy, 18 September 1772.

[156] Mosser, "Menars."

[157] Carmontelle, Prospectus to *Jardin de Monceau*, p. 2.

to Chambers's *Dissertation*.[158] Among the structures Chambers proposed for his summer scenes were some called "Miau Ting," or Halls of the Moon, "of a prodigious size; composed each of one single vaulted room, made in the shape of a hemisphere; the concave of which is art-fully painted, in an imitation of a nocturnal sky, and pierced with an infinite number of little windows, made to represent the moon and the stars, being filled with tinged glass, that admits the light in the quantities necessary to spread over the whole interior fabric the pleasing gloom of a fine summer's night."[159] The Miau Ting is surely related to Boullée's cenotaph to Newton, designed in 1784.

The decoration of the interior of the Miau Ting was equally exotic. Chambers wrote that "The pavements of these rooms are sometimes laid out in parterres of flowers; amongst which are placed many rural seats, made of fine formed branches, varnished red to represent coral: but oftenest their bottom is full of a clear running water, which falls in rills from the sides of a rock in the center; many little islands float upon its surface, and move around as the current directs; some of them covered with tables for the banquet; others with seats for the musicians; and others with arbors, containing beds of repose, with sophas, seats, and other furniture, for various uses." The description may be a source for the interior of the dining hall in the Hameau of Chantilly (Fig. 106), designed only three years after the appearance of Chambers's work, or for the *jardin d'hiver* at Monceau (Fig. 90), which may have been designed contemporane-ously with the publication of Chambers's work.[160] Ganay has noted that the floating islands and underground grottos in at least several of the most important French *jardins anglo-chinois* are related to Chambers's descriptions,[161] and one wonders if the fantasies of Lequeu would have been possible without the previous work of the English architect.[162]

When the reaction against the *jardin anglo-chinois* began, this type of garden was associated with the main figure connected with it: William Chambers. The condemnation of the excesses of both Chambers's descriptions of Chinese gardens and of the *jardin anglo-chinois* was taken up in earnest only after the Revolution,[163] but one early and extreme criticism of his work, delivered somewhat irrationally in 1787 by C. P. A. Lezay-Marnésia, cannot escape comment here. Lezay-Marnésia referred to the English as a melancholy people who, rather than listening to the wise principles of Whately (Wathely), turned to the gigantesque ideas of Chambers (Chambertz), who, seduced by the oriental taste, had destroyed all proportions and forced

[158] Wiebenson, " 'L'Architecture terrible.' "

[159] *Dissertation* (1st ed.), pp. 30-31.

[160] L. V. Thièry, *Guide*, I, pp. 65-66: "Parmi les arbustes groupés sur ces roches sont des raquettes & des coraux factices, dont les tubes creusés servent à placer des bougies le soir. . . . Sur le mur du fond de cette galerie . . . sont peints des marroniers d'Inde chargés de fleurs: de l'autre côté, sont de pareils arbres: leurs troncs sculptés & colorés servent de supports au vitraux, & leurs branches s'étendent pareillement sur la voute peinte en ciel. De distance en distance sont des lanternes de cristal censées suspendues à leurs rameaux." For Chantilly, see also chapter v, note 58 and (for bibliog-raphy) note 99.

[161] Ganay, *Les Jardins à l'anglais en France*, II,

p. 368.

[162] See J. J. Lequeu, *L'Architecture*, collection of drawings by the architect on deposit at the Biblio-thèque Nationale, Ha.80-Ha.80.d.

[163] For the decline of interest in the Chinese garden, and the coupling of Chambers's name with that of the *jardin anglo-chinois*, see E. von Erdberg, *Chinese In-fluence on European Garden Structures*, Cambridge, Mass., 1936, p. 40, n. 4, who cites H. Repton, *Art of Landscape Gardening*, Cambridge, Mass., 1907, pp. 166, 239, n. 38; G. W. Johnson, *A History of English Gar-dening*, London, 1829, p. 212; and P. Boitard, *Traité de la composition et de l'ornement des jardins*, Paris, 1825 (3rd ed.), pp. 3, 5-6.

all effects. The great and the beautiful had been changed by him into the ridiculous. In fact, according to Lezay-Marnésia, Chambers had prescribed the impossible and piled up exaggerations which would be repulsive in the Thousand and One Nights.[164]

In England, opposition to Chambers's *Dissertation* began with the anonymous publication in March, 1773, of *An Heroic Epistle to Sir William Chambers*, written by William Mason.[165] The controversy that this work stirred up was intense enough to cause friends to write to Chambers offering to defend the *Dissertation*.[166] But Chambers declined help, declaring that the *Epistle* was "not worth the answer,"[167] that defense would "keep up the ball longer,"[168] and that "the great torrent of [Masons's] wit is aimed at what doth not belong to me; that is, Peking in miniature, taken from Father Attiret's account."[169] He also felt that Mason's "nonesense makes mine circulate; this first Epistle has sold a large quantity of my dissertations, and I think a second equally seasoned with abuse and wit, would sell the whole second Edition, directly."[170] But Chambers was not unaffected by the debate. In a letter to Lord Grantham, he wrote, "Last year I had prepared a copy of my little book on gardening then just published for your Lordships perusal: but the claps and hisses were for some time so equal, that I grew ashamed of the present, and threw it away, the book [has] however, in less than a year, been damned through two English editions, and applauded through one in french; and while furiously abused by some connoisseurs of the age, it has been as furiously defended by others."[171]

Mason had begun publishing a long poem on the English garden in 1768, and the work—modeled, according to Mason, in part on the principles of Rousseau—would achieve considerable popularity in its French translation in 1788.[172] Mason's *Epistle* was, however, not a critique of gardening but a satire in which Chambers's *Dissertation* was used as an excuse for discussing primarily political topics. However, Mason did make several specific statements about Chambers's work. He complained that "it is the author's profest aim in extolling the taste of the Chinese, to condemn that mean and paltry manner which Kent introduced; which Southcote, Hamilton, and Brown followed, and which, to our national disgrace, is called the English style of gardening,"[173] and he poked fun at Chambers's enchanted scenes,[174] his interest in monumentality and grandeur,[175] his advocating of straight lines in planning,[176] and his extending of the possibilities of garden design to include urban as well as rural situations.[177]

[164] Marquis C. F. A. de Lezay-Marnésia, *Essai sur la nature champêtre*, pp. 34-35.

[165] [W. Mason], *An Heroic Epistle to Sir William Chambers*. The 13th edition (London, 1774) will be cited here.

[166] Chambers, Correspondence, British Museum, MS. Add. 41.334, pp. 21b/21c, n.d., correspondence between Chambers and Goldsmith; pp. 19 r, v, 24 March 1773, correspondence between Leake and Chambers.

[167] *Ibid.*, p. 21b.

[168] *Ibid.*, p. 19 r.

[169] *Ibid.*, p. 19 v.

[170] *Idem.*

[171] *Ibid.*, p. 33 v., Chambers to Lord Grantham, 13 August 1773.

[172] See Mason, *The English Garden*, 1778 ed., bk. 4,

p. 20, where Mason notes that Acander's garden was modeled on Rousseau's description of Julie's garden in *Héloïse*.

[173] Mason, *Epistle*, Preface, p. 3. For the quarrel, see also R. C. Bald, "Sir William Chambers and the Chinese Garden," esp. p. 92; I. W. U. Chase, "William Mason and Sir William Chambers' *Dissertation on Oriental Gardening*," (excluding discussion of the political side of the quarrel); and J. Draper, *William Mason, a Study in Eighteenth-Century Culture*, New York, 1924, pp. 232-246 (political analysis).

[174] Mason, *Epistle*, p. 10.

[175] *Ibid.*, p. 13.

[176] *Ibid.*, pp. 13-14.

[177] *Ibid.*, pp. 4, 14.

The point of view to which Mason subscribed may have originated some twenty years before he wrote his *Epistle*. During the 1750s and 1760s a group of dilettantes were formulating a theory of garden design that was based on the claim of an English origin for the picturesque garden. Early indications of this nationalist viewpoint appeared in the *World* from 1753 to 1755. They centered around the essays of three contributors: Horace Walpole, Richard Owen Cambridge, and Francis Coventry.[178] Of their contributions, one by Cambridge, published on 3 April 1755, is the most significant for our purposes. It has approximately the same relationship to Walpole's history of gardening ("On Modern Gardening") as Chambers's "Art of Laying out Gardens" has to his later *Dissertation*. In the article, Cambridge discussed the historical development of garden design: he considered the gardens of antiquity to be unimpressive, and the gardens of "LeNautre" to be "shackled by lines and regularity . . . elegance and taste . . . overlaid by magnificence."[179] In contrast to Chambers, who, in his *Designs* and later in his *Dissertations*, thought contemporaneous English methods of gardening were defective, Cambridge stated that "It is the peculiar happiness of this age to see these just and noble ideas brought into practice, regularity banished, prospects opened, the country called in, nature rescued and improved, and art decently concealing herself under her own perfections." And, finally, Cambridge stressed the importance of the original English contribution to the picturesque garden when he maintained that "Whatever may have been reported, whether truly or falsely, of the Chinese garden, it is certain that we are the first of the Europeans who have founded this taste." Walpole had already remarked in the *World* that "Kent, the friend of nature, was the Calvin of this reformation [in gardening] . . . ,"[180] implying that the picturesque garden had a purely English origin.

We catch only glimpses of the development of these ideas on gardening during the 1760s. In 1762 Walpole wrote to George Montgomery that he had turned from the Chinese to the Gothic taste.[181] And in 1763 Thomas Gray wrote to William Taylor How, ". . . the only taste we can call our own, the only proof of our original talent in matters of pleasure; I mean, our skill in gardening, & laying out grounds. that the Chinese have this beautiful Art in high perfection, seems very probable from the Jesuit's Letters, & more from Chambers's little discourse publish'd some few years ago, but it is very certain, we copied nothing from them nor had anything but nature for our model. It is not forty years, since the Art was born among us; and it is sure, that there was nothing in Europe like it. & as sure, we then had no information on this head from China at all."[182]

Now, Walpole was in correspondence with William Mason about Chambers's *Dissertation*, and he was connected with Mason's production of the *Epistle*.[183] And Walpole, not Mason,

[178] E. Manwaring, *Italian Landscape in Eighteenth-Century England*, p. 143. It is interesting to note that these English garden views of the 1750s attracted some attention in France: see "Variations dans le goût des Jardins de l'Angleterre" (translation from the *World*) in *Journal Oeconomique*, January 1754, no. 66, pp. 171-174.

[179] *World*, III, no. 118, pp. 84-89, 3 April 1755. Also see R. Cambridge, *Works*, London, 1803, pp. 476-481.

[180] *World*, I, no. 6, p. 37, 8 February 1753. Also see Walpole, *The Works of Horatio Walpole, etc.*, London, 1798-1815 (9v.) (ed. R. Berry), I, pp. 148-150.

[181] Walpole, *Letters*, v, p. 274, 24 September 1762.

[182] T. Gray, *Correspondence of Thomas Gray* (ed. P. Toynbee and L. Whibley), Oxford, 1971, II, p. 813, 10 September 1763.

[183] See W. Mason, *Satirical Poems*, pp. 10-17.

was the major figure of the opposition to Chambers's gardening system. Walpole's "On Modern Gardening," in which his point of view is thoroughly aired, was first published in 1771,[184] but it was a product of many years of thought, and it probably circulated widely before its publication.[185] Walpole's orientation was national. Like Cambridge and Gray he looked no further back for the source of the picturesque garden than Kent, who "leaped the fence, and saw that all nature was a garden."[186] Walpole was critical of the formal garden; his comments are similar to those of Whately: "Art . . . became the means of opposing nature."[187] At the same time, recalling Addison, he remarked that the "good sense in this country had perceived the want of something at once more grand and more natural."[188] In his essay on gardening, Walpole presented a consistently negative picture of the earlier suggested models for the picturesque garden that had been recorded in gardening literature. According to Walpole, Alcinoüs's garden was small and utilitarian,[189] the hanging gardens of Babylon were "trifling, of no extent, and a wanton instance of expence and labour," as well as being "anything but verdant and rural;"[190] and, in spite of Castell's remarks on Pliny's Tuscum in 1728 (where Castell described an area devoted to the artificial imitation of nature),[191] Walpole asserted that Pliny's garden was wholly based on the "Dutch principles" of the condemned topiary garden.[192] He was even critical of the more artificial early eighteenth-century English gardens; later, in his notes to Mason's *Satirical Poems*, he would single out for criticism for its expense and fantasy an earlier English experimental garden, Woburn Farm.[193] And, finally, Walpole noted that the Chinese garden had "no more pretention to be deemed natural than a lineal terrass or parterre."[194] He criticized Attiret's description of the emperor of China's garden in terms which recall the *jardin anglo-chinois*: ". . . except undetermined irregularity, I can find nothing in it that gives me any idea of attention being paid to nature; . . . this pretty gaudy scene is the work of caprice and whim, and . . . presents no image but that of unsubstantial tawdriness. . . . This is the childish solace and repose of grandeur, not a retirement from affairs to the delights of rural life."[195]

While, on the one hand, Walpole divorced himself from older gardening literature with its accounts of historical precedent, he is, on the other hand, the first writer to consider the recent origins and development of the picturesque garden. His analysis is simplistic but basic. He marks as stages in the origin and development the "garden that connects itself with a park" (following the invention of the ha-ha),[196] the recognition of rural vocabulary within a garden (Woburn Farm), to the development of the truly "natural" or "savage" forest—a "kind of alpine scene."[197] Walpole's interpretation of history, in which he specifies the differences

[184] For the date of the editions of Walpole's essay on gardening, and its various titles, see Chase, *Horace Walpole*, pp. xix-xx.

[185] Dr. Michael McCarthy has noted a French translation of Walpole's history, dating from around 1770, at the Henry E. Huntington Library, San Marino, California.

[186] Walpole, "On Modern Gardening," p. 138.

[187] *Ibid.*, p. 124.

[188] *Ibid.*, p. 126.

[189] *Ibid.*, p. 119.

[190] *Ibid.*, p. 120.

[191] R. Castell, *Villas of the Ancients*, pp. 116-118.

[192] Walpole, "On Modern Gardening," p. 121.

[193] Mason, *Satirical Poems*, pp. 39-40.

[194] Walpole, "On Modern Gardening," p. 134.

[195] *Ibid.*, pp. 134-135.

[196] *Ibid.*, p. 137.

[197] *Ibid.*, p. 143.

of periods and places, predicts nineteenth-century historicism, while Chambers's work, echoing Burke (and recalling Castell's study in which different stages of the development of the garden were presented simultaneously), still implies a composite, universal knowledge.

Walpole was not wholly opposed to the point of view expressed in Chambers's *Dissertation*. His theories and those of Chambers came from a common background. Thus, like Chambers, Walpole divided gardening into three types based on Addison's categories of the imagination: a garden which connects itself with a park (beautiful), an ornamental farm (uncommon), and a forest or savage garden (grand).[198] He chose not to adopt Whately's four functional categories—although he favorably mentioned Whately,[199] and considered it necessary to justify the fact that his types differed from those of Whately by noting that he had chosen them as "being in the historic light."[200] Walpole had approved not only Whately's work, but also the anonymously published *Rise and Progress of the Present Taste in Planting Gardens* of 1767, a work which appears to have been influenced by Chambers's *Designs* and is related to his *Dissertation*,[201] referring to them as acceptable and even commendable garden treatises.[202] And, as we have seen, he anticipated with pleasure the turning of the whole countryside into a landscape garden, one of Chambers's main theses in the *Dissertation*.[203]

Moreover, Walpole was not opposed to the use of the artificial style in an urban setting, precisely the situation for which Chambers had recommended it (and which, as we have seen, seems to have been generally acceptable for the *jardin anglo-chinois*). Walpole recommended artifices such as trellis work, espaliers, vases, fountains, and caryatides as being "elegantly symmetrical, and proper for the narrow spaces allotted to the gardens of a house in a capital city."[204] Indeed, the one real and irreconcilable difference between the two theories is between Chambers's stress on tolerance, scope, and contrast, and the view expressed by Walpole in the statement that: "there is a more imminent danger that threatens the present . . . I mean the pursuit of variety. . . . We have discovered the point of perfection. We have given the true model of gardening to the world; let other countries mimic or corrupt our taste; but let it reign here on its verdant throne, original by its elegant simplicity, and proud of no other art than that of softening nature's harshness and copying her graceful touch."[205] Walpole is writing as an amateur, and deliberately turning from the internationally oriented professional training which Chambers considered to be essential to garden designers.

In 1794, Sir Uvedale Price remarked, "It seems to me that there is something of patriotism in the praises Mr. Walpole and Mr. Mason have bestowed on English gardening; and that zeal for the honour of their country has made them, in the *general* view of the subject, overlook defects which they have themselves condemned. My love for my country is, I trust, not less ardent than theirs, but it has taken a different turn; and I feel anxious to free it from the dis-

---

[198] *Ibid.*, p. 145.
[199] *Ibid.*, p. 144.
[200] *Ibid.*, pp. 144-145.
[201] See note 52 above.
[202] Chase, *Horace Walpole*, p. 16 (note by Walpole to the 1782 edition of his essay on gardening), and p. 150 (where Chase notes that the *Rise and Progress*

is included by Walpole in his *Collections of the Most Remarkable Poems Published in the Reign of George III*, Strawberry Hill, 1767).
[203] See p. 54 above.
[204] Walpole, "On Modern Gardening," p. 122.
[205] *Ibid.*, pp. 146-147.

grace of propagating a system, which, should it become universal, would disfigure the face of all Europe."[206] Price surely put his finger on the conscious national bias to Walpole's concern about gardening, for Walpole himself had written in 1779 in his Notes to Mason's *Satirical Poems*, "the reason why Taste in Gardening was never discovered before the beginning of the present Century is, that it was the result of all the happy combinations of an Empire of Freemen, an Empire formed by Trade, not by a military and conquering Spirit, maintained by the valour of independent Property, enjoying long tranquility after virtuous struggles, & employing its opulence & good Sense on the refinements of rational Pleasure. Let it be considered that the Composition of our Gardens depends on Wealth, on extended possession, on the beauties & animation of Agriculture, Farming, and Navigation. Walls are thrown down to admit the prospect of inclosures, villages, great roads & moving life. What would be the View from a Nobleman's gardens in an arbitrary monarchy, if views of the country were called in? —Desolation, poverty, misery, barren rocks, & plains covered with thistles."[207] Perhaps it is in this sense, of peace and plenty within a republican system of government, rather than as an aesthetic decision that we must consider Walpole's statement: "Prospect, animated prospect, is the theatre that will always be the most frequented."[208]

However, in spite of Walpole's considerable national bias against French and for English gardening, his essay seems to have played an important role in French gardening theory.[209] It received its official translation by the Duc de Nivernais in 1784, and it would strongly influence Hirschfeld in his five-volume *Theorie der Gartenkunst*, which began publication in 1779 in both French and German, at the moment of the French reaction to the overly elaborate *jardin anglo-chinois*.

[206] U. Price, *Essay on the Picturesque*, 1, p. 275.
[207] Walpole, Notes to Mason's *Satirical Poems*, p. 44.
[208] Walpole, "On Modern Gardening," p. 146.
[209] See note 185 above; and M. J. Dumesnil, *Histoire des plus célèbres amateurs françaises*, Paris, 1858, 1, pp. 211-212, for a French translation by J. P. Mariette of Walpole's *Lives of the Painters*, begun in 1764.

CHAPTER IV

Gardening Theory: France

French works on gardening theory published after 1770 must be considered within the context of the English publications. They fall into two groups: those that absorbed Whately's method within a particularly French context, and those that developed the theatrical and universal concepts of Chambers. Of these, the two most important works in the field, and, indeed, the bulk of the written material produced, fall into the first category.

The first French work on picturesque gardening to be published was Watelet's *Essai sur les jardins*. The author intended the book to be a part of a larger aesthetic treatise in which rules of taste would be set out for all the arts.[1] The *Essai* appeared in 1774,[2] and it was important enough to permit Hirschfeld to state that the work caused French gardens in the new style to be submitted to the rules of good sense and of taste,[3] and for Le Camus de Mezières to dedicate his own work on architectural decoration to Watelet, whose "Essay on gardens recalls the Golden Age."[4]

The topics discussed by Watelet in his book are similar to those mentioned by Whately, and also common to both authors is the belief that works of art should not only please the senses but should also produce sentiments and form impressions on the spirit and the soul.[5] But the French author's work is considerably different in its method and emphasis from that of its English predecessor. First, as opposed to the strong impact the philosophy of Burke had on English gardening theory, Watelet was influenced by the philosophy of Rousseau. Second, Watelet's work is a contribution to a French effort to relate new concepts of nature to the French tradition of formal gardening. And, finally, Watelet wrote his work for those who amused themselves with the embellishing of their gardens—that is, for the amateur[6] (indeed, much of his work is based on observations he made while designing Moulin-Joli). Thus his account is looser and more personal than that of his English colleague. In the *Essai*, the author has attempted to merge several theoretical systems which are related to French academic training and architectural theory, but not with complete success: the many characters and subjects, genres and characteristics are not clarified or related in a single system. But whatever its de-

[1] Grimm, *Correspondance littéraire*, x, p. 522, December 1774.

[2] For Watelet, see Bibliography: Individual Gardens. Moulin-Joli.

[3] Hirschfeld, *Art des jardins*, i, pp. 153-154.

[4] N. Le Camus de Mezières, *Le Génie de l'architecture, ou l'analogie de cet art avec nos sensations*, pp. iij-iv.

[5] Watelet, *Essai*, p. 2.

[6] *Ibid.*, p. 3.

fects, the work occupies a position in the forefront of the development of French picturesque gardening design and theory.

Watelet began his book with a discussion of the historical development of the garden from natural, to artificial, to natural-artificial, which is rooted in early eighteenth-century gardening theory, but to which is added a new socially oriented interpretation. Watelet stated that the first rural establishments were purely utilitarian, that they were subject to the unchanging laws of nature, and that they were the least influenced by the mechanical arts.[7] But with the introduction of industry and power, inequalities were produced in society and in the ownership of land. Then only the richest estate owners possessed an excess of wealth and the leisure with which to enjoy it.[8] The "turbulent occupations" by which the powerful maintained their wealth did not transform deserts into cultivated land, or the countryside into a garden—it was the cultivators of the land (the workers) who achieved this.[9]

Watelet was of the opinion that gardening had developed in two directions, toward the natural and toward the artificial. But unlike Chambers, who in making a similar distinction earlier explained it on the basis of topographical characteristics, the French writer interpreted the two currents as a reflection of social contrasts related to the differences between rural and city life. This social opposition gave rise to the establishment of two kinds of gardening. The older (rural) kind was related by Watelet to, for instance, the orchard and kitchen garden of Alcinoüs,[10] and was governed by laws of hospitality, expressing a sentiment springing from nature. The most recent (urban) kind was based on "ostensive vanity," an artificial sentiment springing from society.[11] These mechanical and artificial gardens were located in the dwellings of the great, inhabited by people of an artificial sensibility. Their estates resembled cities to Watelet,[12] who expressed his repugnance for urban society, where "phantoms pass for reality ... the delerium of pride, ambition, and cupidity is the most natural state."[13] Later in the *Essai* he would say that cities ("des Capitales") were the "... foyers of accelerated movement, laboratories for the composing of artificial pleasures for men who are separated from Nature. Here is found in the greatest abundance, superfluity, which is badly used, leisure, which is often lost, imaginary passions, infinite needs, exhausted desires, pretentions substituted for real sentiments."[14]

Watelet considered that picturesque, poetic, and romantic inventions were generally used to enrich gardens. But he believed only pastoral inventions were suitable for embellishing the country.[15] Although the older type of pastoral embellishment, the *pastoral ancien*, was outmoded, its modern equivalent, the *pastoral moderne*, could be applied to a country residence, where there would be a combination of utilitarian structures designed also to be agreeable,[16] and with which the modern owner, by means of modern industry and with developed taste

---

[7] *Ibid.*, p. 10.
[8] *Ibid.*, p. 11.
[9] *Ibid.*, p. 12.
[10] *Ibid.*, p. 17.
[11] *Ibid.*, pp. 17-18.
[12] *Ibid.*, pp. 91-92: "La plupart [des maisons de plai-
sance des grands] ... deviennent de petites villes peuplées d'habitans la plupart inutiles...."
[13] *Ibid.*, p. 43.
[14] *Ibid.*, p. 90.
[15] *Ibid.*, p. 19.
[16] *Ibid.*, p. 20, and see chapter v, pp. 103-104.

("un économe industriel et sensuel"),[17] could take advantage of nature both for his needs and for his pleasures. The physical characteristics of this country estate, or *ferme ornée*, the modern equivalent of the *parc ancien*, or ancient park, were then spelled out in detail. It was to be composed of orchards, vegetable gardens, flower gardens, a farmyard with farm buildings, a cow barn, a dairy (probably a *laiterie d'agrément*), a menagerie, an aviary, an aquarium, an oratory in the form of a temple, a retreat (*asile*) in the form of a hermitage, a hospice including a garden of medicinal herbs, a housekeeper's lodge, a laboratory and a medical library, and beehives—all were designed in a "natural," but still at least partially symmetrical, arrangement. And the buildings were to be studied for contrasts of natural materials—stone and brick —rather than, for instance, for difference in color, as Whately had suggested.[18] Later on, Watelet would endorse a regional style ("établissemens conformés à la nature du pays").[19] Watelet's *ferme ornée* is, then, very different from the *ferme ornée* as it was described by Whately. It recalls an idealized past, and it is close to the spirit of the early eighteenth century in France. The French amateur's use of the term is one of the first in French literature, and it suggests developments in French gardening which were only just beginning.

Having discussed the rural gardens, Watelet turned to the artificial ones. His criticism of the *parc ancien*, which he associated with an "urban," or architectural, setting, is similar to criticism of the formal garden by Huet, Laugier, and Whately. Watelet described the park as a vast enclosure, symmetrically planned, without variation in its design, and surrounded by walls. Like Laugier, Watelet believed that the sentiment such a park inspired would be serious, and sometimes even sad, and that promenades in such a garden would not be enjoyed, since there would be little shade or freshness where the trees were clipped and the water stagnated in canals. Moreover, Watelet also thought that such a park was a remnant of feudal pride,[20] and he complained that it would take a large section of the land from useful employment. Like Whately, he would permit formal gardening only in cities, where the "disposition [of a garden] belongs particularly to Architecture."[21] In a comment which seems as close to Chambers's work as to Le Nôtre's designs, Watelet noted that in these parks effects were created by means of theatrical illusion, so that the resulting scenes were far removed from the spectacle of simple nature.[22]

It is not surprising to note that Watelet, like Rousseau, was as opposed to the imitation of the English garden as he was to that of the formal one: both types were artificial. He commented that "the parks that are disposed according to the new principles are designed under the name of a Nation that we imitate with an affectation which is often ridiculous; and this Nation borrows ideas for its gardens from the Chinese, a people too distant, too different from us, too little known not to cause us to hold extraordinary opinions and to invent fables concerning them."[23] And he then mentioned three types of character, similar to, but not identical

[17] Watelet, *Essai*, pp. 20-21.
[18] *Ibid.*, pp. 27-28; and Whately, *Observations*, p. 126.
[19] Watelet, *Essai*, p. 52.
[20] *Ibid.*, p. 48.
[21] *Ibid.*, pp. 8-9.
[22] *Ibid.*, pp. 53-54. It is possible that Watelet may be

the "modern" French writer whom Walpole, "On Modern Gardening," p. 146, quoted as saying: "l'ennui du beau amene le gout du singulier."
[23] Watelet, *Essai*, p. 50; and see chapter II, note 72, on Chinese gardens and Kent.

with, Whately's characters—the terrible, pathetic, and emblematic genres—presumably used in the *parcs anciens*, and which Watelet maintained were produced by an industry which was not applied to useful objects, and which could only produce a momentary, unenduring admiration.[24] Watelet, like Rousseau, would prefer effects which were simply human, such as hamlets, the inhabitants of which, by their wellbeing, would reflect the bounty of their owner.[25]

Watelet then discussed the *parc moderne*, or modern park. He resigned himself to the fact that, although these parks were not formal, they also were not utilitarian, and that they were thus artificial. For this type, Watelet introduced three "genres" which suggest a second, substantial reworking of Whately's characters: picturesque, romantic (both of these are close to Whateley's character "original"), and poetic, or mythological and imitative (a combination of Whately's characters "emblematic" and "imitative"),[26] which he suggested were suitable for the *parc moderne*. However, he warned the reader that these genres required the introduction of inventions which were marvelous and fictitious rather than natural, and he recognized the fact that two of these genres would require artifice in order to create the desired effect.[27] Indeed, he remarked that here "the Gods of the theater, of illusions," were summoned.[28] The exception, the picturesque genre, was not discussed in detail by Watelet, who was concerned with the two other genres, for like Whately, he felt that painting was not an adequate model for gardens, since paintings were viewed from only a single point of view.[29] Of these, the poetic genre was related by him to ancient or foreign mythologies, customs and costumes,[30] which would make it possible by means of art (artifice) for the spectator to transport himself in imagination to a distant time and place.[31] But Watelet cautioned that since ideas of distant places were vague, few details should be included; moreover, if the accessories were imperfect, the imitation would be apparent, and the effect would be ridiculous.[32] As an example, Watelet then analyzed the city in the emperor of China's garden, which had been described by Attiret and mentioned by Chambers. He noted that such a design required people to represent the inhabitants, because "without such a pantomime, there would be only the spectacle of an abandoned village."[33] And Watelet maintained that "mouvement" (the original actions of the people in the spectacle) would be impossible to imitate.[34] For these reasons he considered this genre to be generally undesirable for use in garden design. He associated it with the work of an "ingenious critic of an English artist, distinguished by his knowledge and his talent"— surely Chambers—and he noted that the gardens that this artist described embraced all of

---

[24] Watelet, *Essai*, p. 60 (probably criticizing Chambers): "Quant aux caractères qui résultent des différentes dispositions de ces matériaux, ils seroient nombreux; s'il étoit, comme dans les Romans & les Drames, des moyens de préparer aux impressions qu'on auroit dessein de produire ou si dumoins les scènes qu'on disposeroit, ne devoient s'offrir qu'à des yeux clairvoyans, à des imaginations flexibles; & sur-tout à des Spectateurs libres de soins & d'intérêts particuliers: mais de ces secours, les uns n'existent pas, les autres se présentent rarement. Il est donc plus sûr en général de se restraindre à des caractères très-prononcés."

[25] *Ibid.*, p. 52.

[26] Watelet, *Essai*, pp. 19, 55.

[27] Watelet, *Essai*, p. 19.

[28] *Ibid.*, p. 53.

[29] *Ibid.*, pp. 55-56.

[30] *Ibid.*, p. 78.

[31] *Ibid.*, p. 79.

[32] *Ibid.*, pp. 80-81.

[33] *Ibid.*, p. 82: "C'est ainsi qu'en Chine la partie intérieure du palais, où l'on exécute le spectacle d'une ville, est dit-on, remplie de gens qui représentent aussi des habitans de tous les états: on y trouve toutes les occupations, & même tous les accidens civiles."

[34] *Ibid.*, p. 83.

nature; they "exhaust all genres, all effects . . . and it is only the Fairies who will execute and maintain them."[35] This is the first declared opposition by a Frenchman to Chambers's work; all later oppositon would be based on Watelet's point of view.

The romantic genre was less specific than that of the poetic: it embraced all that had been imagined, and all that could be invented. But its effects were uncertain, and from the infinite number of romantic inventions, only a small number were generally used, according to Watelet. Romantic ideas were vague, and they tended to be too personal, so that they could not be comprehended by anyone but their creator.[36] But extraordinary illusions could be produced with this genre, even if they were based on "puerile" ideas. To illustrate this point, Watelet introduced a scene similar to Whately's description of the New Weir on the Wye. It was a wild spot, with forges, the noise of hidden machinery and of rushing water, all of which produced effects which, heightened by imagination and illusions, permitted the spectator to believe himself "in the desert of Demons, magicians and monsters."[37]

Watelet did include the abstract characters developed by Addison which stand behind English picturesque gardening theory. But they were transformed, and he devoted little attention to them.[38] The familiar Addisonian trio of grand, uncommon, and beautiful now became noble, rustic (equated with liberty and fantasy), and agreeable. Watelet added to these a list of characters suggesting an association with the architectural characters listed by Blondel in the first volume of his *Cours*, published in 1771, just three years before Watelet's work appeared,[39] as well as an association with the many characters of the satiric theatrical scene. These include delightful (*riant*), and two others, serious (*sérieux*) and sad (*triste*), which indicate a shift in French taste toward the English melancholic and sentimental. ("Sad" may correspond to Chambers's description of autumn and melancholy mentioned in chapter III: Watelet recommended that it be employed only with reserve, for he considered that it indicated a situation of imperfection and disorder.[40]) Also included were three other characters—magnificent, terrible, and voluptuous—about which Watelet remarked only that they required accessories belonging to artifice and to industry.[41]

Watelet's discussion of gardening materials is influenced by Whately. But although the French author took from the English one the basic materials which compose a garden, he

[35] *Ibid.*, pp. 84-85.

[36] *Ibid.*, pp. 86-87.

[37] *Ibid.*, pp. 88-89: ". . . lieu très-sauvage où des torrens se précipiteroient dans des vallons creux; où des rochers, des arbres tristes, le bruit des eaux répété par des antres multipliés, porteroient dans l'ame une sorte d'effroi; où l'on appercevroit des fumées épaisses, des feux sortant de quelques forges, de quelques verreries cachées; où l'on entendoit les bruits de plusieurs machines, dont les mouvemens pénibles, & les roues gémissantes rappelleroient les plaintes & les cris des esprits mal-saisans. Ces images d'un désert magique, d'un lieu propre aux évocations, auxquelles se joindroient les accidens & les sons qui leur conviennent, présenteroient un romanesque auquel la pantomime même ne seroit pas nécessaire. En effet l'imagination émue seroit prête à la suppléer; & dans l'instant où le jour s'obscurciroit, où les ombres de la nuit répandroient la tristesse qui leur est propre, & les illusions qui les accomagnent; peu s'en faudroit qu'on ne crût voir dans ce désert des Démons, des Magiciens & des monstres."

[38] *Ibid.*, pp. 75-77.

[39] Blondel, *Cours*, I, pp. 377-447, including the characters of: sublime, pyramidale, vraie, vraisemblable, belle, noble, livre, symbolique, mâle, légere, champêtre, naïve, féminine, mystérieuse, grande, hardie, terrible, naine, frivole, licensieuse, dissemblable, amphibiologique, vague, barbare, asservie, méplate, futile, pauvre. See also G. Boffrand, *Livre d'architecture*, Paris, 1745, p. 16, for a more traditional discussion of characters. Also see chapter VI, n. 15.

[40] Watelet, *Essai*, p. 77.

[41] *Ibid.*, p. 61.

added to them many others, and devoted to all only brief and unsystematic remarks. He mentioned ground, plans, exposure to sun and to light (*exposition*), trees, water, spaces, grass, flowers, prospects (*aspects extérieurs*), rocks and grottos (which he noted served as a transition from natural to artificial objects), and natural accidents (*accidens naturels*).[42] And in the very brief development of these materials,[43] in which he suggested only the main contribution that each "material" made to the scene, plans is included with ground, grass with spaces, and prospects and natural accidents are omitted.

The Frenchman's work seems to belong to the romantic, emotionally oriented theory of the years after 1770, while the work of his English counterparts is related to the more systematic and formal tradition that was dominant before this date. However, Watelet's work is surely influenced by the thinking of J. F. Blondel. Not only does the French amateur recall Blondel's characters in his work, but also he includes a passage close to one published by Blondel the year before the publication of the *Essai*.[44] Blondel had recommended a relaxation of symmetry at the periphery of a garden,[45] and Watelet wrote that in the remote corners of the artificial gardens nature was permitted to flourish: he strongly recommended employing picturesque and poetic genres in these spots.[46]

At the end of this rambling discussion of characters, genres, and materials, Watelet returned to the three genres of the *parc moderne* to discuss some of the materials with which they should be composed. To create the picturesque genre, Watelet suggested that the main emphasis should be on the mingling of objects of curiosity with objects that invite attention.[47] He emphasized the importance of movement, accident, and inequality in landscape,[48] and he was opposed to garden architecture (*objets factices*) because "a profusion of ornaments is indicative of the sterility of creativity."[49] On the other hand, the poetic genre required the introduction of statues of famous men and equestrian statues; of temples dedicated to the virtues, sciences, arts and "sentimens agréables"; and of inscriptions engraved on trees (recalling Moulin-Joli), columns, and obelisks.[50] (However, the genre did not, according to Watelet, require a "mausoleum to a favorite dog"—possibly referring to the one to Signor Fido at Stowe[51]—or a monument to the memory of a bird.)[52] Watelet even recommended the mechanics of the romantic genre here, although he warned that artifices and refinements would not produce simple pleasures.

The final two chapters, on a description of a Chinese garden translated from the Chinese (which would seem from the description to contain many of the elements of a French garden)[53] and on a French garden (his own Moulin-Joli),[54] are illustrations of what Watelet

[42] *Ibid.*, pp. 59-60.

[43] *Ibid.*, pp. 60-61, 62-74.

[44] In a description similar to that of Blondel in 1752 (mentioned in chapter I, pp. 14-15), Watelet noted that in the dwellings of the great, trees were shaped into walls and ceilings, and that there was a proliferation of marble, bronze and vases.

[45] Blondel, *Cours*, IV, pp. 5-6.

[46] Watelet, *Essai*, pp. 97-98.

[47] *Ibid.*, p. 105.

[48] *Ibid.*, p. 109.

[49] *Ibid.*, p. 111.

[50] *Ibid.*, pp. 113-114.

[51] See Hunt, "Emblem and Expression," p. 300, on the Fido monument at Stowe.

[52] Watelet, *Essai*, p. 115.

[53] *Ibid.*, pp. 125-137. Watelet notes that the author was Seé-ma-Kouag, but the chapter is taken from a description of the garden of another author, Liu-Chou (translated by P. M. Cibor), later published as "Essai sur les jardins des Chinois" in *Memoires concernant l'histoire . . . des Chinois*, VIII, 1782, pp. 301-326. Bald,

considered to be the correct way to design such a *lieu de plaisance*, or modern retreat, where the charms of nature, the sweetness of study, and the conversation of a chosen society could be enjoyed.

Watelet's gardening treatise is related to the philosophy of Rousseau, whom he knew. The writer of the other major work falling within this group of gardening treatises associated with Whately and Rousseau, the Marquis de Girardin,[55] also knew Rousseau. He published his own treatise, *Composition des paysages*, three years after Watelet's *Essai* appeared, in 1777.[56] Like Watelet, the Marquis wrote as an amateur, and he used his experience with the designing of his own estate in the development of his theories on gardening. There are many other similarities between the two works. The *Composition* begins with a brief account of the history of garden design. Girardin, elaborating on Watelet's historical description, stated that "A garden was the first present of Heaven, the first dwelling of man; this idea, sacred in all nations, was inspired even by nature, which indicated to man the pleasure of cultivations, as the most certain way to avert all the evils of the body and the mind."[57] The Marquis then noted that the next stage of development was that of the gardens of the ancients (similar to Watelet's *parcs anciens*), which were remarkable only for their size and expense;[58] they displayed imagination and variety, but "the delightful retreats of nature were unknown."[59] However, unlike Watelet, Girardin's opposition to formal gardening was based on aesthetic rather than social grounds. He criticized the fact that the formal garden was separated from nature: like Whately and Burke he noted that its design was subjected to the compass, and that it was closed off from the surrounding country.[60] He remarked (in a passage similar to the comments of the early eighteenth-century playwright Marivaux on *beauté* and *je ne sçais quoi*), "A handsome man or woman is often only a statue . . . ; the most disagreeable thing in a countenance is the want of animation and expression; as in the ground being enclosed with walls, and disfigured by the rule and compass."[61] Thus, conventional beauty, "though it varies in different places and at different times, is . . . an inanimate" kind of perfection (or, by implication, disagreeable), while picturesque beauty is "animated, and gives motion, character, and expression to the physiognomy of all objects."[62]

Girardin's opposition to artificiality in any type of gardening design, including that of the *jardin anglo-chinois*, is surely related to the thinking of Watelet and Rousseau. The Marquis noted that "Natural taste led people at first to suppose, that in order to imitate nature, it was sufficient to banish even lines, and to make serpentine walks instead of straight ones; they thought to produce a great variety, by crowding into a small space the production of all climates and monuments of all ages, bringing the whole world together within four walls: not per-

"Chambers and the Chinese Garden," p. 92, maintains that Chambers's essay in the *Designs* is similar to descriptions of Chinese gardens, in particular Liu-Chou's essay.

[54] *Ibid.*, pp. 138-160.

[55] For Girardin, see A. Martin-Decaen, *Le dernier Ami de J.-J. Rousseau: Le Marquis de Girardin* (with bibliography).

[56] Originally intended to be published in 1775: see

Girardin, *Composition*, "Avis à l'éditeur," p. iij, r. All further references are to the English translation by D. Malthus, unless otherwise noted.

[57] *Ibid.*, p. 1.

[58] *Ibid.*, p. 2.

[59] *Ibid.*, p. 3.

[60] *Ibid.*, pp. 3-4.

[61] *Ibid.*, p. 75.

[62] *Ibid.*, pp. 138-139.

ceiving, that if such an incongruous mixture was capable of any beauty in the detail, the whole could never have any truth or nature."[63] But Girardin was more sensitive to the actual beauties of nature than were these two men. He further noted that "When you are sensible that there are landscapes of all sorts—the sublime, the magnificent, rich, beautiful, soft, solitary, wild, severe, peaceful, verdant, simple, rural, rustic, &c. [a list which recalls both Watelet's and Blondel's numerous "characters" as well as the infinite number of scenes possible in the satiric drama], you will be convinced that it is not necessary to have recourse to fairy-land and fable, (which are always as far below the imagination, as falsehood is inferior to truth;) nor to employ machinery, which always fails in its effect; nor stage tricks, which always shew the cords and pullies."[64]

Now, a reference to Chambers's discussion of the Chinese garden may be implied here. And it would surely seem from this statement that Girardin was opposed to all theatrical effects. But Girardin then compared the painting of theatrical scenery to the designing of a landscape, and he referred in particular to the work of Servandoni, the best-known and the most elaborate in style of all contemporary theatrical designers, and famous for his ability to construct natural effects by means of artifice.[65] The gardener was also advised to have several paintings made of the result he wished to achieve.[66] It is in these practical suggestions, by means of which Girardin suggested a way in which landscape painting effects could be transferred to the landscape garden, that the Frenchman moved beyond the philosophically oriented treatise of Whately.

The sensitive and personal reworking of existing theoretical gardening concepts which is exemplified in the beginning of Girardin's book can be observed throughout the work; in particular, in the modification of the ideas of the main source for gardening treatises— Whately's *Observations*. Thus, the chapters of the *Composition* were, in contrast to Whately's methodological organization, and even to Watelet's complex categorizations, based on practical application alone and organized to proceed from general to specific topics.[67] Girardin declared that he would not consider historical gardens, natural gardens, or garden divisions

[63] *Ibid.*, pp. 12-13.

[64] *Ibid.*, p. 92. Girardin was even opposed to Chambers's straight roads (*ibid.*, p. 236).

[65] *Ibid.*, pp. 23-26, and see chapter v, p. 97 and note 86. Morel also mentions Servandoni in this context in the 1802 edition of *Théorie des jardins*, II, pp. 209-210, n. 7 (although he is opposed to the effects the decorator produced): "Les représentations en tableaux mobiles et en personnages muets que Servandoni donnait aux Tuileries, malgré leur surprenante illusion, malgré la perfection du jeu des machines, le prestige des effects, n'aurait pas soutenu un quart-d'heure l'attention des spectateurs, si le spectacle n'eût pas présenté une succession des scènes, et si l'auteur n'y eût pas joint une action."

[66] Girardin, *Composition*, pp. 26-29.

[67] The chapters read: "Introduction: Of Landscapes, or Chosen Spots" (pp. 1-6); Chapter I: "An attempt to define and determine the difference between a garden, a country and a landscape" (pp. 7-15); Chapter II: "Of the whole" (pp. 16-35); Chapter III: "On the con-nexion with the country" (pp. 35-41); Chapter IV: "Of the inclosing border of the landscape" (pp. 41-44); Chapter V: "Of the difference between a vague geographical view, and a limited picturesque view, such as is suited to a dwelling house or habitation" (pp. 45-47); Chapter VI: "Of the different parts" (pp. 47-73); Chapter VII: "Of the possibility of improving all sorts of situations" (pp. 73-90); Chapter VIII: "Of the adaption of this style to all kinds of proprietors" (pp. 91-93); Chapter IX: "Of imitation" (pp. 94-96); Chapter X: "Of plantations" (pp. 97-101); Chapter XI: "Of water" (pp. 102-111); Chapter XII: "Of the course of valleys, the deception in perspective, and the effect of light" (pp. 111-114); Chapter XIII: "Of buildings and edifices of all kinds" (pp. 114-128); Chapter XIV: "Of the choice of landscape as appropriated to the different hours of the day" (pp. 129-133); Chapter XV: "Of the power of landscape over the senses, and, through their interposition, over the soul" (pp. 134-147); Chapter XVI: "Of the means of uniting pleasure with utility, in the general arrangement of the country" (pp. 148-160).

(and he specifically mentioned Whately's four divisions), but that he would "only treat of the methods to embellish or enrich nature, the combinations of which, varied to infinity, cannot be classed, and equally belong to all ages and all countries."[68] His only deviation from this aim was in the discussion of his own estate, Ermenonville, where he wrote that it was divided into four sections, based on the use and the topographical condition of the land: woods, forest, meadow, and farm (a division into elements which he defined, in contradiction to his thesis, as "characters").[69]

Although Girardin, like Whately, considered natural materials, he thought of them purely as elements of vocabulary which could be shaped by the designer. For this reason, he omitted the categories of ground and rocks: "The materials employed in landscape are wood, water and buildings. Rocks and mountains are not to be commanded, and the trifling removal of earth is never worth the expence which it occasions."[70] The final "material" considered by Girardin consisted of buildings, which he recommended should be adapted to their site (that is, designed in a regional vernacular style),[71] rather than imitate other structures (that is, exotic styles), or be developed symmetrically. Girardin concluded his discussion of buildings with an important statement for its date: "It is in consequence of the custom of hearing and seeing only by habit, without entering into the reason of any thing, that it became an established rule to cut according to the same pattern the two sides of a house. This is called symmetry; Le Nôtre introduced it in gardens, and Mansard in buildings." Girardin disliked symmetry because he saw it as primarily associated with the techniques of painting: "The central point, which is the fundamental point in symmetry, necessarily makes the objects appear flat, because the surfaces only are seen." And he felt that "It is from the picturesque effect that buildings must receive the charm which pleases and attracts the eye; and to effect this, the best point of view must be chosen to show the object, and the different fronts should as much as possible be presented."[72] Not only is this statement in opposition to the generally established view that formal gardening should be retained near the house,[73] but, if Girardin can be assumed to have formulated this concept in the 1760s by the time he began work on Ermenonville, his commitment to asymmetry in architecture may predate that of the English.[74] It is surely one of the earliest examples of consideration being given to the purely picturesque aspect of architecture, carried to its logical, asymmetrical conclusion. Girardin's concept of asym-

[68] *Ibid.*, pp. 8-9.

[69] *Ibid.*, pp. 89-90.

[70] *Ibid.*, p. 97. But Girardin is not wholly consistent, for he recommends the breaking-up and mending of rock to form a grotto (*ibid.*, pp. 64-65), as he had done at Ermenonville.

[71] *Ibid.*, pp. 94-96.

[72] *Ibid.*, pp. 123-125.

[73] Listed by R. J. Gennett, "Beckford's Fonthill: The Landscape as Art," *Gazette des beaux-arts*, LXXX, December 1972, pp. 335-336, as preferring regularity next to the house are: Chambers, *Dissertation* (1772), pp. 16-17; (1773), pp. 18-19; H. Repton, *Art of Landscape Gardening*, London (1907 ed.), p. 132; Walpole, "On Modern Gardening," p. 143; and Price, *Essays*, II, p. 177. Also see Home, *Elements*, III, p. 305.

[74] See J. Summerson, *Architecture in Britain, 1530-1830*, London, 1963 (4th ed.), pp. 289-290, where he notes that the first irregular buildings in England were Walpole's round tower at Strawberry Hill (irregular, according to Summerson, as a result of being extemporized over a number of years) of 1759, and Payne Knight's Downton Castle, of 1774-1778 (the first planned irregular permanent structure of any size). See also Girardin, *Composition*, p. 127, where he says that the ruin has a "picturesque effect" and could be given some "emblematical character," while it serves also some useful purpose. Perhaps Monville had Girardin in mind when he created the house in the form of a column at Retz (see O. Choppin de Janvry, "Le Désert du Retz").

metry may be related, not to English development, but to the observing, collecting, and illustrating of rural scenes with rustic buildings by such Frenchmen as Boucher, Watelet, and Robert, which had already begun by the 1740s in France.

In his consideration of genres and the role of association in garden design, Girardin superbly demonstrated that he could combine an intelligent and interpretative summing up of existing published theory with the introduction of new, imaginative material—and this in a field in which five major works had appeared in the previous five years. The chapter titled "Of the Power of Landscape over the Senses and through their Interposition, over the Soul," is based on Whately's Burke-oriented philosophy. However, in considering genres Girardin turned to Watelet and his picturesque, poetic, and romantic types rather than to the original, emblematic, and imitative ones of the Englishman. Yet, he did not, like Watelet, consider these genres to represent different but equal means for achieving the emotional heightening of natural effects. For him, they were part of a developmental process which moved toward a single aesthetic goal. Thus, picturesque scenes were merely pleasant to the eyes; poetic scenes, on a more complex level, recalled "all the attributes of such a spot, which poetry has rendered sacred."[75] Girardin's notion of the poetic recalls both the Leasowes and Moulin-Joli: the distinguishing elements included "inscriptions on the bark of ancient oaks; urns in the wood; in the consecrated grove, a rustick temple; in the orchard, under the shade of fruit-trees, a neat cottage; groups of cattle feeding in the meadows; the chorus of the shepherds, assembled round the living spring, while every maid of the village becomes a wood nymph."[76] He saw romantic scenes as surpassing even poetic ones because they appealed directly to sentiment: ". . . all the force of that analogy is felt, which subsists between physical and moral impressions. Here the mind wanders with pleasure, and indulges those fond reveries, which become necessary to such as are open to soft affections, and know the just value of things: we wish to dwell in these scenes for ever, for here we feel all the truth and energy of nature." But, he added, these scenes were rarely found, "except in the bosom of those immense ramparts, which seem intended by nature as the last asylum of peace and liberty."[77] In an allusion to Chambers, who in large part was responsible for popularizing, in garden design, romantic character (composed of strong contrasts) and the Chinese garden, Girardin cautioned: "If the food is not seasoned with the poisons of the east, the quality of it is excellent, and the taste wholesome and pure."[78]

Girardin's work is an exception to other French gardening treatises in having what seems to be a link with one English source. It has been suggested that Girardin designed Ermenonville with William Shenstone's *Unconnected Thoughts on Gardening*, published in 1764,[79] at hand, and that he visited Shenstone's Leasowes in the early 1760s.[80] The approach to garden design in the theoretical works of these two men places the principal emphasis on the achieve-

[75] Girardin, *Composition*, p. 141.

[76] *Idem.*

[77] *Ibid.*, p. 147.

[78] *Ibid.*, p. 146.

[79] E. Malins, *English Landscape and Literature, 1680-1840*, London, 1966, pp. 76-77. Shenstone's work does not figure among the major English treatises on gardening and thus is not mentioned in chapter III.

[80] J. Boulenger, *Au Pays de Gérard de Nerval*, pp. 106-107; and Martin-Decaen, *Girardin*, pp. 10-11, quoting from a letter from Girardin to his parents: "Mon Leasowes vous ne m'en dites rien, de cette composition vraiment charmante et poétique. . . . L'aurait-on gâtée depuis que je ne l'ai vu; . . ." as opposed to Blenheim and Stowe, where there was "certainement plus de magnificence que de conséquence et de vérité."

ment of pictorial effect—on the final picture—rather than on the organization of the garden vocabulary of contemporary treatises. Girardin's major contribution to French gardening may be his development of precisely these picturesque effects: their study is the major object of his book. Similarities between the works of the Englishman and the Frenchman are sometimes very close. Both men divided the historical stages of gardening into similar categories: kitchen gardening (useful), parterre gardening (formal), and "landskip" or "picturesque gardening" (picturesque).[81] Both preferred the variety of intimate scenes to the grand view of large prospects.[82] Like Girardin, Shenstone suggested that there were alternatives to Addison's trio of unusual, great, and beautiful.[83] And, again like Girardin, the Englishman recommended that "Art should never be allowed to set a foot in the province of nature."[84]

It may be the similarity between the two works which recommended Girardin's to the English—it was, indeed, the only French eighteenth-century work on picturesque gardening to be translated into English, in 1783.[85] (Of course English interest in, and sympathy with, the philosophy of Rousseau, which was represented in Girardin's work, surely also helped prompt the English translation.) But there are also basic differences between the two. Shenstone's essay consists of casual observations and reflections, while Girardin's treatise offers a completely developed concept of the design and philosophy of the picturesque garden. In contrast to Shenstone's and later English garden theory, the French amateurs held the picturesque garden to be a synthesis of both spiritual and physical reality. It should be recalled that English designs —those of Brown, for instance—reflected only the tangible and visual form of the garden,[86] and also that they were being executed at the very time that Girardin was expressing his desire to compose landscape not as an "architect or a gardener, but as a poet and a painter," so that both the "understanding and the eye will be pleased."[87]

There is no doubt that Girardin's views are based on French philosophical tenets, and that they are related to those expressed by Rousseau in *Héloïse*. Like Rousseau, the Marquis would even "abolish those great prospects over the countryside because they soon tire the sight" (Shenstone also favored the close picturesque over the distant sublime view),[88] and Girardin was surely influenced by Rousseau in his equating for admiration "the picturesque landscapes which please the sight" and "the moral landscapes which delight the mind."[89] Moreover, in

[81] W. Shenstone, "Unconnected Thoughts on Gardening," p. 77; Girardin, *Composition*, pp. 1-6.

[82] Shenstone, "Unconnected Thoughts," p. 79; Girardin, *Composition*, p. 65.

[83] Shenstone, "Unconnected Thoughts," pp. 85-86; Girardin, *Composition*, pp. 8-9.

[84] Shenstone, "Unconnected Thoughts," p. 84; and Girardin, *Composition*, pp. 18-19 (for instance).

[85] D. Malthus, the English translator of Girardin's work, was an enthusiastic admirer of Rousseau and Home (*Biographie Universelle*, XXVI, pp. 279-287, biography of F. Malthus). W. Mason spoke favorably of Girardin's work in his 1778 (third) edition of his *English Garden*, p. 13; and he modeled several of the buildings in book IV of this work on descriptions from the *Composition* (*English Garden*, bk. IV, pp. 13, 21).

[86] D. Stroud, *Capability Brown*, London, 1950, p.

199, quotes from letter of December 1782 from Hannah More to her sisters: "I took a very agreeable lecture from him [Brown] in his art, and he promised to give me taste by inoculation. He illustrates everything he says about gardening by some literary or grammatical allusion. He told me he compared his art to literary composition. 'Now *there*,' said he, pointing his finger, 'I make a comma, and there,' pointing to another spot, 'where a more decided turn is proper, I make a colon; at another part, where an interruption is desirable to break the view, a parenthesis; now a full stop, and then I begin another subject.'"

[87] Girardin, *Composition*, p. 15.

[88] See note 82 above and the reference to Rousseau cited in chapter II, note 35.

[89] Girardin, *Composition*, p. 150.

the original French edition there are two long passages, missing from the English translation, in which Girardin embarked on a lengthy discussion of Rousseau's social contract,[90] and a consideration of Rousseau's ideas on the redistribution of land.[91]

For the French, Girardin's work was "a classic work which will always be studied."[92] But, in spite of the fact that it was the most English in tone of any of the French publications on the subject, Girardin's moral and social philosophy were satirized by one English garden theorist, Horace Walpole, in the 1782 edition of his history of modern gardening,[93] and he also ridiculed the Marquis's book in his correspondence.[94] Walpole was, in the long view, correct. The improving of nature was a pragmatic, visual undertaking; elements such as poetry, social philosophy, and morality were extraneous to the art, and, as picturesque garden design developed, they would disappear. Girardin's was the last major work on gardening to attempt to achieve these high-minded ideals, which had their roots in earlier gardening tradition. But in his work the Frenchman also emphasized the direction garden design would take—it would concern itself increasingly with the vocabulary and the methods for composing purely visual picturesque effects.

The majority of contemporary French works on gardening follow the direction indicated by Watelet and Girardin. They reflect the desire for a retreat from sophistication and worldliness to the simple and rural life and a reaction against the theatrical, the artificial, and the bizarre which were so apparent in the "Chinese" style of gardening. Among them, the most comprehensive theory was formulated by J. M. Morel, in his *Théorie des jardins*, published in 1776. Morel was an architect who specialized in gardening—his biographer credits him with work on some forty estates,[95] and he was employed by Girardin at Ermenonville, where his position seems to have been similar to that of François Barbier at Retz, who was a technical consultant and architect of individual structures rather than a designer responsible for the master plan of the estate.[96] Morel may be a defector from the camp of Chambers and the Chinese garden, for it is possible that he translated into French Chambers's "Art of laying out Gardens among the Chinese."[97] His own book, although important for its lengthy descriptions

[90] *Ibid.* (French edition, 1777), pp. 140-146.

[91] *Ibid.* (French edition, 1777), pp. 148-158.

[92] Lezay-Marnésia, *Essai sur la nature champêtre*, p. 35.

[93] Chase, *Horace Walpole*, p. 23 (quoting from the 1782 edition of Walpole's "On Modern Gardening"): ". . . The French, indeed, during the fashionable paroxysm of philosophy, have surpassed us, at least in meditation on the art [of gardening]. I have perused a grave treatise of recent date, in which the author, extending his views beyond mere luxury and amusement, has endeavoured to inspire his countrymen, even in the gratification of their expensive pleasures, with benevolent projects. He proposes to them to combine gardening with charity, and to make every step of their walks an act of generosity and a lesson of morality. In stead of adorning favourite points with a heathen temple, a Chinese pagoda, a Gothic tower, a fictitious bridge, he proposes to them at the first resting place to erect a school; a little farther to found an academy; at a third

distance, a manufacture; and at the termination of the park to endow a hospital. Thus, says he, the proprietor would be led to meditate, as he saunters, on the different stages of human life, and both his expence and thoughts would march in a progression of patriotic acts and reflections. When he was laying out so magnificent, charitable, and philosophic an Utopian villa, it would have cost no more to have added a foundling-hospital, a senate-house and a burying-ground."

[94] Walpole, *Letters*, XII, pp. 381-382, Walpole to Mason, 7 December 1782.

[95] For Morel, see S. de Fortair, *Discours sur la vie et les oeuvres de Jean-Marie Morel*.

[96] For Retz, see Choppin de Janvry, "Le Désert de Retz."

[97] Fortair, *Morel*, p. 34, who says that in 1757 Morel gave to the Société d'Agriculture d'Histoire naturelle et Arts utiles de Lyon a work entitled *Art de distribuer les Jardins suivant l'usage des Chinois*. This book cannot be located. A work of the same title, published in

of Guiscard and Ermenonville, is a well-considered synthesis of the works of Whately and Watelet, and it adds no new material to our knowledge of French gardening theory. Indeed, the architect did not travel even to England until many years after the publication of his work.[98] Watelet, on the other hand, had benefited from an extensive stay in Italy,[99] and Girardin from a trip to England, Germany, Switzerland and Italy,[100] before writing their books or designing their gardens. So Morel was unable to profit from the kind of direct observation that aided the formulation of the theory and practice of picturesque gardening in France.

One other synthesis of the social ideas of Watelet and the picturesque theories of Girardin may be mentioned. In a short section on gardening in his *Discours sur le goût*, F. M. Lecreulx strongly criticized the artificial garden, including in the term both the traditional formal garden and the irregular Chinese garden, at the time in vogue. He stated that the artificial gardens were restricted to a privileged society, were enclosed, and followed the caprices of luxury and novelty, while an architect instructed in the particulars of his art would work for all classes and for all social needs.[101]

In contrast to these many high-minded Rousseauian interpretations of the picturesque garden—they were realized in comparatively few examples—the philosophy behind the *jardin anglo-chinois* produced only one major written work on gardening. This was the Introduction to the description of the park at Monceau by the amateur, dilettante, and playwright Carmontelle.[102] In the Prospectus to his publication on the Parc Monceau (an early version of the Introduction), Carmontelle endorsed an approach to gardening precisely the opposite of that of the writers considered above. It was one that had been discussed in detail by Chambers, whom Carmontelle cited in recalling the English architect's protest against the monotony

London in 1757, and written by an N. Morel, is listed in F. Janne, *L'Art et la théorie des jardins: Bibliographie*, Liège, 1966 (2v.), I, p. 131, as located in the Bibliothèque des Arts décoratifs in Paris, although no such work is listed in the catalog of that library, and an intensive search has not located it there. Hautecoeur, *Histoire de l'architecture classique*, V, p. 11, also mentions a work of the same title published in London in 1757, and written by a Jean-Marie Moreau. This work too has not been located.

[98] Fortair, *Morel*, pp. 12-13.

[99] Watelet, *Recueil de quelques ouvrages de M. Watelet*, Paris, 1784, "Note sur Silvie," p. iv.

[100] Martin-Decaen, *Girardin*, p. 8.

[101] F. M. Lecreulx, *Discours sur le goût*, pp. 34-38, 41-49. The *Avertissement* states that the author wrote some of his reflections twenty-five years previously, or in 1753.

[102] For Carmontelle, see "Un gentilhomme artiste: Carmontelle. D'Après deux documents inédits," *Gazette des beaux-arts*, XL, 1908, pp. 254-260; L. Vauxcelles, "Avant-propos," *Louis Carmontelle, lecteur du Duc d'Orléans*, Paris, 1933 (exhibition catalog), pp. 3-13; and A. F. F. de Frénilly, *Souvenirs du Baron de Frénilly, pair de France (1768-1828)*, Paris, 1908 (quoting from *Recollections of Baron de Frenilly, Peer of*

France (1768-1828), London, 1909), p. 5, where the author recalls that Carmontelle began his career as tutor to the children of the Marquis d'Armentières. Then

> he became reader to the Duc d'Orléans. His ambition went no further. . . . He designed and planted gardens that were somewhat extraordinary, for they were not French, and he got angry if you called them English. He planted my father's garden at Saint-Ouen and the famous one of Mousseaux, on the wall of which he had written: "This is not an English garden."
>
> His proverbs . . . had been performed at the Villers-Cotterets. . . . Thence they passed into every *salon*; nothing else was played there and thus Carmontelle became the Scribe of his Epoch.

Métra, *Correspondance secrète*, I, pp. 201-202, 18 February 1775, criticized Carmontelle's *Proverbes dramatiques* "que la mode répandit & fit jouer dans la plupart des Sociétés." But Carmontelle's "Théâtre de Campagne" "paroissent destinées uniquement à amuser ceux qui trouveront plaisir à les représenter" but it was "sans chaleur, sans énergie." See also O. Siren, *China and Gardens of Europe in the Eighteenth Century*, New York, 1950, p. 121.

which resulted from too great attention to nature and too little to imagination and artifice.[103] Carmontelle wished for "not a *Jardin Anglois* ... but precisely what has been said in criticism of it, to reunite in one garden all times and all places."[104]

To be sure, Carmontelle endorsed the writing of Whately (indeed, he considered the *Observations* to be the fundamental work in its field),[105] and Girardin's Ermenonville, although he considered this garden to be a unique product of a unique situation—one which made it possible to embellish a countryside with "much talent and taste,"[106] instead of requiring the creation of an artificial landscape. However, the playwright thought that most French sites had neither the character nor the extent in which to develop such a design, and that they must be developed artificially to create a countryside of illusions where nature would be imitated by means of art. He wrote, "... all precepts which constrain the imagination should be avoided. ... In a garden one expects to discover what would not ordinarily be seen. If what belongs to Princes cannot be had, the greatest efforts of Art, at least those qualities which are uncommon should be found there."[107]

For Carmontelle, the French picturesque garden had a very different character from that of the English one: "... our new gardens are not always badly made, if they do not resemble those of the English. We love this happy liberty [of the English garden] which produces new and unusual effects; but although the course of the flow of water can be changed, its quality cannot be changed."[108] Carmontelle considered that for the French the charms of nature were good cheer, the hunt, games, concerts, and spectacles. Although philosophical conversation would not be banished, it would not be austere or somber; instead of dreaming alone (and here Carmontelle surely had in mind the French interpretation of the English garden as melancholic), the French sought company for conversation.[109]

Carmontelle also argued against the concept of utility associated with the agreeable. According to him, rural life did not suit French taste for society, pleasure, and dissipation: "the description [of rural life] is loved more than the practice,"[110] for the French only knew the shepherds of *Astrée*, of Fontenelle, of Boucher, and of the Opera; to depict the country as it was would destroy for the French the taste they believed they had for it.[111] Carmontelle, using Laugier's argument but reaching opposite conclusions, recommended that this taste would be satisfied by an art which held the visitors by means of the variety of the objects, without which they would seek in the country what they missed in the garden, the image of liberty.[112]

The same philosophy was endorsed by the architect N. Le Camus de Mezières who, in his *Génie de l'architecture*, recommended the study of Servandoni's theatrical decorations to both

---

[103] Carmontelle, Prospectus to *Jardin de Monceau*, p. 2. For the quote, see chapter III, p. 37.

[104] *Idem.*

[105] Carmontelle, *Monceau*, "Avertissement": "On n'a pas la prétention d'offrir ici une théorie, ni des préceptes; ce seroit un ridicule, connoissant l'Ouvrage publié en Angleterre, par *Sir Thomas Wathely* (*sic*), sous le titre modeste d'*Observations sur l'Art de former les Jardins modernes*. Ce Livre contient les véritables élé-

ments de ces sortes de Jardins"; and Prospectus, pp. 2-3.

[106] Carmontelle, *Monceau*, p. 5.

[107] *Ibid.*, p. 4.

[108] *Ibid.*, p. 5.

[109] *Ibid.*, p. 4.

[110] *Ibid.*, p. 5.

[111] *Idem.*

[112] *Ibid.*, p. 6.

architects and garden designers.[113] But the architect also endorsed Watelet's *Essai* when he dedicated his own book to the amateur, and he praised Girardin's Ermenonville—although in terms which are closer to Laugier's description of a "Chinese" garden than to Girardin's intention to blend his estate with the surrounding region: "All has been forseen here . . . one believes himself to have wandered into one of those gardens where the Fairies display their enchantments, although on reflecting one sees only the simple and the natural. . . ."[114]

A combination of the Watelet-Girardin and Carmontelle themes is that of the botanist A. N. Duchesne,[115] who in 1775, one year before Morel's work appeared, published his *Sur la Formation des jardins*, in which he carefully and impartially balanced the merits and demerits of the regular ("régulier") and free ("naturel") genres of gardening. He asked: "Does one of these two sentiments merit preference to the exclusion of the other? It is this question which will be examined in this book."[116] Duchesne stated that he saw Watelet's *Essai* only after his own work was completed, and that he agreed with its thesis.[117] But where Watelet was restrictive in his attitude toward the picturesque garden, Duchesne was comprehensive. Thus the botanist considered the strong emotions associated with the sublime, although he felt that they should be experienced only in areas of uncultivated nature ("Nature livrée"), including mountains, precipices, rapid torrents, enormous heights, immense forests, and arid deserts, where (in a passage surely influenced by Burke) "a frightful silence, interrupted only by the cries of wild animals, spreads terror in these deserted places. . . ."[118] In contrast to this type of nature, Duchesne recommended "the fruit of human Industry"[119] for cultivated land, where both uniformity and irregularity played their part, each having its own merits, and farther on he gave as models for this design the work of two masters of the artificial imitation of nature, Kent and Dufresny, who, he said, introduced "a wise liberty" into garden design.[120] Indeed, for Duchesne the free genre was (in contrast to its association with simple nature by Girardin and Watelet) the *style Chinois*. He related it to the wilderness: "Oriental gardens . . . consist only of a confused jumble of trees, without Parterres, Allées, or 'rooms' of foliage or arbors . . . they resemble Groves more than Gardens."[121] However, he criticized the introduction of excessive garden structures,[122] and even too much diversity in planting,[123] and he recommended the *jardin chinois* only for areas of a large extent.[124]

Like Watelet, Duchesne was interested in the *ferme ornée*, which he said was generally

[113] Le Camus de Mezières, *Génie de l'architecture*, pp. 4-6, and see chapter v, pp. 97-98.

[114] *Ibid.*, p. 78. Compare with Laugier's statement in chapter i, p. 22.

[115] A short biographical notice on Duchesne is in A. N. Duchesne, *Voyage de Antoine-Nicolas Duchesne au Havre et en Haute-Normandie, 1762*, n.p., 1898, P. D. Bernier, "Notice sur Antoine Duchesne et sur Antoine-Nicolas son fils," pp. 3-9. See also H. Jadart, *Relation du voyage à Reims d'Antoine Duchesne*, 1902, mentioned in Hautecoeur, *Histoire de l'architecture classique*, v, p. 18, n. 2.

[116] Duchesne, *Sur la Formation des jardins*, pp. 2-3.

[117] *Ibid.*, p. 86, n. 1.

[118] *Ibid.*, p. 7.

[119] *Ibid.*, p. 8.

[120] *Ibid.*, p. 55, and p. 54, where Duchesne mentions Attiret's description of the Emperor of China's garden in Peking.

[121] *Ibid.*, p. 53.

[122] *Ibid.*, p. 60 and n. 1.

[123] *Ibid.*, pp. 68-69.

[124] *Ibid.*, pp. 92, 99-100. Also see pp. 84-85, where Duchesne contrasts the garden at Stowe with the garden of the Emperor of China: the first was contained in too small an area (and thus "Il y deviendroit trop difficile de dissimuler que cette prétendu liberté de la Nature, n'est qu'un ouvrage humaine; une copie servile & défiguré; ou pis encore, l'effet du caprice"), while the other was a garden of great extent.

found in gardens of the "new style," where it was introduced in order to recall "the rustic life of our virtuous ancestors."[125] His description of the farm marks a stage in the transition between the older traditional type and the modern hamlet, just being created at Chantilly. Duchesne's farm was to be situated in an enclosure formed by ditches, hills, and planting, in which were orchards, a lawn full of animals and birds, and separate buildings which were placed at the center of the complex. These would consist of the main house ("corps-de-logis"), granges, carriage-house, forge, and small "gardens" for vegetables or wheat. Duchesne noted that the only innovation necessary to turn this older type of farm into a modern one was the addition of some kind of ornamental planting, such as cabinets, rotundas, colonnades, and the composition of interesting perspective views.[126]

The anonymous author of a pamphlet on the *jardin anglais*, which appeared simultaneously (October 1775) in the *Journal Encyclopédique*,[127] also described and endorsed both the ornamental and the pastoral styles of garden design.

Whatever the differences between the two approaches to the picturesque garden, both were concerned with one major French question: the relating of this type of garden to the French gardening tradition. Ganay has shown that the *jardin français* was never wholly abandoned in the eighteenth century, and, indeed, symmetry was often included in the new *jardins anglais*.[128] Among the theorists, Blondel, surely influential, was committed wholly to symmetrical gardens. Blondel was not alone. In 1775 M. Chabanon, an amateur and a classical scholar,[129] published an amusing poem, *Epitre sur la manie des jardins anglois*, in which, in defending the gardens of Le Nôtre, he posed a question which must have been asked by many Frenchmen: "Without art, what could be created which would please or be admired?"[130]

Other studies following these, although popular, are either too personal or too late (De Ligne's *Coup d'Oeil sur Beloeil*, published in 1781, and De Lille's *Les jardins: un poème*, published in 1782) to be of influence on the forming of the picturesque garden. However, one final, comprehensive, and probably definitive statement on the picturesque garden was made by C. C. L. Hirschfeld in his five-volume work, the *Theorie der Gartenkunst*, which appeared beginning in 1779 in French and in German (but not, interestingly, in English). It also demonstrated the extent to which the *jardin anglo-chinois* had fallen out of favor. Although the author devoted a large portion of one volume to citing from Chambers's *Designs*,[131] his preference was for Walpole's theory. He considered that Chambers's work was not based on a

---

[125] *Ibid.*, p. 57. Duchesne further qualified the *vie rustique* as related to the description of the fourteenth-century Bolognese writer, Petrus de Crescentiis, whose standard agricultural work, *Ruralium commodorum librum* (1495), was published in a French translation (*Le Livre des prouffitz champestres et ruraulx*) by 1529, with many later editions.

[126] Duchesne, *Formation des jardins*, pp. 58-59.

[127] L.L.D.G.M., *Lettre sur les jardins anglois*, Paris, 1775; "Lettre aux auteurs de ce journal sur les jardins anglois," *Journal encyclopédique*, VIII, October 1775, pp. 132-142. See also chapter V, p. 99.

[128] Ganay, *Les Jardins à la française*.

[129] Bachaumont, *Mémoires*, I, pp. 167-168, 20 November 1762, notes that Chabanon, then 35, resolved to merit a literary title, was admitted to the *Académie des Belles-Lettres*, and that his translation of Pindar assured him a brilliant future. Thus, Chabanon was in the company of De Lille, who translated the Georgics (*ibid.*, I, p. 170, 28 November 1762), and Watelet, who read a free translation of Tasso (*ibid.*, I, p. 194, 22 January 1763).

[130] M. Chabanon, *Epitre sur la manie des jardins anglois*, p. 5.

[131] See chapter III, note 12.

knowledge of the Chinese garden,[132] which Hirschfeld maintained was in reality of a tasteless sterility and simplicity, causing neither admiration nor surprise.[133] And, following Walpole rather than the French, Hirschfeld attributed the invention of the picturesque garden not to the Chinese, but to Kent, who was "the creator of gardening art in England and the first who planted gardens which would be considered to be in good taste."[134]

[132] Hirschfeld, *Art des jardins*, I, p. 154.　　　　[134] *Ibid.*, IV, pp. 3ff.
[133] *Ibid.*, I, pp. 117-118.

CHAPTER V

French Picturesque Garden Types:
The Pastoral Farm, the Jardin Anglo-Chinois,
and the Ferme Ornée

The first fully irregular French garden has yet to be identified.[1] One of the earliest, however, is Ermenonville, which was owned by the Marquis de Girardin. It has been assumed that the Marquis began work there in 1766,[2] but recently discovered documents indicate that he may have acquired his inheritance on 23 July 1762, and that he added to his estate (suggesting that he was following a specific plan for the development of the property) from 23 May 1764 to 3 May 1778.[3] Ermenonville is also one of the best known of the new picturesque gardens. It even has been considered by some critics to be the most outstanding of the type.[4] The owner was, like Watelet, a wealthy amateur. But, unlike Watelet, Girardin's interest was in social as well as cultural reform.[5] His enlightened and philanthropic philosophy was similar to that of Rousseau, who spent his last months at Girardin's estate, and who was buried there.

We are fortunate to have accounts by Girardin, by Morel (who worked on the estate), and by Girardin's son, as well as considerable visual material which help in the reconstruction of the original design. Ermenonville comprised a château and extensive grounds. In contrast to many French parks—which were flat, dry, and without variety—this one contained a wide

[1] Among the candidates are: the garden at Chauvry, attributed by Pérouse de Montclos (*Boullée*, p. 85) to Boullée, and illustrated in Le Rouge, *Nouveaux Jardins à la mode*, cahier xi, pl. 15; cahier xii, pl. 15 (cahiers dated 1784), and designed at some time after the remodeling of the estate in 1764; the garden of the lawyer Gerbier at Aulnay (Petit de Bachaumont, *Mémoires secrets*, iv, pp. 337-338, 19 August 1769, and v, pp. 217-218, November 1770, who describes it as designed by an English gardener); the garden of Mme. la Princesse de Montmorency at Boulonge-sur-Seine (Duc de Croÿ, *Journal*, ii, p. 272, 14 April 1767, and p. 316, 27 July 1768; De Ligne, *Beloeil*, p. 26); the garden of M. le Premier (Croÿ, *Journal*, ii, p. 316, 10 July 1768); and a garden in the old Hôtel de Bourbon (Croÿ, *Journal*, ii, p. 320, 27 July 1768, described it as already being replaced).

[2] Based on the date when Girardin was believed to

have acquired his inheritance, in 1766. See Martin-Decaen, *Le Marquis de Girardin*, pp. 10-11; and Boulenger, *Au Pays de Gérard de Nerval*, p. 107, who also notes that Girardin bought out the coinheritors at this time.

[3] Information from "Acquisitions et propriètès des biens de Mr. de Girardin," deposited at the Musée Jacquemart-André at Châalis, Doc. xxii-6. I am extremely indebted to M. Pierre Marot, Conservateur of the Musée for his kindness in locating and transferring the documents to the Bibliothèque de l'Institut, and to Mme. Hautecoeur, Directeur de la Bibliothèque de l'Institut, for permitting me to look at the documents there.

[4] For Ermenonville, see Bibliography: Individual Gardens.

[5] For Girardin, see Martin-Decaen, *Le Marquis de Girardin*.

assortment of landscapes, from irregular, hilly terrain to marshy flatland, and there was a good existing water supply, including a stream and a lake. Thus the Marquis was able to carry out what must have been a predetermined goal—the preservation of the regional character of the site. Indeed, the general subdivision of the property into four natural sections of meadow, woods, forest, and farm (mentioned by Girardin in his *Composition*), reflect the owner's concern that the local characteristics of the area be maintained (Fig. 54). Moreover, he developed the area without greatly disturbing the natural configuration of the land, and in keeping with this goal, his "embellishments" were designed to heighten the effects of existing natural situations rather than to create new and purely artificial ones.

At the time that Girardin acquired the estate, the grounds had been developed in a regular, formal manner (Figs. 52, 53). The Marquis destroyed a large, square kitchen garden, irrigated by canals, which existed to the south of the château.[6] He drew the water from the existing lake and stream into two succeeding cascades, which then became a meandering stream on the north side of the château, where originally there had been a canal terminating in a small, regular pond. Some elements of the earlier estate seen to have been retained; the woods may recall an earlier wilderness or riding with a rond-point now transformed into a meeting place; an allée of trees which connected the southern garden with the woods appears to have belonged to the earlier plan (as did two mills on the estate);[7] and the area of the Wilderness was left almost entirely in its original undeveloped state. The village dependent on the château seems to have been "improved" by Girardin (Fig. 55), in a manner which may have its source in theatrical designs, such as the backdrop for a pastoral opera, mentioned in chapter 1, which is believed to have been designed by Boucher (Fig. 56). And the walls shutting off the château and the grounds from the road were pulled down so that, according to a contemporary account, a "scene of perpetual movement" was created along the road when it was viewed from the château.[8]

One of the main characteristics of Girardin's design was his concern with the "pictures" that could be created from the natural surroundings. Even the views from the north and south sides of the château were composed as if they represented different styles of landscape painting. Thus, the view to the south of the château (Fig. 57) was designed in the manner of the sunlit brilliance of an Italian landscape, as it might have been painted by Claude Lorrain.[9] It consisted of a lake, framed by wooded hills, with a wide "Arcadian" field in the background, and in the foreground the cascade and grotto. In the lake were two islands, one ringed with poplars. Rousseau's tomb was added here only after his death in 1778 (Fig. 82). The other island

[6] For the original condition of the site, see *ibid.*, pp. 17-18, and note 9 below.

[7] *Ibid.*, p. 17.

[8] Morel, *Théorie*, p. 246.

[9] According to S. Girardin, *Promenade*, p. 9. For a description of the view, see A. Laborde, *Description*, p. 85: ". . . The part to the south which forms this view, exhibits on the left the fall of the lake, where are collected all the rivulets which water the south. Above it are seen the hills covered with trees, and in the midst of them a temple of nearly the same form and in the same situation as that of Tivoly. One is apt to think of one's self transported to that ancient country seat of the Romans, and that one hears the noise of the Arno, which falls down the rocks: it is particularly when the rising sun lights up this scene that the illusion is most complete. This picture is still better enjoyed when one reflects that it replaces stagnated ponds, kitchen gardens, and stone terraces, in the room of which M. Girardin has substituted this enchanting prospect."

contained the tomb of the painter George-Frédéric Mayer, placed there shortly after 1778. The major architectural addition to the natural setting was the Temple of Modern Philosophy.

The view to the north of the château (Fig. 58) was of a flat field, with a "melancholy and gentle" stream winding down the center of the composition.[10] Far in the distance could be seen the ruins of the tower of Mont-Epilay.[11] This view was pastoral, and it is surely to be associated with that of pastoral and meditative northern landscape paintings, although this association is not explicitly suggested in any contemporary text. As opposed to the pastoral and classical southern view, the northern one contained local and rural accessories: the "picture" was terminated by a rustic mill, and in the middle ground was a structure designed to resemble an ancient tower. Two small islands near the tower were noted by Le Rouge as allocated, respectively, to sheep and goats. Although "views" are a common element of garden design, Girardin's son wrote that even in England no garden composition had yet been designed to resemble a painting when seen from the house, and that Girardin, "who had not attempted to imitate the English style in his compositions," was the first to conceive the idea.[12]

The concept of the picture was continued throughout the park with small, picturesque views which may have been developed from the "views" of pictures obtained at the ends of axial vistas in the early eighteenth-century formal parks, and which made up much of the charm of Moulin-Joli. They could be observed while walking through the park, and they provided a series of contrasts—open to closed, wild and rocky to pastoral and rural, rough to tame—which were often noted by Girardin's son, in his text to Mérigot's guide, to be in the style of particular painters: one was in the style of Hubert Robert,[13] another in the taste of Salvator Rosa,[14] and a view toward the Abbey of Châalis recalled the landscapes of Ruysdael and Van Goyen.[15]

The effect of these views might be created solely with local natural materials, including rocks which were transported to effective visual locations: appended to many of the views were numerous literary references and inscriptions (indeed, so numerous that one visitor noted that they tyrannized thought),[16] often from pastoral poetry, both ancient and modern, and, as at Moulin-Joli, recalling sentimental, moral, and pastoral associations. Altars and other memorials further heightened the pastoral and elegiacal character of the estate. Among these were the Altar of Reverie, added in the late 1770s, and a brick obelisk, which was designed in this material because of the relation of its color to the surrounding greens,[17] but also possibly because of Watelet's recommendation of natural materials.[18] Each face of the obelisk was dedicated to a different poet (Fig. 59)—one to William Shenstone. Nearby was a stone inscribed to this English poet and garden designer, with a reference in verse to his design of the Leasowes, which may be evidence that Girardin had this English pastoral farm in mind when designing Ermenonville.

One memorial deserves particular mention. It was inspired by a discovery made by workmen of a prehistoric burial pit (now the Dolmen), which was transformed by Girardin into an area

[10] *Ibid.*, p. 11.
[11] A. Laborde, *Description*, p. 92.
[12] Girardin, *Promenade*, p. 13.
[13] *Ibid.*, p. 19.
[14] *Ibid.*, p. 47.

[15] *Ibid.*, p. 53.
[16] Quoted in Ganay, "Ermenonville," p. 4.
[17] Girardin, *Promenade*, p. 33.
[18] See chapter IV, p. 66.

devoted to meditation on death. The visitors entered the burial pit, or "catacomb," through a door which Girardin's son described as a "monument of barbarism which recalls a period of horrors and calamities...."[19] A Latin inscription above the entry referred to past deeds of war and death. But this was not an imitation of the English melancholy-religious garden, such as Tyers's Garden of the Valley of Death. The Hermitage (Fig. 60) which Girardin placed next to the cave (and which, in contrast to some English and French ones, was not intended to be inhabited) was furnished with simplicity, and not, as was noted, with the bad taste which placed all the "monastic utensils" from hourglass to death's head in such a place. It is possible that the Hermitage was intended to be an answer to an English allegorical garden. It also may have represented a type diametrically opposed to the French rustic hut with its elaborately elegant interior, which was intended not for solitary meditation but for entertainment, and which produced striking theatrical effects through the strong contrast between exterior and interior style.[20]

Some of the monuments at Ermenonville were simple picturesque compositions formed from materials in the natural environment. These included the cascade and grotto (Fig. 61), the Monuments of Old Loves in the Wilderness (Fig. 62), the Green Grotto, and, above all, the stark, uncultivated, and primitive Wilderness (Fig. 63), with rocky eminences, rugged trees, sandy soil, and a large lake. All were similar to areas of the Forest of Fontainebleau, which was considered by such early advocates of nature as the Abbé Le Blanc to be preferable in its grand simplicity to either the formal gardens of France or to the artificially natural gardens of England.

Among the structures included in the park were some that reflected the most primitive and basic constructions of man; a hut in the wilderness, the earliest of the garden structures built at Ermenonville, and which was little more than a cave with a thatched roof (Fig. 64); the Rustic Temple (Fig. 65) where tree trunks were substituted for columns (perhaps under the influence of the concept of the primitive hut referred to by Vitruvius and popularized by Laugier); huts for fishermen and a charcoal-maker (the latter constructed of tree stumps, and it may have been a prototype for Ledoux's later design for a charcoal-maker's hut [Fig. 66]); the Hermitage, and the House of Philemon and Bauchis in the Arcadian Fields (Fig. 68); which was intended to recall the habitations of the golden age.

Some of the structures were permeated with the pastoral and arcadian atmosphere which was directly related to the sentimental and romantic world of Rousseau's *Héloise*. The Rustic Temple and the Monuments of Old Loves were both intended to recall specific locations in Clarence, the estate described in Rousseau's *Héloise*, as was the Orchard of Clarence and the Tower of Clarence (Fig. 70), a *maisonnette en colombe* built for Rousseau, but unfinished at the time of his death.[21] Incidentally, this last structure is also similar to rural buildings in Boucher's landscapes (Fig. 71). Another type of structure on the estate was related to one of Girardin's main concerns in the development of Ermenonville: to improve the living conditions of the inhabitants of the region and to increase agricultural productivity. Thus Girardin

[19] Girardin, *Promenade*, p. 36.   [21] Ganay, "Ermenonville," p. 13.
[20] See p. 100 below.

built a grange at the rond-point in the woods, where peasants gathered for festivities, over which the Marquis and his guests presided (Fig. 67). Several cottages for agricultural workers are mentioned by Girardin's son, although only one, the House of the Vinegrower is illustrated or included in the plan of the estate. There was also a model farm, where the Marquis could attempt agricultural experiments in which he hoped to approach the English in "an art that they had so greatly perfected,"[22] and, near the Wilderness, a charming picturesque hamlet, remodeled from one of the old mills (Fig. 69).

This was, then, the general character of the design of Ermenonville. All the structures discussed conformed to Girardin's theories, and they were designed in a regional, vernacular style. In addition, there were four larger and more individual garden structures on the estate. Of these, the best known and the most prominent, and possibly the most traditional in terms of classical form and iconographical content, was the Temple of Modern Philosophy (Fig. 72). It was designed with reference to the Temple of the Sibyl at Tivoli (Fig. 73), although, in contrast to the antique ruin, this building was intended to appear to be in an unfinished state.[23] The other three structures were stripped of both iconography and of classical form. These three garden buildings were similar in rural style, rustic materials, and asymmetrical composition.[24]

Two of them were major accents in the "picture" on the north side of the château. One, the Tower of Gabrielle (Fig. 79), was designed as if it were an ancient monument recalling to the imagination the age of chivalry.[25] (It may have been the only structure on the estate that was dependent on theatrical "props" for its effects, for the tower was alleged to have belonged to the mistress of Henry IV, the "belle Gabrielle," and it contained furnishings which evoked historical recollections of the period of this famous early seventeenth-century romance.)[26] The other structure designed for this view was the so-called "Italian" mill (Fig. 80),[27] which terminated the stream on the north side of the château. In spite of the Italian designation, the style was also close to that of the vernacular style of the mill at Moulin-Joli, but Laborde noted that it "calls to mind the handsome structures of Italy; the composition of it is due to Mr. Girardin, who had acquired this good taste during his travels in that country."[28]

Finally, there was the Brasserie (Figs. 74, 77), an old mill which had been converted into a gameroom.[29] According to a contemporary source, Hubert Robert was responsible for the design of at least the game room:[30] a drawing of the mill by the artist (Fig. 75), in which a

[22] Girardin, *Promenade*, p. 65, n. 1. According to Girardin's son, the Marquis intended to build small farms for members of the parish, where he hoped through the establishing of a prize, to encourage agricultural experiments and emulation of the English.

[23] For a description of the iconography of the Temple of Philosophy, see Girardin, *Promenade*, pp. 38-40; and Ganay, "Ermenonville," p. 6. The six standing Tuscan columns were dedicated to famous men who had made useful contributions to knowledge by writings or by discoveries: Newton—light, Descartes—no void in nature, Voltaire—irony, William Penn—humanity, Montesquieu—justice, J. J. Rousseau—nature. The Temple was dedicated to Montaigne, "who said everything." At the entrance was a broken column with the inscription "Qui l'achèvera?" and more col-

umns were left on the ground, as if to be added to those in place and awaiting the privileged geniuses who were yet to appear.

[24] For Girardin's views on asymmetrical buildings, see chapter 1, pp. 72-73.

[25] Attributed by A. Thiébaut de Berneaud, *Voyage d'Ermenonville*, p. 175, to Morel.

[26] For the Tower of Gabrielle, see descriptions in Girardin, *Promenade*, pp. 61-65; and A. Laborde, *Description*, p. 93.

[27] For the Italian Mill, see description in Laborde, *op. cit.*, p. 94.

[28] *Idem.*

[29] For the Brasserie, see descriptions in Girardin, *Promenade*, p. 19; and Laborde, *Description*, pp. 87-88.

[30] Villeneuve, *Vues pittoresques*, p. 9.

section of the later structure is missing, suggests that he may have added this, too. Moreover, a painting by Robert of the "Italian Park," now in Lisbon, is modeled on the Brasserie and shows the artist's familiarity with it (Fig. 78). The simple colonnaded entrance to the structure (Fig. 77) is similar to one in the backdrop for the pastoral opera attributed to Boucher and referred to earlier (Fig. 56). Both porches are composed of two primitive "Tuscan" columns supporting a flat porch roof. Laborde noted that the Brasserie called to mind the sites of Italian villas.[31] He was referring to the view from the Brasserie down the allée of trees which does indeed recall the allées of towering trees recorded by both Fragonard and Hubert Robert during their stay at the Villa d'Este in 1759 (Fig. 76).

What were the sources for this garden? It has been noted that the Marquis hired "a band of Scotch gardeners,"[32] and Girardin's son mentions a Scotch head gardener who was responsible for the lush English appearance of the lawn for which Ermenonville was famous.[33] Now, both Ermenonville and Moulin-Joli, in their picturesque and literary character, resemble the Leasowes, which may have been the first garden of this type. However, not only was the English garden not seen by Watelet, but also there is no indication at present of French knowledge of this garden prior to the time that it was published by Whately, with the possible exception of Girardin's undated recollection of having visited it. How much of this visit might have inspired the Marquis, and how much merely reinforced his own concepts is not now known. But it is certain, from the statements of Girardin's son, that only the "fabrique gothique" or Keeper's Lodge, which was situated in the corner of a little *jardin anglais* (Fig. 81) seems to have been intended to recall English gardening.[34] Although it was considered by Laborde to "resemble those appropriated to the same use, which are found in many parks in England," he designated it, more generally, as "in the rural style."[35]

Whatever the English influence, the designing of the park was undertaken by French and not by English garden designers. The candidate most often connected with Ermenonville is the architect Morel, who maintained in his *Théorie des jardins* that he formulated the design concept.[36] But his contributions to the estate are limited, according to Girardin's son, to two bridges, and to the *Bocage* or grove in the bed of the stream on the north side of the château (Fig. 83).[37] The *Bocage* has been described in detail, and a recapitulation of the description will give us some idea of Morel's style. It was designed like a maze, with winding paths and streams which recall, possibly deliberately, the *Bosquet des Sources* at Versailles (Fig. 2). Within it were a circular structure (the Temple of the Muses), a grotto, a sandy bank, a small murmuring cascade and the inevitable inscriptions. The *Bocage* seems old-fashioned in its smallness and its closeness to the traditional enclosed maze when it is compared with the design of the rest of the estate. Girardin's son noted that the grove was intended to be poetic

[31] A. Laborde, *Description*, p. 88.

[32] Martin-Decaen, *Girardin*, p. 19; Boulenger, *Gérard Nerval*, p. 106, n. 6. See also Girardin, *Promenade*, p. 28, and n. 1.

[33] Girardin, *Promenade*, p. 28, n. 1.

[34] Ganay, "Ermenonville," p. 13, citing Villeneuve, *Vues pittoresques*, p. 3.

[35] Laborde, *Description*, p. 86.

[36] Morel, *Théorie*, pp. 256-257.

[37] For a comprehensive presentation of Morel's participation in the designing of Ermenonville, see Ganay, "Ermenonville," pp. 16-17; see also Siren, *China and Gardens of Europe*, pp. 125-132. Morel is credited by Girardin, *Promenade*, p. 58, n. 1, with only the design of the *Bocage* and two bridges on the north side of the château. But see note 25 above.

rather than picturesque—that is, to arouse the emotions and revery.[38] It may be possible to infer that Morel was more inclined to follow the earlier poetic ideas of Watelet as they were developed at Moulin-Joli rather than to develop the carefully worked out picturesque scenario of Girardin's later design. Perhaps Morel's ideas were too conventional for Girardin. There is, in any case, no other source than Morel's own statement to credit him with a larger part in the designing of the estate. And Girardin's son hints that the structure designed by Morel had fallen into ruins, due to deliberate neglect on the part of Girardin, to indicate his displeasure at Morel, who had published his claim to have been the creator of the entire estate at Ermenonville.[39]

There is no doubt that the design of Ermenonville was formulated by Girardin. But there is another possible candidate who is associated with the designing of the estate, one who would have worked in harmony with the concepts of Girardin: Hubert Robert. We know that this artist was responsible for the design of Rousseau's tomb (1778-1780) (Fig. 82), and for the design of a section of the Brasserie. He may also have had a hand in the designing of the southern "picture," for later the artist would paint a similar "picture" of Méréville (Fig. 113), which included another imitation of the Temple of the Sibyl.[40] We have already seen that this type of composition had previously been adopted by Boucher (Fig. 33). It is of interest that Robert began to be influenced by the work of Boucher, the designer of Watelet's *maison bourgeois*, shortly after his return from Italy in 1765.[41] Thus, Robert may represent a link between Moulin-Joli, where Boucher had worked, and Ermenonville. The painter Hubert Robert became friends with Watelet in 1763 during Watelet's second trip to Rome, and there are illustrations by the artist of the mill at Moulin-Joli which he would have made after his return from Italy in 1765, while visiting the amateur (Figs. 24, 29). Whatever the connection may be, these two gardens are remarkably close in spirit. Both are unusual in their austerity, high-minded purpose, and literary associations among the French picturesque gardens of the second half of the century. Moreover, Ermenonville was praised in terms close to those of the critics of Moulin-Joli: it was a garden "which pleased the meditative and philosophical, because it spoke to the soul, it stimulated sentiment, flattered the senses, and stirred the imagination."[42]

But there is one element in which the garden at Ermenonville differs from that at Moulin-Joli—the style of the buildings. At Moulin-Joli the structures have prototypes which can be associated with specifically French architecture, while most of those at Ermenonville are in a universal anonymous vernacular style. As we have seen, at least one of Girardin's garden structures—the mill—was associated by Laborde with the Italian style. This critic was surely not referring to the Italian style of either the classical Roman past, or of the Renaissance and Baroque Italy of modern times. The term must have been intended to refer to the indigenous, rural style of the buildings of the Italian countryside. It should be remembered that the north-

[38] Girardin, *Promenade*, p. 58.
[39] *Ibid.*, p. 59: "Il tombe en ruine; l'on ne paroît pas disposé à le faire rétablir: on sent combien il est déplacé."
[40] For Méréville, see J. de Cayeux, "Hubert Robert dessinateur de jardins et sa collaboration au Parc de Méréville"; and O. Choppin de Janvry, "Méréville."
[41] Cayeux, "Robert a pris modèle sur Boucher," *Connaissance des Arts*, October 1959, pp. 100-107.
[42] P. M. de Valenciennes, *Elémens de perspective*, 1800, pp. 344-345.

ern visitor to Italy was increasingly impressed during the eighteenth century with the beauty of the Italian countryside, in which the villa or farm was integrated with an exceptionally picturesque setting. A return to the idealized, simple country life which the Italian country estate represented would surely have been considered desirable by not only the eighteenth-century English amateur, but also by his enlightened French counterpart. In 1774 Watelet would remark that whoever has traveled to Italy must know the attraction which very common objects derive from the simplicity of their masses and the happy relation of their parts.[43] It is a functionalist observation, in which beauty is seen as the result of the use of the object, but it is also a record of the new attitude of the Frenchman toward Italy, now seen not only for its great monuments, but for the picturesque effects produced by everyday objects in a verdant, natural landscape.[44] The Italian rural architecture may have represented for the northern traveler a universal architectural style, applicable to utilitarian structures of all countries and all times. It is surely within this context that an inscription at the entrance to Ermenonville was intended:

> *La Nature et le paysage*
> *Sont de tout temps, de tout pays*[45]

If I am correct, when the concept of the Italian style entered the mainstream of French architecture, it seems to have been associated not only with the rural architecture of Italy, but, more specifically, with the work of Palladio. The transition between the eccentric creations of the amateur and the professional essays of the architect may have commenced with a work of the architect M. J. Peyre, the villa, or so-called "Folie," of the Baronne de Neubourg on the outskirts of Paris, which he designed in 1762 (Fig. 84). The architect published an illustration of the Folie in 1765, in his *Oeuvres d'architecture*, which contained his Roman studies. Like Watelet's *maison bourgeois*, the building contained only the simplest and most rudimentary architectural vocabulary. In the explanation attached to his illustration, Peyre stated: "I have ornamented this facade with columns forming the peristyle, as they are found in most of the larger structures ("Cazins") in Italy, in order to create the play and movement which make their general effect very agreeable." And he added, "This effect is seen in a great number of examples of the works of Palladio."[46]

Surely the simplified style and the Palladian motifs of French architects after the mid-1760s, and in particular the work of the architect Ledoux, must be seen with the foregoing in mind.

---

[43] Watelet, *Essai*, p. 28.

[44] See, for instance, A. Laborde, *Description*, p. 48: "Il faudroit que l'art des jardins devînt populaire en France, comme l'architecture l'est en Italie: chaque maison, dans ce dernier pays, a son principe de construction qui se rattache à une école pure: les moindres métairies sont ornées d'un petit porche, d'un toit bien fait, ou d'une galerie à jour qui sert à sécher les légumes; enfin on remarque partout un ensemble qui présente de jolies lignes et se groupe agréablement avec ce qui l'entoure. Chaque maison devroit être accompagnée d'un jardin soigné, de fleurs, de beaux

arbres, et n'être séparée des autres habitations que par un fossé ou un haie, afin de servir ainsi mutuellement de point vue. Le pays se trouveroit alors former une réunion de demeures agréables, de tout genre."

[45] Ganay, "Ermenonville," p. 4 (from Girardin, *Promenade*, pp. 14-15).

[46] M. J. Peyre, *Oeuvres*, p. 7 and pl. 12: "J'ai orné la Façade de Colonnes formant le Pérystile, comme le sont la plûpart des Cazins Italiens, afin de lui donner le jeu & le mouvement qui rendent en général l'effet de ces sortes de Bâtimens très-agréables on en voit un très-grand nombre d'exemples dans Palladio."

The speculative luxury housing that Ledoux designed for the West Indian planter Hosten in 1792 (Fig. 85) is almost without ornamentation, with the exception of some Palladian motifs. The irregularity of the siting of the houses is close in concept to the picturesque irregularity of the buildings of Girardin's farm-hamlet (Fig. 69): it may be that Ledoux had such an idealized farm in mind when designing his project.

The French publications on Italian vernacular architecture follow, rather than initiate, this development. From 1791 to 1793 François-Louis Seheult drew Italian buildings but did not publish them until 1821 in his *Recueil d'architecture, dessiné et mesuré en Italie . . .* ; Percier and Fontaine also probably did not begin their series of illustrations for the *Palais, maisons et autres édifices modernes dessinés à Rome* (published in 1798) until 1792; Pierre Clochard published his *Palais, maisons et vues d'Italie* in 1809, and Famin and Grandjean de Montigny published *Architecture toscane* in 1806. By this time Durand's *Précis des leçons* had already appeared (1802-1805), with many Italianate examples (Fig. 86).

Precisely what the connection of this style was with similar English architectural developments cannot be determined now. But it has been suggested by Summerson that the 1811 promotional drawings for Nash's Regent's Park project, which contained asymmetrical Italianate country villas, were by a French artist (Figs. 166a-f).[47] And already by 1802 Nash had designed Cronkhill. The portico of this country villa is close to the simple country portico of the Folie Neubourg; the dovecote-like tower, the asymmetry and the idealized "Italian" style perhaps recall the character of the garden structures at Ermenonville, and the spirit behind the simple country house in which Watelet lived.

Returning to the picturesque garden, if Ermenonville represents the pastoral aspect, the opposite is represented by the *jardin anglo-chinois*. According to Métra, this latter type of garden was owned by wealthy eccentrics who wanted to have English gardens, but who arranged them in their own manner. He gave as early examples two Paris gardens which had been developed on flat, marshy terrain on the northern edge of Paris. They were Boutin's Tivoli and the Duc de Chartres's Monceau. Both were considered by contemporary critics to be models for later gardens in this style. Of the two, Tivoli (Fig. 87 and text ill. 1) is slightly earlier: it was completed by 1771.[48] Métra maintained that it was the first of these gardens to be executed "en grand,"[49] and De Lille asserted that it was "the first in France to suggest the model [of a fully-developed picturesque garden]."[50]

However, Tivoli was still a preliminary statement of the "new style" of garden, the *jardin anglo-chinois*. We know little about the appearance of the garden structures, but we can assume that they were designed in the *style français*. For, although the spirit of Tivoli was contrary to that of Moulin-Joli, many of the elements of this garden were related to those of the earlier one. For instance, the approach along an allée defined by small individual buildings

---

[47] J. Summerson, "Introduction," to T. Davis, *The Architecture of John Nash*, London, 1960, p. 13, who notes that there are a few French words on one of the panoramas, and suggests that the French artist was Charles Augustus Pugin. A. Saunders, *Regent's Park, A Study of the Development of the Area from 1806 to the Present Day*, Newton Abbot, Devon, 1969, p. 86,

notes that Pugin was Nash's assistant for some years.
[48] For Tivoli, see Le Rouge, *Nouveaux Jardins à la mode*, cahier i, p. 26.
[49] Métra, *Correspondance secrète*, i, pp. 146-147, 2 January 1775.
[50] De Lille, *Jardin*, p. 14.

was similar to the approach at Moulin-Joli, although in the later garden multiple and elaborate structures replaced the single earlier one. They included "stables for different animals" (possibly a menagerie?), a dairy (*laiterie d'agrément*), a cow barn, and a stable, all similar to structures at Moulin-Joli, as well as a dovecote, a gardener's hut, and, nearby, two belvederes, an aviary, and a greenhouse.[51]

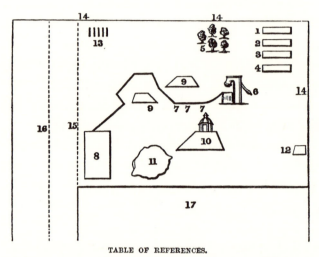

TABLE OF REFERENCES.

1. Slip of corn. 2. Do. of grass. 3. Do. of weeds, very rural. 4. Do. of oats. 5. Irregular grove. 6. A well and pump that furnishes the river. 7, 7, 7. A serpentine river in a stone channel, four feet wide. 8. A canal. 9, 9. Two mountains, twelve feet high, in the shape of a tansy-pudding, but not so green as the river. 10. Mount Olympus, with a temple on it. 11. An irregular piece of turf. 12. A fairy, with an Italian front. 13. Slips of grass. 14, 14, 14. The wall. 15. Terrace commanding a superb view over the hot-houses and dunghill. 16. Kitchen-garden with melon frames. 17. French garden.

text illus. 1   Diagram of Tivoli. From Walpole, *Letters*, VIII, p. 69.

The garden proper was designed in three sections: the largest was a kitchen garden; the two smaller areas were designated *jardin italien* and *jardin anglois*. The *jardin italien*, with its changes of level and its pronounced symmetrical axis within a small and busy design, is reminiscent of contemporary French rococo gardens rather than of the grandeur and simplicity of Italian ones. Although the *jardin anglois* was asymmetrical, its smallness and busyness are similar to that of the *jardin italien*. It was described by Le Rouge as including twisting paths, a winding artificial river with two islands, a cascade, irregular groves, mounts, bridges, an antique tomb with cypresses, a sheepfold, and rare flowers and shrubs.[52] Horace Walpole, who saw the *jardin anglois* in 1771, noted that Boutin had "taken a piece of what he calls an English garden to a set of stone terraces, with steps of turf. There are three or four very high hills,

[51] Le Rouge, *Nouveaux Jardins*, cahier i, p. 26.   [52] *Ibid.*, p. 25.

almost as high as, and exactly in the shape of, a tansy pudding. You squeeze between these and a river, that is conducted at obtuse angles in a stone channel, and supplied by a pump; and when walnuts come in, I suppose it will be navigable." Walpole also noted in this garden "a strip of grass, another of corn, and a third *en friche*, exactly in the order of beds in a nursery."[53] Some suggestion of agriculture may have been attempted here by Boutin, and this might account for the inclusion of not only the kitchen garden, but also of a dairy and a cow barn as prominent elements in his city garden. However, this is a very artificial creation of a pastoral environment. When Roucher in his poem *Les Mois* referred to a garden near Paris where nature appeared in masquerade, he surely meant Boutin's.[54]

The qualities of utility, formality, and artificial naturalness, which occurred separately in Boutin's garden, were combined into a unified whole at Monceau. This park was begun around 1773, although, as with Ermenonville, the idea for it may have begun to take shape earlier, in 1771, when the Duc de Chartres began acquiring property at the site.[55] The park contained almost all of the thematic motifs which would be present in the fully developed picturesque gardens of the late 1770s and 1780s (Fig. 88).[56] Many of these are illustrated by the designer of the park, Carmontelle, in his 1779 publication of Monceau. Again, the account of the structures in Carmontelle's description, and in a contemporary guidebook, Thièry's *Guide des amateurs*, permit us to discuss its appearance and origins in detail.

Thièry described Monceau as containing a "quantity of curious things," which he then discussed in the sequence in which they would be seen.[57] The visitor entered the garden through a Chinese gate. Next to the gate was a "Gothic" building, which served as a chemical laboratory, according to Carmontelle. The visitor then proceeded through colored pavilions and greenhouses to a narrow mirrored pavilion through which (by pushing a button which opened one of the mirrors) he entered the *Jardin d'hiver* (Fig. 90). This building was filled with exotic plants, and the floor was covered with fine red sand which formed an irregular, winding path. Trees were painted and sculpted along the walls; their branches extended into the vaulted ceiling, where crystal lanterns were suspended. There was also a waterfall, which was illuminated at night by candles hung from imitation coral. The gallery was glazed on one long side and it was lit by a clerestory on the other so that daylight conditions were close to those of the exterior.[58] At the far end of this well-lit and plant-filled gallery there was a deep rock grotto, where the Prince gave dinner parties: musicians played in a room above the grotto, and the sound of music filtered through openings in the vault to the diners below.

---

[53] Walpole, *Letters*, VIII, pp. 64-65, Walpole to John Chute, 5 August 1771; also see *ibid.*, pp. 67-70, 11 August 1771, Walpole to the Countess of Upper Ossory.

[54] Roucher, *Les Mois*, chant iii, p. 183.

[55] Dacier, "Le Jardin de Monceau," p. 51, proposes 1771 as the date when the design of Monceau was begun. He cites as evidence the "Copie du procès-verbal de l'estimation de Mousseaux," an xiii, p. 3r, deposited at the Bibliothèque Historique de la Ville de Paris (MS 935), where it is noted that the Duc de Chartres began acquiring property for the developing

of his site by 28 June 1771. See also the allotment plan for the park (Archives Nationales, Seine III 868, *Plan géometral d'un jardin et de plusieurs pièces de terre adiacentes situées sur le terroir de Monceau*).

[56] A. Laborde, *Description*, p. 117.

[57] Thièry, *Guide*, I, pp. 64-73.

[58] The room surely was an influence on the Dining Hall in the Hameau at Chantilly: both contained sanded floors, tree-painted walls, and a contrast of simple rustic exteriors with elaborate and exotic interior decoration. See chapter III, note 160.

On leaving the grotto the visitor found himself within the precinct of a rustic farm (Fig. 89) and next to a cabaret. The sociable function of the cabaret may have been planned in deliberate contrast to that of the dairy (*laiterie d'agrément*), further on, which was a garden structure traditionally associated with meditation. The cabaret was included in the design of the farm buildings, all of which were constructed, like a stage set, against the exterior wall of the park. From here a path led to the Ruins of the Temple of Mars (Fig. 103), where there once stood a statue of Mars, no longer there by the time Thièry described the place. Beyond the Ruins stretched a field and a winding river, in which was located the Island of Rocks (Fig. 91). On the opposite bank was a Dutch mill which moved a pump for a waterfall. Close by, on the highest spot of ground, was a reservoir which furnished all the water for the flat garden site. Beyond the mill was the dairy (called the *Maison rustique du Meunier*, possibly in reference to Moulin-Joli and its *belle meunière* Marguerite Le Comte). Thièry neglected to mention a large flower garden placed in the center of the park, which was composed of complex geometric patterns of beds of red, yellow, and blue flowers. Between the flower beds were statues of Meleager, Hymen, and Friendship. The guide also omitted mention of the two French pavilions there, which were flanked by statues of Marriage and Friendship (by the sculptor Pigalle), and the small Grove of Sycamores and Ebony Trees, which joined the flower garden.

Thièry did notice another flower bed, the Flower Marsh, which was divided into small regular plots. He noted that to the north there was a stream issuing from a fountain situated beside a rock basin. Following the bank of this stream the visitor came to a mount (Fig. 92), on the summit of which was a Turkish pavilion or "minaret," according to Carmontelle,[59] or a small pavilion in the gothic style, according to Thièry.[60] It also functioned as a belvedere with an unlimited view. At the base of the mount and on its far side was a rock cave which was the entry to the icehouse.

Keeping the stream which circles the garden to the right, and proceeding through the Flower Marsh, the visitor arrived at the Wood of the Tombs (Fig. 97), which was planted with Italian poplars, sycamores, plantanes, cypresses, and Chinese cedars. Within the woods was the tomb of a young girl, a pyramid (the interior of which contained eight granite columns, one-third buried and with capitals formed of Egyptian heads, a painted domical vault, and tombs, niches, and a basin with a statue along the sides of the hall), an urn, a fountain, and a tomb with a "ruined pyramid" above it.

The visitor next came to the Italian Vineyard, in which there was, appropriately, an antique statue of Bacchus, and then, following the path and crossing the stream, he entered a wood, called the *Bois irrégulier*, on the opposite bank. This wood contained several clearings including openings for a resting place in which were found a statue of Mercury and an altar, two ruined monuments (one with a fire pump above which was a small room decorated à la chinoiserie), a bell tower, and a fountain (the Fountain of the Bathers) composed of a basin with a sculptural group by Houdon.

---

[59] Carmontelle, *Monceau*, p. 8.   [60] Thièry, *Guide*, I, p. 67.

Leaving the *Bois irrégulier* by a ruined gate, the visitor entered the area of the Naumachia (Fig. 93). Here a ruined Corinthian peristyle stood along one end of an oval pool, in which an obelisk was situated on a rock island. The visitor then crossed a wooden bridge that spanned the stream on the north side of the garden; nearby was the Military Column, beyond which the visitor passed in succession a small botanical garden, a Fountain of the Nymph (at the "source" of the stream), a statue of Paris, a Turkish tent (Fig. 94), a marble monopteral circular temple (now located on the Ile du Pont at Neuilly), a Chinese bridge, the *Bois régulier* (next to the main pavilion), and a ruined castle (in which were stairs leading to a platform and to a belvedere from which the whole garden could be seen) (Fig. 95). A water mill was situated on the other side of this ruin. Close by, water cascaded over rocks through the main arch of a stone bridge; just beyond the castle was an island of sheep (Fig. 89). Next to it were the "farm" and the cabaret.

The visitor had now regained the garden side of the main pavilion, before which there was laid out an elegantly planned formal garden which included a large aviary (noted by Carmontelle to be of a "type difficult to represent in a view"). To one side of the main pavilion was a *jeu de bague* (Fig. 96), that is, a kind of maypole with seats attached to it which were turned by servants so that the seated guests could attempt to catch rings which were suspended from above them. Beyond this elaborate object were two Turkish tents, the *Salle des maronniers*, in which was placed a statue by Bouchardon (from the antique), and a field with farm animals which was separated from the main garden by a ditch.

This was indeed a garden containing a "quantity of curious things!" As we have seen in chapter II, Monceau was often paired with Stowe (Figs. 88, 36) by the French, who criticized both these gardens for their expense and artificiality, and for their excessive number of structures. When Alexandre Laborde described Monceau as "one of the first essays in France of the English manner of laying out gardens," he cited as an example of its English quality, not its irregularity, but the "profusion of buildings."[61] But in spite of the fact that there is no doubt about English influence on Monceau—it should be recalled that its owner, Philippe-Egalité, was an ardent anglophile[62]—its character and even the very number of its structures are rooted in French garden design and theory. According to its creator, Carmontelle, the park was designed in the French manner to achieve diversity of structures and entertaining effect rather than in the English manner suggesting closeness to nature and meditative associations.[63] And the general arrangement of Monceau was related to that of traditional French gardens: the elaborate regular planting next to the house recalls the complex patterns of the formal French parterre, groves now are modified into an irregular series of open and closed scenes rather than planned in a geometrical configuration, and the mazelike "wilderness" at the base of the garden can be related to the outlying park of French tradition.

There are more specific instances at Monceau of references to traditional French gardening. Not only do the regular, "architectural" sections of the garden, such as the geometrically

[61] A. Laborde, *Description*, p. 117. See also Morel, *Théorie*, p. 355, n. 1, for criticism of this type of garden.
[62] Britsch, *Philippe-Egalité*, pp. 382-432, chapter XI:

"La seconde réputation du Duc de Chartres: l'Anglomanie."
[63] See chapter IV, pp. 76-77.

shaped flower bed, recall this tradition, but also the kitchen garden and the vineyard suggest the simpler, more utilitarian gardening of the period prior to that of Louis XIV. And the regular square beds of the Flower Marsh recall the square patterns of sixteenth-century gardens. The rocky hermit's mount at Gaillon, designed in the mid-sixteenth century, and illustrated by Du Cerceau, may be one source for Monceau's rocky island and for the many later ones which proliferated in French picturesque gardens, as well as for later eighteenth-century hermitages.[64] The monopteral circular temple, which was a common structure in French eighteenth-century picturesque gardens, and which was represented at Monceau by the minaret (Fig. 92) as well as by the marble temple, may have originated in such a sixteenth-century example as the one at the Bâstie of Honoré d'Urfé.[65] Statues of classical gods, placed in locations where, by their allegorical references, they would represent the character of the site, were also a part of French formal gardening vocabulary. The colonnade of the Naumachia at Monceau is surely an updated and classicized version of the Colonnade at Versailles (Figs. 93, 4).[66] The relation of the *Jardin d'hiver* grotto to the earlier Kiosk at Lunéville had been mentioned in chapter 1. Even the main pavilion of Monceau follows a traditional plan established for villas and hunting lodges—as, for instance, for Malgrange in 1711—by the late 1680s.[67]

But these associations can only suggest a strong French tradition for the French picturesque garden. A more accurate assessment of the roles of France and England in the evolution of this type of garden is not possible without a thorough study of garden structures in both England and France. To date, no such study has been made; thus far, there is only one article on one garden type, the dairy. It indicates the possible direction, between France and England, which the sequences of steps marking the development of the picturesque garden may have taken. According to its author, the dairy (*laiterie d'agrément*) was introduced in France in the sixteenth century, when it was incorporated with the menagerie. It was isolated as a separate structure in England, possibly first at Richmond in the 1730s, and it reappeared as an isolated garden structure in France after 1769 at Le Raincy and Beloeil. It is possible that the dairies at Monceau and at Tivoli are very early appearances of this type as a single structure in French gardens. The dairy at Moulin-Joli was incorporated with the cow barn—a possible transitional stage between the dairy associated with the menagerie and the independent dairy of the *ferme ornée*. The ultimate development of the dairy, when it was incorporated with the grotto, occurred at Rambouillet and at Méréville.[68]

An investigation of the history of one of the "scenes" from Monceau, the Wood of the Tombs (Fig. 97), suggests some of the implications of looking to French sources for the

[64] Gothein, *History of Garden Art*, I, pp. 47-48. From J. A. Du Cerceau, *Le premier Volume des plus excellents Bastiments de la France*, Paris, 1607, pp. 3-4.

[65] Mentioned by Hautecoeur, *Histoire de l'architecture classique*, V, p. 31; and reproduced in Stein, *Jardins de France*, pl. 96 (from P. Vitry, "Le Château de las Bastie d'Urfé," *Les beaux Monuments historiques de la Plaine du Forez*, Saint-Etienne, 1937, opp. p. 16). Hautecoeur also mentions, as possible sources for the monopteral circular temple, illustrations in Perrault's

Vitrivius and sixteenth-century illustrations of landscapes.

[66] Blunt, "Hypnerotonmachia Poliphili," pp. 126-128, relates the sources for the Versailles Colonnade to Colonna's work.

[67] For a discussion of this plan type, see R. Pommer, *Eighteenth-Century Architecture in Piedmont: the Open Structures of Juvarra, Alfieri and Vittone*, New York, 1967, pp. 68-71.

[68] J. Langner, "Architecture pastorale."

French picturesque garden. This particular type of "scene" was popular in the French *jardin anglo-chinois*. It may have originated only several years before the development of Monceau, in 1771, in the single tomb at Boutin's Tivoli as described by Le Rouge. By the late 1770s there was an Island of Tombs at Bagatelle, a Valley of Tombs at Betz,[69] and tombs at Armainvilliers and other gardens.[70] Indeed, by 1781 the Prince de Ligne would criticize the abuse of this type, which he said was used for kitchens, wine cellars, larders—and even lower functions.[71] Now, the French tombs are designed as imaginative, inventive essays in heterogeneous styles which are an extension of the vocabulary of traditional ornament, rather than, in the English fashion, as memorials. Similar designs for tombs were invented by Piranesi (ca. 1750) for his imaginary reconstruction of the Appian Way (Fig. 157).[72] These designs are related to the publications of architectural ornaments which appeared in the late 1760s by, for instance, Delafosse, Legeay (Fig. 98), and Cuvilliès (Fig. 99).[73] At the same time (1769) Piranese included in his *Diversi maniere d'adornare i cammini* an imaginative and inventive use of heterogeneous styles. In his introductory remarks to this publication, he summed up the rationale behind the use of the new, exotic ornament. For him, objects which had no functional or structural restrictions requiring a traditional use could be enriched by this extended and diverse field of ornamentation.[74]

The popularizing of historical styles of ornament in order to increase the number of models to which artists might refer may have begun with Caylus's *Recueil d'antiquités*, which began to appear in 1752, and was published with this purpose in mind.[75] But behind this interest in historical and exotic styles is surely Fischer von Erlach's *Entwurff einer historischen Architectur*.[76] The work was in preparation from 1705, although it was not published until 1721 in German and French. It was translated into English by 1730. It was thus available to artists and amateurs early in the century, and, indeed, it was designed for this audience. The comprehensive scope of its architectural examples and the emphasis on colossal scale were influ-

---

[69] Ganay, *Les Jardins à l'anglaise en France*, II, pp. 506ff.

[70] R. Lanson, *Le Goût du moyen âge en France au XVIIIe siècle*, Paris, 1926, p. 40.

[71] De Ligne, *Beloeil*, p. 286. See also Tschoudy, *Encyclopédie*, 1776, mentioned in chapter II, p. 28.

[72] For the dating of Piranesi's *Appian Way*, see Hylton Thomas, *The Drawings of Piranesi*, London, 1954, pp. 45-46, and pl. 32. This reference has been kindly communicated to me by John Wilton-Ely.

[73] See Y. Sjöberg, biography of Legeay, *Inventaire du Fonds Français: graveurs du XVIIIe siècle*, Paris, 1974 (Bibliothèque Nationale), pp. 507-508, and J. M. Le Magny, "Jean Laurent Le Geay," *Nouvelles de l'Estampe*, 1967, pp. 311-313, who mentions J. C. Delafosse, *Nouvelle Iconologie historique*, Paris, 1768; J. L. Legeay, *Fontane* (1767), *Vasi* (n.d.), *Rovine* (1768), *Tombeaux* (1768); F. Cuvilliès, *fils, Architecture bavaroise*, 1769-1772.

[74] G. B. Piranesi, *Diversi manieri*, p. 7: "I am rather inclined to think that chimneys form a particular class in architecture by themselves, which class has its own particular laws, and properties, and is susceptible of all the embellishments, and variety which the *small* architecture can furnish."

[75] Comte de Caylus, *Recueil d'antiquités egyptiennes, étrusques, grecques et romaines*, Paris, 1752-1767 (7v.), I, p. ij: "Les monumens antiques sont propres à étendre les connoissances. Ils expliquent les usages singuliers, ils éclaircissent les faits obscurs ou mal détaillés dans les Auteurs, ils mettent les progrès des Arts sous nos yeux, & servent de modèles à ceux qui les cultivent." For French interest in the history of architecture, see Nyberg, "Meissonnier," pp. 10-11, and note 15.

[76] For Fischer von Erlach's *Entwurff einer historischen Architectur*, see G. Kunoth, *Die historische Architektur Fischers von Erlach*, Düsseldorf, 1956. It should be recalled that at the same time that Fischer's work was published, Juvarra was producing his *Capricci architettonici* (ca. 1720) in England, one of the *capricci* shows a similar interest in the ornamental possibilities of tomb architecture.

ential for such important artists as Piranesi[77] and Boullée.[78] Fischer's section on China and other oriental countries has been associated with the eighteenth-century picturesque garden (Figs. 101, 102). The first book of the *Historischen Architectur* contains designs for Egyptian tombs and pyramids (Fig. 100) which resemble the tombs and memorials illustrated by Piranesi in his reconstruction of the Appian Way, and those that appear in the garden of Monceau. It should be noted also that the Ruins of the Temple of Mars at Monceau (Fig. 103) recalls Fischer's illustration of the Ruins of Palmyra (Fig. 104),[79] to which Carmontelle may have referred specifically when creating this "scene" at Monceau.

Fischer's work is a cumulative and comprehensive exposition of the architecture of the past and of distant lands synthesized with contemporary architecture. It presents, indeed, one aspect of a "world image"—a concept recently investigated by Susi Lang, in a study of the gardens of Stowe, for its relevance to the design of the early eighteenth-century English picturesque garden.[80] Lang identifies at Stowe an underlying program specifically designed to recall distant times and places (a program which, incidentally, is associated with the iconography of Hadrian's Villa). Indeed, she suggests Stowe to be the most comprehensive eighteenth-century English exponent of the "world image" concept. The Chinese gate, the Turkish tent, and probably also the Gothic ruin at Monceau are surely designed within the tradition of a "world image."[81] In contrast, by the 1770s when Monceau was designed, such exotic structures were presented less as a scholarly exposition of accumulated knowledge and more in a spirit of delight in adventure and travel to the fantastic and illusory lands of distant times and places.

The theme of the tomb in the garden also may have had an additional source. Carmontelle specifically related a scene from *Pyramus and Thisbe* to his "scene" of the *Wood of the Tombs* at Monceau.[82] His reference to the theater was not unique. In 1806 Laborde, writing of the Pyramid at Maupertuis, acknowledged the association of this garden type with the theater as follows: "This custom of tombs, in gardens, dates from the latter times that preceded the Revolution. . . . Dramas were wanted on the stages, tombs in gardens."[83] It is possible that the development of theatrical concepts would eventually permit the expansion of the "picture" or scene into a total theatrical environment—Bélanger, in a post-Revolutionary letter to a client, would speak of such a garden as having been designed as a "moving picture."[84] Moreover, the

---

[77] M. Binney, "Megalomania and Melancholy: Piranesi at the British Museum," *Country Life*, CXLIV, 12 December 1968, p. 1593.

[78] D. Wiebenson, review of J. M. Pérouse de Montclos, *E. L. Boullée*, in *Journal of the Society of Architectural Historians*, XXX, October 1970, pp. 250-251.

[79] The ruins of Palmyra were illustrated in the seventeenth century by Jean Marot, although the English illustrations by Wood and Dawkins (*Ruins of Palmyra*, London, 1757) are considered to be the immediate source for later French interest in Palmyra, as reflected most notably in Soufflot's architectural ornament for Sainte-Geneviève (see Wiebenson, *Sources of Greek Revival Architecture*, London, 1969, p. 66). There is another possible prototype for the Ruins of the Temple of Mars. Duchesne, *Sur la Formation des jardins*, p. 60, observed that this area of Monceau was

modeled on paintings. He may have been thinking of painted theatrical backdrops in public pleasure gardens, such as the scene of the ruins of Palmyra in the London Vauxhall which were installed by 1754 (Wiebenson, *Sources*, p. 63).

[80] S. Lang, "Alexander Pope and the Gardens of Stowe," paper read at Dumbarton Oaks, 12 March 1974. This iconography may have been national. For instance, Dennerlein has noted (*Gartenkunst*, pp. 154-155, and 218-220, nn. 441, 442) that Chinese pavilions occurred mainly in England and Germany in the first half of the century, but seldom in France.

[81] A. Britsch, *Philippe-Egalité*, pp. 420-421.

[82] Carmontelle, *Monceau*, p. 10, and see note 90 below.

[83] A. Laborde, *Description*, p. 157.

[84] Stern, *Bélanger*, I, p. 30.

very function of the French garden, as a site for fêtes and other theatrical entertainments, suggests a traditional connection between theater and garden. The transposition of natural effects into the French picturesque garden would not have been possible had not the designers been thoroughly familiar with the techniques of stage decoration. Indeed, French garden designers had links with the theater and even with the related art of painting. Dufresny was a playwright, Carmontelle was an amateur dramatist, François Boucher was associated with the *Comédie française*, and, above all, Servandoni, who was responsible for the designing of structures in several eighteenth-century gardens,[85] is best known for his innovative work in theater design.[86]

In particular, there seems to have been some influence of effects from the medium of the opera on the *jardin anglo-chinois*. Opera was a composite medium which drew on effects from all the arts—and even from the sciences—to produce facsimiles of not only historical and geographic places but also natural phenomenon. It was precisely such effects that some contemporary French garden critics were demanding. As we have seen in chapter IV, Carmontelle himself wished to create "a country of illusions." He wrote, "Our gardens should transport us through the scenes of an Opera, we should create the illusion of a reality from what the best Painters can offer as decorations." And, since nature was variable according to the climates, Carmontelle even suggested that it would be possible to vary climate within the garden or to cause one to forget the real climate altogether.[87]

Carmontelle was not alone in his views. By 1770 even Walpole had observed, "Watteau's trees are copied from those of the Tuilleries and Villas near Paris; a strange scene to study nature in! There I saw the originals of those tufts of plumes and fans, and trimmed-up groves, that nod to one another like the scenes of an *opera*. Fantastic people! who range and fashion their trees, and teach them to hold up their heads, as a dancing-master would, if he expected Orpheus should return to play a minuet to them."[88] And, as we have seen in chapter II, the anonymous writer who had associated Monceau with Stowe also related gardens of this type to the opera.[89] It is possible that when Carmontelle suggested that the Wood of the Tombs recalled a scene from *Pyramus and Thisbe*, he was referring to a scene designed by Servandoni for the 1726 production of that opera.[90] In 1780 Le Camus de Mezières recommended that Servandoni's elaborate and extreme theatrical effects be imitated in the context of garden design. Le Camus wrote that it was the ability to improvise, based on known theatrical techniques, which formed the basis of the method for the creating of both operatic scenes and the *jardin anglo-chinois*. He observed:

> What are the causes of different effects? . . . Let us turn our eyes to our Theatres, where
> the simple imitation of nature determines our affections. Here is the enchanted Palace

[85] Gallet, *Demeures parisiennes*, p. 184, lists a chapel in the gardens of the Hôtel de la Live de Jully, rue Cambon; a temple in the park of Gennevilliers (engraving, Le Rouge); and a fountain in the cloister of Sainte-Croix de la Bretonnerie (drawing, Musée Carnavalet).

[86] For Servandoni, see D. Oenslager, *Stage Design: Four Centuries of Scenic Invention*, New York, 1975, pp. 84-85; and P. Bjurström, "Servandoni décorateur de théâtre." Also see chapter IV, p. 71.

[87] Carmontelle, *Monceau*, p. 4.

[88] Walpole, *Anecdotes of Painting*, IV, pp. 35-36.

[89] See chapter II, pp. 35-36.

[90] *Mercure de France*, October 1726, p. 2341. In the fifth act, "le Théâtre représente un bois épais: on voit à travers des arbres, les Tombeaux des Rois d'Assyrie." The opera opened on 17 October 1726.

of Armida; all is magnificent and voluptuous; one believes that Love built it. The scene changes; it is the dwelling of Pluto that brings terror to our souls. Do we see the Temple of the Sun? It produces admiration. The sight of a Prison causes sadness. Apartments arranged for a festival, surrounded by gardens with fountains and flowers, make us happy and prepare us for pleasure. At the sight of the forest of Dodona, the soul is moved; we are seized by the sacred terror of the woods.

The famous Servandoni, of whom the fertile genius and the knowledge of the secrets of his Art have surprised us on the stage [and here Le Camus specifically referred the reader to a *Représentation en machines*, produced at the Salle des Machines in the Tuilleries in 1741], knew, in a wordless Spectacle, how to create the effect of the burning warmth of the Sun. The Camp of Godefroy was seen threatened by the fires of the Canicule; nearly without shade, a reddened sky, dry earth, an effect of light which recalled that of firey winds; all this produced an illusion from which no Spectator could shelter himself; all believed himself to suffer, all submitted to the powers of art. It would be possible, without doubt, and with as much success, to create the illusion of a smarting cold, if we were presented with the image of those climates where some stripped birches were the only vegetation growing from the rocks covered with eternal snow; an overcast day and a pale and uniform sky are indications of new frost. Stiff, icy flowers, streams surprised and captured in their course, present to us nature deprived of life and movement. This spectacle would make us shudder. What could we not attempt. . . ."[91]

Perhaps Carmontelle was thinking of Servandoni's work when he suggested the production of artificial climates in gardens.

One other "scene" at Monceau, the *ferme ornée*, became a common element in the later *jardins anglo-chinois*. The background of the *ferme ornée* is complex. The type may have developed from the menagerie. Loisel, in his comprehensive study of menageries, notes that there was one at the Château de Monceau in the Faubourg du Roule (later, Monceau) from the time of Louis XIV, and he has suggested that it might have developed into the later areas for a farm for domestic animals when the estate was transformed into a *jardin anglo-chinois*.[92] With this theory in mind, it is possible to suggest that Watelet's cow barn at Moulin-Joli, and Boutin's "stables for different animals" at Tivoli represent transitional stages in the development from elaborate shelter for exotic beasts to rustic farmyard for domestic animals.

On the other hand, discussions of the *ferme ornée* in contemporary gardening theory and other literature suggest an English origin for it.[93] Whately's description of Woburn Farm, which he classified as a *ferme ornée*, is the best known and possibly the earliest one of the type.[94] What is more, Whately's work appeared in a French translation in 1771, just before the

---

[91] Le Camus de Mezières, *Génie de l'architecture*, pp. 5-6. Incidentally, he also noted that the English gardens were truly Chinese in origin, although the method used to create them was drawn from nature (*ibid.*, pp. 14-15).

[92] G. Loisel, *Histoire des ménageries de l'antiquité à nos jours*, II, p. 266, where he notes a document on the earlier menagerie in the Archives Nationales (O¹ 1246).

[93] See W. Mason, *The English Garden*, 1778 (3rd ed.), p. 33. "Mr. Southcote was the introducer, or rather the inventor, of the *Ferme ornée*, for it may be presumed that nothing more than the term is of French extraction."

[94] Whately, *Observations*, pp. 177-182.

ferme ornée achieved its popularity in France. Whately's description suggests, however, that to the English the *ferme ornée* was composed of a series of rural pictures to be viewed by the visitor, while to the French the *ferme ornée* was a theatrical stage set in which the visitor could play at rural life.

One final possibility for the origin for the term, *ferme ornée,* is its use in connection with the traditional French estate. It seems to have been applied originally to a French country estate that was designed to be both useful and ornamental (in the manner of the ideal early eighteenth-century estates discussed by Nourse and Addison). Such an estate was described by Mme. de Genlis in her *Mémoires,*[95] as the *ferme ornée* of M. Joui at Chevilly, near Paris, which she had visited in her youth, around 1761. It consisted of a complex of buildings (known as *La Ferme*) with a dairy (*laiterie d'agrément*) decorated with shells, white marble and porcelain vases. The terraced garden, of about forty acres, was planted with fruit trees and roses and contained trellises. It was walled off from the surrounding countryside, and there was a pavilion at the bottom of each of its terraces. In the middle of the orchard was a large pavilion, decorated with mirrors, white marble, and frescoes of landscapes. The type is surely related to the *ferme ornée* which Watelet discussed extensively in 1774.

Whatever its origin, by 1775 the *ferme ornée* had assumed its particular character. We have already discussed the short description of it by Duchesne in his work on gardening theory and noted the author's remark that the type had just come into fashion.[96] At precisely the same time that Duchesne published his description, the hamlet (*hameau*) also achieved independent status and its definitive form as an independent element in the picturesque garden. From this point on, it is difficult to separate the farm and the hamlet in the new gardens. Indeed, it is the hamlet and not the *ferme ornée* which appears to have been representative of the new style of garden. The hamlet is described in the *Lettre sur les jardins anglois* which was published anonymously on 11 October 1775, and republished almost simultaneously in the *Journal encyclopédique* (as mentioned in chapter IV).[97] The anonymous author comments in passing that both poetry—citing Milton—and the operatic decorations for *Castor and Pollux* inspired the taste for modern gardens. He describes a country estate which had no château, but rather, twenty cottages, dispersed in a grove and with rustic exteriors and well-appointed interiors. To each cottage was joined a garden, stable, orchard, kitchen garden, parterre, trellis, espalier, and each ensemble differed from the other according to the conditions of the soil and the orientation. Freedom was enjoyed by all, for each inhabitant believed himself to be the owner of his own cottage and farmed his property as he pleased. Each cottage even had its own small private library, for which the principal cottage (*salon*) maintained a general catalog of holdings so that the books could be borrowed. But the author of the letter also remarked that there was no shelter from the weather because there was no enclosure between the buildings, and, moreover, that dampness made the garden unsuitable for women.[98]

[95] Mme. Brulart de Genlis, Marchioness de Sillery, *Mémoires*, Paris, 1825-1826 (8v. in 4) (6th ed.), I, pp. 108-111.

[96] See chapter IV, pp. 78-79.

[97] See chapter IV, note 127.

[98] *Journal encyclopédique*, VIII, October 1775, pp. 136-142. The last sentence is contained only in the pamphlet, pp. 14-15.

In 1775 the hamlet at Chantilly was begun (Fig. 105). It would become, as the Prince de Croÿ observed in 1778, a model for all later hamlets.[99] It was made up of seven detached rustic cottages—a mill, a stable, a dairy, a kitchen, a dining hall, a billiard room, and a grange. On the site were a kitchen garden and an orchard. But the rustic simplicity of the cottages was deceptive, for the interiors were richly decorated. In a contemporary guide, it was noted that the kitchen contained utensils for the multiple needs of opulence; the dining hall (Fig. 106) was decorated as if it were a leafy wood—the seats were imitations of tree trunks, flower banks and trees lined the walls, branches covered the ceiling; and the garage contained a "large and superb salon" ornamented with coupled Corinthian pilasters and a richly decorated frieze, a painted ceiling, mirrored walls and drapes of rose-colored taffeta.[100]

The *ferme ornée* and the hamlet were included separately or in combination in most of the major picturesque gardens after 1775, and the exotic structures of the *jardin anglo-chinois* were replaced first with imitation huts, and later with cottages where the employees of the estates lived. At Betz there was a small farm which was composed of rustic buildings and inhabited by the gardener.[101] De Ligne built a village of huts for his herdsmen at Beloeil.[102] A *ferme ornée* was planned at Méréville, but only the dairy was built,[103] although a sheepfold still exists which may have been designed as a separate and unrelated structure. There was a farm at Bellevue built between 1780 and 1781 which contained a mill and "village houses and several other analogous structures in these picturesque gardens, but of a new genre."[104] (Fig. 107). There was, of course, the Hameau at the Trianon, built between 1778 and 1782, which was linked with a Norman farm begun in 1783.[105] At Franconville there was a Swiss village with cows and chalets, which was inhabited by the Count d'Albon and his wife (Fig. 108).[106] At Malmaison there was a Swiss hamlet, added, however, after the Revolution.[107] At Le Raincy— which was probably the largest and the most committed to irregularity of the pre-Revolutionary picturesque parks, as it was remodeled by Philippe-Egalité between 1786 and 1793—there were both a farm and a hamlet, and all the structures in the park were designed for use. A "Russian" coffee house, designed of simulated logs painted on stucco, as were many of the structures in hamlets, including those at Chantilly, was considered to be both useful and

[99] Croÿ, *Journal*, IV, p. 130, 18 June 1778. However, the dating of the Chantilly hamlet varies; De Ligne, *Beloeil*, p. 161, notes that it was built nearly eight years before the publication of his book (in 1782); Thièry, *Guide aux environs de Paris*, p. 226, notes that it was constructed in less than three months in 1780, in "une immense prairie," by the architect J. F. LeRoy. See J. A. Dulaure, *Nouvelle Description . . . de Paris*, I, p. 66 (who also says the hamlet was begun in 1780); and G. Macon, *Les arts dans la Maison de Condé*, Paris, 1903, pp. 98-121, where work on the *jardin anglais* is said to have been finished in 1773 (p. 111), and the hamlet built in 1774 and inaugurated in April 1775 (p. 112).

[100] Dulaure, *Nouvelle Description*, I, pp. 67-71.
[101] For Betz see Bibliography: Individual Gardens.
[102] Mornet, *Sentiment de la nature*, part I, chapter II:

"Plaisirs rustiques," pp. 98-131; and De Ligne, *Beloeil*, pp. 7-8.
[103] A. Laborde, *Description*, p. 104. For Méréville, see also Siren, *China and Gardens of Europe*, pp. 153-158; see note 40 above, and works cited in Bibliography: Individual Gardens.
[104] Thièry, *Guide à Paris*, II, p. 676. The property was subdivided early in the nineteenth century, so that the individual buildings of the hamlet could be sold as residences.
[105] Nolhac, *Le Trianon de Marie Antoinette*, chap. III: "Le Jardin de la Reine," pp. 43-81. For the hamlet, see *ibid*., pp. 148-158.
[106] Dulaure, *Nouvelle Description*, I, p. 177.
[107] G. Riat, *L'Art des jardins*, Paris, 1900, p. 346; A. Laborde, *Description*, pp. 66-67.

agreeable (Fig. 109).[108] Indeed, as at the Ermenonville farm, picturesque composition was as important as the use of the structure: the site of the cow barn was "composed in imitation of valleys of Switzerland."[109] These structures were created in a spirit of play, reflecting not only Carmontelle's precepts for a French picturesque garden, but also Walpole's observation, already in 1771, in his comments on the Emperor of China's garden, which he seems to have associated with the French ones, that "Here too his Majesty plays at agriculture; there is a quarter set aside for that purpose."[110]

It should be insisted that the *ferme ornée* and the hamlet were more than ephemeral curiosities. The kind of architecture which was developed in these artificially rural types, and which was composed of the most basic elements of architectural vocabulary—unfluted Tuscan columns, brick arches, rubble walls, wooden superstructures—was combined in these gardens in an unceasing number of variations to delight the eye, by major architects (Fig. 112). The resulting style was to lead directly into the domestic architecture of nineteenth-century France.

Not all eighteenth-century farms attached to the new picturesque gardens were developed in the spirit of entertainment and play which Carmontelle recommended. Some had a more serious purpose, one having to do with agriculture and its role in improving the national welfare. During the first half of the eighteenth century France had witnessed an increasing deterioration of the traditional economic and social fabric on which the ancien régime depended. It is within this context that the two opposing eighteenth-century views of China must be seen. In the first, China was seen as a philosophically oriented dictatorship: its emphasis on agriculture and rural life made this country of particular interest to the French neomonarchists, who were concerned with reform within the existing French system. They endorsed an enlightened despotism represented by a French monarchy relieved of its fiscal and feudal dependencies. For these reformers China was an example of a peaceful, stable, and affluent nation, free from the privileges of nobility and church, and administered by an enlightened bureaucracy of scholar-philosophers. Libertarian reformers, however, saw China as an example of an authoritarian and dictatorial system, which imposed an inflexible government on a cowed and passive population. This group was concerned with increasing popular power, and it turned to such models as the British constitutional monarchy, based as it was on parliamentary control, or to the concept of a republic in the Roman tradition.

Thus the interest in China, and even the fashion for chinoiserie, may be associated with the commitment to the preservation and the reform of tradition. On the other hand, Rousseau, for instance, who was outspokenly hostile to China, is linked to the opposing attitude.

The opinions of two groups which became active around 1750 and which were interested in promoting agriculture can be related to these political views on China. One group, the

---

[108] A. Laborde, *Description*, p. 141. For Le Raincy, see Bibliography: Individual Gardens.

[109] *Ibid.*, p. 139.

[110] Walpole, "On Modern Gardening," pp. 134-135. In spite of Chambers's sympathy with the principles of the *jardin anglo-chinois*, he described his design of the village at Milton Abbas (Chambers, Correspondence, on deposit in the British Museum, MS. A.D. 41,134, p. 20v., 7 April 1773, Chambers to Lord Milton) in terms similar to that of Nourse's description of a village on a country estate, written almost a century before ("An Essay of a Country House," *Campania Felix*, 1700, pp. 297-344).

Physiocrats,[111] was concerned with the underlying political and social implications of agricultural reform; the other, the Agronomes,[112] was concerned with practical experimentation with new agricultural methods. The first group turned to China, the second to England, for a model.

The Physiocratic movement has been linked with the *jardin anglo-chinois* by several scholars.[113] Like the *jardin anglo-chinois*, the movement was not without some spirit of fantasy. For example, a story about the emperor of China having assisted in the ritualistic spring plowing of a field as an indication of his support for the peasant-farmer was illustrated in the first edition of Mirabeau's *Philosophie rurale*, published in 1764 (text fig. 2).[114] The same event was reenacted literally or pictorially at least three times—by Louis XV in 1756,[115] by the Dauphin in 1768,[116] and by the Emperor Joseph of Austria in 1764.[117]

text illus. 2   Ceremonial plowing by the Emperor of China.
From Mirabeau, *Philosophie rurale*, frontispiece.

[111] For the Physiocrats, see Maverick, "Chinese Influences upon the Physiocrats," *Economic History* (London), III, no. 13, February 1938, pp. 54-67; and "The Chinese and the Physiocrats; a Supplement," *Economic History*, IV, no. 15, February 1940, pp. 312-318.

[112] For the Agronomes, see A. J. Bourde, *The Influence of England on the French Agronomes, 1750-1780*, and *Agronomie et agronomes en France au XVIIIe siècle*.

[113] A. Reichweine, *China and Europe*, New York, 1925, pp. 101-109. (the English translation of *China und Europa*, Berlin, 1923); and Siren, *China and Gardens of Europe*, pp. 5-7.

[114] V. Riquetti, Marquis de Mirabeau, *Philosophie rurale*, Amsterdam, 1764.

[115] Reichweine, *China and Europe*, p. 106.

[116] Maverick, "Chinese Influences," pp. 125-126.

[117] *Idem*. The poet Roucher eulogized the ceremony of the "Prince Laboureur" in his poem *Les Mois*, p. 23. He also included in his notes to the poem an explanation of Turgot's agrarian program and of the "commerce des blé."

The Physiocratic movement has also been connected with the policies of Turgot, the short-lived Minister of Finance (1774-1776).[118] With his fall began the decline of the influence of the Physiocrats and of interest in China as a model of government. From this point in time, the French turned to the immediate and tangible example of their prosperous neighbor across the Channel. The visits of Voltaire, Montesquieu, and Le Blanc to England in the 1720s and 1730s, and the Abbé LeBlanc's high praise of English agriculture had been early instances of French interest in agricultural science. The extent to which English successes could be paralleled by French failures is brought out in a comparison of the two countries by one French visitor to England in 1785. He noted with approval the high English regard for agriculture, which was considered to be the main source of the country's well-being, and he compared the English supportive tax system, which by its leniency encouraged development of the land (fields and cattle were not taxed at all), with the French system, where agriculture was almost the sole support of the state. Farmers and landowners were rich in England, poor in France. There were rarely complaints about taxes in England, and the writer added, in a statement in which in its mingling of attitudes regarding English and Chinese gardens and agriculture illustrates the impossibility of clearly distinguishing among eighteenth-century attitudes about China, England, and France: "If the English imitate the Chinese in culture and the arrangement of their gardens, they imitate them equally in their concern for Agriculture by honoring and appreciating this first of the arts."[119]

Real concern in France with English agricultural methods developed suddenly, in 1750, the year of publication of the first volume of Du Hamel de Monceau's revised and enlarged translation of Jethro Tull's treatise on agriculture, *Horse-hoeing Husbandry*.[120] This work dealt with experimental methods of farming, and mainly with recent French experiments such as the rotation of crops and improved methods of plowing. One of the chief advances of the Du Hamel-Tull system, the drill, was considered to be a Chinese rather than an English invention, illustrating once more how complex and confused the relationship between England and China was seen to be.

After this date some members of the French nobility made efforts to set an example for the improvement of agriculture and manufacture on a national scale by developing model farms on their own estates. Fresnais de Beaumont's *La Noblesse cultivatrice*,[121] published in 1778, was written with this role of the nobility in mind. But the new agricultural systems were too out of step with both traditional agricultural methods and traditional economic policy to move beyond the experimental stage. And the experiments were in general those of amateurs interested in the theory rather than in the practical application of agricultural reforms.[122] Girardin's farm at Ermenonville was an early example of the interest in improving agriculture as well as in increasing the rural character of the area by the addition of picturesque effects. As we

[118] For Turgot, see D. Daikin, *Turgot and the Ancien Régime in France*, London, 1939.

[119] F. de Hartig, *Lettres*, pp. 93-94.

[120] Du Hamel de Monceau, *Traité de la culture des terres*.

[121] Fresnais de Beaumont, *La Noblesse cultivatrice, ou moyens d'élever en France la culture . . . au plus haut degré de production*, Paris, 1778.

[122] See Young, *Travels*, pp. 15-16, June 1787, on the Society of Agriculture at Limoges, where they "meet, converse, offer premiums, and publish nonsense." For less serious manufacturing efforts, see Hautecoeur, *Histoire de l'architecture classique*, v, p. 183.

have seen, the Marquis intended to introduce in his park new improved methods of agriculture, thus placing his farm within the tradition of Montesquieu's Labrède and Voltaire's Ferney, where Voltaire established a model factory and a model village—and this, it should be noted, during the 1760s, or precisely the years during which Girardin was designing Ermenonville.[123] But chief and foremost among those interested in agriculture was the Duc de Liancourt, who began to establish a farm on his estate around 1770.[124] Liancourt's general plan was inspired by those of the English country estates he had seen in 1768. It included a farm and a school, to which was added later a village for the housing of workers engaged in the manufacture of linen.[125] Liancourt, like Girardin, was concerned with beauty as well as with utility, and his factory was designed as a picturesque garden structure (Fig. 110). Other estate owners, though less dedicated than Liancourt or Girardin, also indicated concern for the improvement of agriculture. There was a working farm at Le Raincy, made up of a stable, cow barn, chicken roost, dovecote, and a large grange.[126] There was a large dairy and a sheep farm at Chanteloup,[127] and Ledoux also promoted the cause of agriculture with his projects for a Utopian sheep farm at Le Roche Bernard. Nor was Laborde, the owner of Méréville, insensitive to this potential of the picturesque garden, and he was the first Frenchman to import merino sheep into Europe.[128] The most famous and the most important of the French experimental farms was the farm and sheepfold at Rambouillet (where the sheepfold was not built until after the Revolution, the sheep being first housed in the menagery). This experimental farm was designed by Tessier after the estate was acquired by Louis XVI in 1783 (Fig. 111), and from its inception was intended to promote the national welfare.[129] It is significant that the structures, the planting, and even the land of the fantastic *jardin anglo-chinois* at Rambouillet have all but disappeared, while the utilitarian farm buildings continued in use, uninterrupted, through the course of the Revolution and into the nineteenth century: indeed, they are still functioning today.[130]

These, then, are the major types of French picturesque gardens. All of them, whether pastoral, ornamental, or rural have one thing in common: in all the elements of nature are composed into a series of highly controlled and sophisticated "pictures." Whether this approach to garden design originated in England or in France, precisely how it developed, and in what stages, are not now known. But it is possible that Ermenonville may have been the first French garden to transform the framed "view," as composed in paintings which were perceived by the spectator, into a series of "scenes" in which the spectator participated. The painter Hubert Robert, who knew Ermenonville, may have been at least partially responsible for the transformation of Girardin's ideas into visual reality. Whatever his position at Ermenonville, he was

[123] For Voltaire's model village at Ferney, see F. Caussy, *Voltaire, Seigneur du village*; and H. N. Brailsford, *Voltaire*, chap. VII.

[124] For Liancourt, see Bibliography: Individual Gardens.

[125] Young, *Travels*, p. 56, 16 September 1787.

[126] C. Chavard, *Recherches sur Le Raincy, 1238-1848*, Paris, 1884, p. 104.

[127] Young, *Travels*, p. 52, 10 September 1787. Young suggests that a ploughman was imported, since the farm was "better laid out and ploughed than common in the country."

[128] Choppin de Janvry, "Méréville," p. 96.

[129] For the experimental farm at Rambouillet, see M. Tessier, *Notice relative à l'établissement d'économie rurale de Rambouillet*.

[130] For Rambouillet, see Siren, *China and Gardens of Europe*, pp. 158-162, and Bibliography: Individual Gardens.

surely a key figure in the transition from the gardening vocabulary and painterly techniques developed at Ermenonville to those later stages when the sentimental and moral associations still identified by Girardin with the picturesque garden gave way to theatricality and exoticism.

Robert is associated with many of the late eighteenth-century French picturesque gardens. Among his known, documented works are, first and foremost, Méréville (begun in 1784 by Bélanger for Jean-Joseph, Duc de Laborde, and continued by Robert in 1786),[131] Betz (which was designed by Robert in collaboration with the Duc d'Harcourt from 1780 for the Princesse de Monaco),[132] Rambouillet (with which Robert was associated after its purchase by the king in 1783),[133] and Versailles and the Trianon (where Robert's career as a professional garden designer may have begun in 1778).[134] Robert has been associated with many other gardens,[135] including Moulin-Joli,[136] and, interestingly, Monceau.[137] Of all these gardens, Méréville (Figs. 112-115), with its *grands tableaux* of complex grottos, spectacular cascades, and charming artificial rural scenes, where the simple elements of nature have indeed been transformed into a series of magnificently conceived events in which the spectator is fully absorbed, may be the ultimate example of the picturesque garden in France. Here it should be noted that Robert and Bélanger were at the peak of their garden designing careers at Méréville, and that their work there was carried out about a decade before the controversy over the concept of the picturesque broke out between Repton and Price.[138] It is at this point in time, during the 1780s, that a truly pictorial use of the vocabulary of nature seems to have been achieved in France.

As the techniques for relating the picturesque garden to landscape painting developed, the models for this type of garden changed. The scenes of Italy by Claude and of the northern countryscape by Dutch and Flemish artists which had been adapted at Ermenonville and possibly at other gardens of the 1760s were no longer preferred in the later gardens. The pastoral character of Italian and northern rural landscapes did not offer the variety and extreme contrast sought after by the 1780s. Indeed, even the most popular publication of illustrations of Italy—the *Voyage pittoresque* of the Abbé de Saint-Non, who had traveled with both Robert and Fragonard to Italy in the 1750s and 1760s—presented views of ancient ruins, picturesque views, and the unusual natural effects of Naples and Sicily,[139] rather than scenes of the country-

[131] For Méréville, see Bibliography: Individual Gardens.

[132] For Betz, see Bibliography: Individual Gardens.

[133] For Rambouillet, see Bibliography: Individual Gardens; and Thièry, *Guide aux environs de Paris*, p. 491.

[134] For Robert at Versailles, see P. de Nolhac, *Hubert Robert*, Paris, 1910 (2v.), I, pp. 53-60. Robert was named "dessinateur des jardins du Roi" in 1778.

[135] C. Gabillot, *Hubert Robert et sons temps*, Paris, 1895, pp. 160-168, includes Monceau and Montreuil among the gardens with which Robert had some connection. Ganay, *Jardins à l'anglaise en France*, I, mentions Bellevue (p. 219) and the Château du Val (pp. 220-221).

[136] T. Leclere, *Hubert Robert*, Paris [1926], p. 88. See also Gabillot, *Hubert Robert*, p. 160.

[137] In addition to Gabillot (*op. cit.*, pp. 160-161), Dacier, in "Le Jardin de Monceau," p. 62, cites a family tradition that Robert had collaborated on Monceau. He publishes (p. 53) a view of the Naumachia by Robert which was then at the Bibliothèque d'art et d'archaeologie but is now missing. Nolhac, *Trianon*, p. 58, notes also a tradition connecting Robert with Bagatelle.

[138] Repton's advocacy of traditional gardening design —wanting to preserve it and incorporate it within his gardens—was supported by Malthus (who had translated Girardin's work) and by William Mason (who was sympathetic to Rousseau and opposed to Chambers). See D. Stroud, *Humphrey Repton*, London, 1962, pp. 82-92.

[139] J. P. R. Saint-Non, *Voyage pittoresque de Naples et de Sicile*, Paris, 1781-1786. The volume replaced the projected *Voyages d'Italie* originally undertaken by

side or of the famous Italian gardens such as those Robert and Fragonard had sketched in the 1750s.

Thus Italy was by no means the only or even the main source for the dramatic effects of the later French picturesque gardens. The French increasingly looked to another type of landscape for models. During the eighteenth century there were two major routes to Italy. For one, through France and then by sea to Italy, the scenery was picturesque and rural. The other route was through Switzerland.[140] Here the civilized picturesqueness of the agrarian countryside was replaced by scenic wonders—of rocky mountains, fertile valleys, spectacular cascades, rustic cabins, and bridges of strange design. These would be the inspiration for many of the fantastic and bizarre "effects" which the French garden designer-decorator sought to produce in miniature in the picturesque garden (Figs. 116-118).[141] It would even seem that Swiss "effects" and Chinese "effects" were considered to be interchangeable—Bélanger, for instance, noted that models of bridges could be taken either from China or the Alps.[142] Such effects were used so often and with so little regard for the limitations of setting that the Prince de Ligne warned: "None of these Alps and ridiculous Pyrenees," and he noted that these new "modern" Alps consisted of mountains that could be carried in baskets, and rivers that could be placed in bottles.[143] But not all of these "effects" were in poor taste. Such a pictorial wonder as the "scene" at the grand cascade at Méréville (Fig. 114), with its rustic hut perched high on a rock and its rickety bridge (Fig. 115), which surely originated in the exotic scenery of Switzerland, is one of the most memorable achievements of all the "scenes" of the *jardin anglo-chinois*. But these "scenes" do not appear to have been inspired by painting. Indeed, popular interest in the scenery of Switzerland as a subject for landscape painting begun later, possibly only in the nineteenth century.[144] It may be with these last pre-Revolutionary gardens that the French garden designers abandoned their reliance on painting for a model and turned directly to nature.

J. B. Laborde in 1776. When Laborde, for lack of funds, was unable to complete publication of the series, its financing was assumed in 1783 by Girardin. See L. Guimbaud, *Saint-Non et Fragonard*, pp. 151-168.

[140] The Swiss route also made possible a visit to Voltaire's Ferney. See Guimbaud, *Saint-Non et Fragonard*, pp. 55-56.

[141] See Hirschfeld, *Art des jardins*, v, p. 190, for comments on Swiss landscape. Addison, in his *Remarks on Several Parts of Italy*, may have been the first traveler to write about the rural landscape of Switzerland and Italy. By the mid-century, French enthusiasm for Switzerland was such that Montesquieu could say in his *Essay on Taste* (p. 313): "He who should live for any time in the Alps would come down disgusted with the happiest situations and the most charming prospects." P. J. Grosley, *Nouveaux . . . observations sur l'Italie*, i, pp. 5-6, gives an account of the scenic wonders of the Alps which is very like one by Rousseau (*Héloïse*, letter xxiii). Rousseau was born in Switzerland, the setting for *Héloïse*, and it represented for him a democratic and self-sufficient ideal. Hirschfeld would write (*Théorie de l'art des jardins*, v, pp. 186ff.): "Le caractère tantôt sublime, tan-

tôt romanesque, tantôt doux & seduisant du paysage, compose les plus beaux tableaux qui puissent jamais ravir l'oeil du voyageur, & inviter à l'imitation le génie du paysagiste. Et à ces impressions de site si propres à élever l'âme, à la frapper, à l'animer, se joint encore l'idée variante du bonheur que font goûter à ces villageois leur liberté, leur proprieté assurée, & leurs moeurs presque dignes de l'Arcadie. . . ." The best account of French interest in Switzerland is in *Les Joies de la nature au XVIIIe siècle* (exhibition catalog), Paris, 1971.

[142] Stern, *Bélanger*, i, p. 29, where he also mentions models for bridges, and suggests the suspended bridges of the Pyrenees and the Alps, or the bridge described by Milton.

[143] De Ligne, *Beloeil*, pp. 287-288.

[144] F. Novotny, *Painting and Sculpture in Europe 1780 to 1880*, Baltimore, Md., 1960, pp. 38-39. However, there is a sketchbook in the Cabinet des Estampes (Bibliothèque Nationale) (Ub.43.c) attributed to Robert showing the principal views of Italy, Switzerland, and along the Rhône, similar to those in J. B. de Laborde *Tableaux de la Suisse*, 1784-1788.

The era of the *jardin anglo-chinois*, the pastoral farm, and the *ferme ornée* all came to an end, along with the ancien régime, in 1789. The gardens of the nineteenth century would be in the spirit of the English garden, closely allied with nature and taking into account the practicalities of economy and use. In 1808 Laborde wrote of Le Raincy: "The art of gardening may be divided into two epochs or periods. In this as in the rest, imagination after having preceded taste has been guided by it. All the gardens of the first epoch are loaded with useless and incoherent ornaments; and it is only in those of the second period that sense and utility are found united with elegance. After having for a considerable time considered fabrics as edifices of show, the only aim of which was to form prospects, it was considered proper to give them a designation: and that elegance and luxury which had before been lavished on vain decorations, is now directed on buildings necessary to the settlement."[145] He would also note, in a last reminder of the important role of the painters in garden design, that the taste of Boucher was supplanted by the taste of Greuze.[146] After the coronation of Napoleon in 1804 a more approving eye could be cast on the excesses of the pre-Revolutionary period. Many of these pre-Revolutionary gardens were illustrated by Laborde in his *Description des nouveaux jardins de la France*, published in 1808 and 1815. And Krafft, in his *Plans des plus beaux jardins pittoresques de la France*, published in 1809-1810, praised these elaborate and artificial productions of the ancien régime.[147] However, it is fitting that the last comment to be made here on the *jardin anglo-chinois* should be that of a Socialist-Utopian, an inheritor of the philosophy which underlay much of the French attitude toward both China and England, but who surely would seem to have been in no way associated with any of its manifestations in the pre-Revolutionary picturesque gardens. Charles Fourier, in his *Traité de l'association domestique agricole*, published in 1822, mentioned the Chinese garden briefly. And this radical philosopher was still close enough to the tradition to say that this type of garden, invented by the Chinese and adopted first by the English and then by the French, was very agreeable, although only when appropriately employed.[148]

---

[145] A. Laborde, *Description*, p. 135.

[146] *Ibid.*, p. 41: "Les danses des bergers de Vatteau et de Boucher furent remplacées par les scenes villageoises de Greuze."

[147] J. C. Krafft, *Plans des plus beaux jardins pittoresques*, I, pp. 3-4.

[148] F. M. C. Fourier, *Traité de l'association domestique agricole*, Paris, 1822, I, p. 50.

CHAPTER VI

The Picturesque Garden and Urban Planning

The impact of garden design on Parisian planning began with a revival of interest in the planning of Paris at the end of the War of Austrian Succession in 1748. The new urbanism was an outgrowth of public concern with the embellishing of the city in order to give it an appearance worthy of its significance as a major capital. The most important project connected with the new urban embellishment was the designing of a square for the equestrian statue of Louis XIV. The history of the two competitions for the square has been considered by several scholars.[1] But it can be briefly reviewed here, since the projects and the executed plan were of importance in the realizing of planning concepts in the second half of the eighteenth century.

The first competition for the designing of the square was held in 1748.[2] The architects competing were instructed to choose any site in Paris which they considered to be appropriate, and to develop their schemes in any manner they wished.[3] The competition entries represented a wide range of planning thought, and they were surely well known before 1765, when a selection of them was published by Patte (Fig. 119).[4] Most of these designs were traditional and static, either defined by buildings around a center core,[5] or focused on an open space.[6] Only one project, designed by the architect Boffrand, seems to have had no earlier French urban prototype (Fig. 120). Lavedan has stressed the unique spatial quality of Boffrand's design. It is composed of a succession of interconnecting screened spaces, which are defined by colonnades rather than by architecture, in a manner similar to that of the design of a formal garden.

[1] See S. Granet, *Images de Paris: La Place de la Concorde*, with an extensive bibliography on the Place Louis XV. See also P. Lavedan, "Le IIe centenaire de la Place de la Concorde."

[2] See Grant, *Place de la Concorde*, for bibliography and information on the first competition.

[3] Some of the areas selected by the architects later became sites for public buildings: the Hôtel des Monnaies (Lavedan, "IIe Centenaire," pp. 165-167); the Ecole Militaire (P. Laulan, *L'Ecole Militaire de Paris: le monument 1751-88*, Paris, 1950, p. 1); and possibly the Halle au Blé, since the Hôtel de Soissons was demolished the year of the competition (see F. Boudon, "Urbanisme et spéculation à Paris au XVIIIe siècle; le terrain de l'Hôtel de Soissons," *Journal of the Society of Architectural Historians*, XXXII, December 1973, pp.

267-307).

[4] P. Patte, *Monumens érigés en France à la gloire de Louis XV*. See *Recueil de differens projets et plans provisée pour la construction d'une place publique destinée à la statue Equestre du Roi*, 1749, deposited in the Bibliothèque de l'Arsénal, MS. 3103, for many illustrations and commentaries on projects submitted for the first competition. See also the articles in *Mercure* in 1748 and 1749 on the problem of the Place, many of them by Bachaumont (July, October, December 1748; August 1749), and included in the *Recueil de M. Bachaumont*, Bibilothèque de l'Arsénal, MS. 4041.

[5] Lavedan, "IIe Centenaire," p. 165, suggests that the circular plans were inspired by English examples.

[6] See J. Garms, "Projects for the Pont Neuf and Place Dauphine."

Lavedan has suggested its influence on the planning of the Place Royale at Nancy (1751-1755) (Fig. 121),[7] which in turn was a prototype for many later squares in Europe.[8]

The second stage of the competition was held in 1753. This time all competitors were required to submit designs for a specific site: the area between the Champs-Elysées and the Tuileries, which faced the Seine and the Hôtel de Bourbon-Condé on the opposite bank (Fig. 122). We know considerably less about this stage of the competition than about the first,[9] but the ultimate solution was strongly influenced by the thinking of Marigny, then Director for Buildings, who called for a public square in which the open, parklike character of the site would be retained.[10] There is no doubt that Marigny considered the square not in terms of architecture but in terms of garden design. The completed area was conceived as a formal parterre which was open to the Seine and which was limited by the planting of the Tuileries gardens, by the Champs-Elysées,[11] by moats, and by sentry boxes which recalled garden structures (Fig. 123). The colonnaded facades of the two buildings at the rear of the square form a monumental screen, like a theatrical backdrop, which terminate the space and frame a view of the Madeleine (Fig. 124).

Simultaneously with the designing of the square for the statue of Louis XV a theory of urban planning in terms of garden design was being formulated. In November 1748, five months after the announcement of the first competition for the Place Louis XV, the author of an article in the *Mercure* suggested that defects in the aligning of city streets could be corrected by introducing fountains, columns, or other "ingenious artifacts" similar to those used by Le Nôtre in his garden designs, and that street vistas should be terminated by beautiful houses, churches and other edifices, which, according to the author, would have a function similar to that of the bell towers, houses, mills, canals, groves, and other agreeable views with which garden designers terminated allées. This principle was within the tradition of early eighteenth-century French gardening, as was the author's advice to architects to use as many resources for embellishing the streets of Paris as gardeners and "architects of gardens" used for the embellishment of a garden or a park.[12]

[7] Lavedan, "La Place Royale de Nancy et son influence," p. 254.

[8] Lavedan, *Histoire de l'urbanisme: Renaissance et temps modernes*, pp. 319-326.

[9] Granet, *Place de la Concorde*, p. 130, n. 17, gives information about a collection of drawings for this project. See also *ibid.*, p. 27.

[10] See "Mémoire concernant la Place publique que l'on se propose de construire pour y placer une statue Equestre du Roy," July 1748, and "Observations du Procurer du Roi au Bureau des Finances sur la situation la plus convenable et la plus avantageuse pour la nouvelle Place où l'on doit élever la Statue de Sa Majesté," 1753-1757 (both deposited in the Archives Nationales, O¹ 1585 (docs. 242, 243, 245). The 1753 document has been summarized by the Comte de Fels, *Ange-Jacques Gabriel*, Paris, 1912, pp. 52-56. For the history of the Champs-Elysées area, see L. Petit de Bachaumont, *Essai sur la peinture, la sculpture, et l'architecture*, pp. 57-58. The landscape possibilities of

"cityscape" were considered by the 1730s (see chap. III, n. 134, and Garms, "Projects for the Pont Neuf"). In 1738 the architect of the 1730 project cited by Garms, P. A. Delamair, would comment, in his *Porte d'Honneur ou extrait du livre de la demonstration. Ouvrage contenant des remarquables essentielles sur la meilleure & plus veritable situation de l'Hotel de Ville de Paris*, deposited in the Bibliothèque de l'Arsénal, ms. 2912, on his project for a new Hôtel de Ville on the Pont Neuf: "Puisque sa position est entre deux places publiques . . . et d'un fort beau loingtain de paysages; . . . en un mot situé au milieu de tous les objets qui l'environnent, au centre au chef lieu de tout ce qui les compose et leur faisant face à tous par un prospect, . . . non pas regularisé par l'Art, mais cimetrisé par la nature. . . ."

[11] The Champs-Elysées was replanted between 1765 and 1770. See P. d'Ariste and M. Arrivetz, *Les Champs-Elysées*, p. 40.

[12] *Mercure*, November 1748, pp. 40-49.

Five years later the Abbé Laugier, in his *Essai sur l'architecture*, again compared the design-ing of a city to the designing of a park by Le Nôtre. But Laugier carried the analogy of park to city considerably further than had the earlier author of the *Mercure* article. For Laugier con-sidered the city as a kind of wilderness (he stated: "Il faut regarder une ville comme une forêt")[13] which would be transformed into a park by means of proper subdivision and the design of streets and squares. The result would be a "magnificent whole divided into an infin-ity of different beauties, so that each quarter would have something new, original, and attention catching, but all would fit within an ordered system."[14] Laugier emphasized contrast in his design. The simple and the disordered, the elegant and the magnificent, would be found in this city; and one architectural extreme would be opposed to the other—soft to hard, delicate to strong, and noble to rustic.[15] He maintained that by these means "Paris would no longer be only an immense city, it would be a unique creation, a prodigy, and an enchantment."[16] Laugier's planning suggestions are also within the tradition of French formal gardening,[17] and they were endorsed by such an important figure as Pierre Patte, who recommended Lau-gier's work in his *Monumens de Paris*, in 1765.[18]

But although there was public concern for civic projects, the major areas of physical devel-opment and expansion in Paris during the last half of the eighteenth century were not those of monumental civic centers, but those of the new, fashionable residential quarters (Fig. 125).[19] This was a somewhat later development than the revival of interest in civic projects. Construc-tion on the new residences began in the 1760s, and accelerated in the 1770s; the majority were built in the last decade of the pre-Revolutionary period.[20] By 1782 Sebastien Mercier would

[13] Laugier, *Essai*, p. 259, and p. 263: "Il n'y a point de ville qui fournisse aux imaginations d'un artiste in-génieux un aussi beau champ que Paris. C'est une forêt immense, variée par des inégalités de plaine & de mon-tagne, coupée tout au milieu par une grande rivière, qui se divisant en plusieurs bras, forme des îles de dif-férente grandeur." See also Laugier's later comments, *Observations*, p. 313.

[14] Laugier, *Essai*, p. 262.

[15] *Ibid.*, p. 269. For an even earlier suggestion of Blondel's architectural characters (chapter IV, n. 39), see La Font de Saint-Yenne, *Observations sur les arts*, Leyden, 1748, pp. 136-137. In the July 1748 *Mercure*, pp. 147-153, diversity of building types was suggested within the city, where the purpose was to create "un beau tableau."

[16] Laugier, *Essai*, p. 271. However, as La Font de Saint-Yenne noted in his *Examen d'un essai sur l'archi-tecture . . .*, Paris, 1753, pp. 155-158: ". . . toutes ses réflexions à ce sujet soient un répétition de ce que Vol-taire & avant lui une infinité de bons citoyens en ont écrit. . . ." Among the "bons citoyens" was La Font de Saint-Yenne, who wrote *L'Ombre du grand Colbert le Louvre et le ville de Paris, dialogue*, The Hague, 1749. Laugier's views are an outgrowth of the earlier scenic panoramas projected by Meissonnier and Dela-mair (see note 10 above).

[17] As late as 1773 Blondel would still recommend the formal garden as the only type worthy of being a

model: ". . . c'est dans les jardins de nos Maisons Royales, dans ceux de nos Maisons de Plaisance, enfin, dans les promenades des Maisons de nos riches parti-culiers, à la campagne, & dans le seine des Villes, qu'on peut seul bien apprendre à étudier [le Jardinage]" (Blondel, *Cours*, IV, 1773, p. 99).

[18] P. Patte, *Monumens*, p. 213, n. (a). Also see G. Poncet de la Grave, *Projet des embelissemens de la ville et faubourgs de Paris*, who suggests colonnades and triumphal arches, fountains and even pyramids within the context of a renewed interest in the em-bellishment of a city in a monumental style.

[19] J. G. Legrand and C. P. Landon, *Description de Paris et ses édifices*, I, p. 31, where the authors also mention that the design of the belt around Paris was created "sur les dessins de M. Ledoux."

[20] An incomplete, but typical, distribution chrono-logically of the construction of the new residences can be obtained from J. C. Krafft and N. Ransonnette, *Plans . . . des hôtels construits à Paris. . . .* Of those residences included in this publication, the numbers completed in a given year are as follows: during the 1760s—one in 1762, two in 1767; during the 1770s—two in 1770, four in 1772, two in 1774, two in 1775, two in 1776, one in 1777, one in 1778, one in 1779; during the 1780s—four in 1780, two in 1781, one in 1783, three in 1784, four in 1786, four in 1787, eight in 1788, three in 1789; during the 1790s—four in 1790, one in 1793, four in 1795, two in 1796, one in 1797,

say of the extensive residential building activity, "There is money only for buildings; immense structures rise from the ground as if by magic and new quarters are composed of hôtels of the greatest magnificence. . . ."[21]

If Parisian architecture was designed within the context of the formal seventeenth-century garden, the private residences often were designed within the context of the irregular, picturesque *jardin anglo-chinois*.[22] The characteristics of the *jardin anglo-chinois*—its miniature scale, over-elaboration of effects, and its artificiality and theatricality—were precisely right for the small Parisian lot: tortuous lanes, miniature hills and islands opened up possibilities for the visual expansion of the site far beyond its real boundaries. One of the latest of these gardens, designed by Bélanger in 1790 for the Hôtel Beaumarchais (demolished in 1818), has been recorded in several drawings by the designer and in a plan (Figs. 126-128). Here the varying levels, different "scenes," and the planting of "screens" created the appearance of a space far larger than the actual area, which was only one city block.

The new residences were often designed to appear to be in a large park or rural setting. The very titles by which they were categorized suggest their character: the *pavillon* or *pavillon de chasse* (hunting lodge), the *folie*,[23] and the *maison de plaisance* (pleasure house), the latter being the more general and traditional term for these buildings and the equivalent of the *maison de campagne* (country house).[24] All of these types were sometimes also designated as *petites maisons* (little houses),[25] and these have been compared with garden architecture.[26] Many of them were designed like pavilions, such as those associated with French royal parks. Among these is the Pavillon de la Boissière (designed between 1751 and 1754 and altered in 1767), which was one of the first of the Parisian *maisons de plaisance* (Fig. 129). It was situated, like a French garden pavilion, in a formal garden; and it was praised by Blondel as "one of the prettiest and the most estimable" of this new type.[27] It has a family resemblance, as do many of the new hôtels, to the contemporaneous Petit Trianon. The Hôtel Thélusson (designed by Ledoux and built between 1778 and 1781), with its three interconnecting buildings and grotto (Fig. 142), is similar to an earlier design by the architect Héré for Stanislaus's *Pavillon d'eau* at Commercy (Fig. 143). References to monuments from classical antiquity were incorporated into other hôtels, in the same manner in which antique references appeared in picturesque parks. Thus

two in 1798; during the 1800s—four in 1801, one in 1802.

[21] Mercier, *Tableaux*, I, pp. 277-283 (especially 277-279), chap. LXXXVIII: "On bâtit de tous côtés"; and Watin (ed.), *Etat actuel de Paris*, Preface, pp. i-ii: "Paris cette immense ville, le centre des beaux arts, le rendez-vous de l'Europe, s'embellit & s'aggrandit chaque jour."

[22] Such gardens were even included on the roofs of Parisian houses. Thiéry, *Guide à Paris*, I, pp. 136-137, describes that of the architect André Aubert, at the corner of the rue Caumartin. It was situated in a roof terrace with a 120-yard perimeter and included bosquets, truncated columns, triumphal arches (*en treillage*), pyramids, ruins (which hid chimny pots), and even water surrounding an island connected to the "mainland" by Chinese bridges (the water being reserved for domestic use).

[23] M. Gallet, *Demeures parisiennes*, p. 97, notes that the designation *folie* derives from the original location of the garden building in a wooded area or *feuillage*.

[24] Blondel, *Cours*, I, pp. 388-389; II, p. 252.

[25] For a description of an ideal type, see J. F. Bastide, *La Petite Maison* (for complete reference, see chap. I, n. 83). For further remarks on the relation of the house to the garden, see Le Camus de Mezières, *Le Génie d'architecture*.

[26] For instance, see Gallet, *Demeures parisiennes*, pp. 97-98; and J. Langner, "C. N. Ledoux und die Fabrike," pp. 1-36.

[27] Blondel, *Cours*, II, pp. 251-252.

the Hôtel Brunoy (designed by Boullée in 1774) (Fig. 130) contained a reference to the Mausoleum of Halicarnassos,[28] and the circular monopteral temple was often merged with the garden facade of these new hôtels (Figs. 139, 144). In particular, the entrances might suggest garden structures. At least one Parisian house, the Maison d'Olivier, built only in 1799, but designed in the spirit of the pre-Revolutionary hôtels, was entered through a grotto (Fig. 132), which recalled such earlier ones as the gate to the Désert de Retz (Fig. 133) and the entrance to Ledoux's Salines. In one unexecuted example the entrance facade to a projected hôtel resembled the entrance to a Chinese pavilion (Fig. 134), taken from an illustration in Chambers's *Designs of Chinese Buildings* (Fig. 135).

These hôtels not only were conceived as garden structures, they were also designed within the context of a landscape setting. The most elaborate of them were composed in an exclusive, comprehensive, and enclosed environment, such as those created at the Parc Monceau and at Tivoli. In the Folie Beaujon, located in the same area and begun in 1781, the idea of the self-contained microcosm was carried the farthest of any of these estates. It was designed, according to a contemporary source, as if it were a Dutch farm, with garden, aviaries, an orangerie, a farm, a kitchen, and everything required to make it a self sufficient retreat where the owner could cast off all ties with the outside world.[29] Other gardens, such as Bagatelle and the Folie Sainte-James (both just outside of Paris, and designed by Bélanger beginning in 1777 and 1778, respectively), the Hôtel Beaumarchais, and the Pavillon d'Orléans (the first stage planned by Brongniart about 1770)[30] may have been less comprehensive than were the gardens of Monceau or Beaujon, but they were also landscaped to create a special, idyllic and enclosed environment.

Monceau and Beaujon were large estates: the owner of the small city lot had to be content with the illusion of largeness. One way to achieve this effect was to connect privately owned with public spaces. In the speculative development on the north side of the Champs Elysées the houses were located on land originally intended to form a part of the park.[31] The gardens of these houses faced the park and by the 1770s they were fenced with iron grilles so that the private property might appear to extend unobstructed into the public space.[32] The most important house of this group was the Hôtel Brunoy. Its garden (Fig. 130), designed by Boullée, was separated from the park only by an iron grille, and, in order not to spoil the view into the Champs Elysées, the architect even provided a subterranean promenade in the gardens.[33]

A similar solution for relating public and private property was used in the design of the Hôtel Monaco (by Brongniart, around 1774), where again there was only an iron grille between the garden and the boulevard, so that, according to a contemporary account, the tree-lined boulevards would appear to be a continuation of the private grounds.[34] It is possible that the neigh-

[28] For the incorporation into eighteenth-century architecture of the Mausoleum of Halicarnassos and similar antique motifs, see W. Oechslin, "Pyramide et Sphère: notes sur l'architecture révolutionnaire du XVIIIe siècle et ses source italiennes," *Gazette des beaux-arts*, LXXVIII, April 1971, pp. 207-211.

[29] For the Folie Beaujon, see Watin, *Etat actuel de Paris*, IV, part ii, pp. 29-30; H. L. d'Oberkirch, *Mémoires*, I, pp. 302-303, 14 June 1782.

[30] See M. Hébert, "Les demeures du Duc d'Orléans et de Mme. de Montesson à la Chaussée d'Antin," *Gazette des beaux-arts*, LXIV, September 1964, pp. 161-175.

[31] For accounts of the history of the planning of the Champs Elysées, see J. Mondain-Monval, *Soufflot*, pp. 240ff.; and Petit de Bachaumont, *Essai*, pp. 57-62.

[32] Pérouse de Montclos, *Etienne-Louis Boullée*, p. 107, n. 1.

[33] Thièry, *Guide à Paris*, I, p. 88.

[34] *Ibid.*, II, p. 581.

boring Hôtels de Condé and Masserano (both built in the late 1780s by Brongniart) were designed with similar open vistas onto the boulevard. One further example of the opening-up of the garden to the public space is the Hôtel Tamnay (begun in 1789 by the architect Itasse), where the garden front of the relatively small house acquired the monumentality associated with a public facade (Fig. 131).

The extension of private into public space received critical notice and endorsement. As early as 1751, Petit de Bachaumont suggested not only that grilles be used for this purpose, but that they be painted green, as they were at Saint James's Park in London, so that private and public areas would seem even more closely related; and he proposed as an even simpler alternative that spaces be separated from each other merely by a terrace or a ditch.[35] By 1782 Sebastien Mercier commended the fashion of surrounding houses with iron grilles which ornamented the view without destroying it.[36]

As the dividing line between public and private space grew thinner, Paris became a spectacle for the private citizen, much as the rural countryside had become a spectacle for his landowning country counterpart. A magnificent view of the city could be obtained from the terraces of the Hôtel de Sainte-Foix (built from 1779 by Brongniart) (Fig. 137). One architect, De Wailly, provided his own house on the rue Pépinière (begun in 1776) with a belvedere overlooking the city.[37] And the Hôtel Beaumarchais, although it was built on a low site, had a raised garden and a belvedere (Fig. 128) which doubtless provided a vista over street, canal and the Seine. If the spectator could not find a private viewing point, he might climb to the top of the windmills on Montmartre, as did the Prince de Croÿ in 1764, in order to see Paris at dawn.[38]

While the architect was able to achieve the illusion of extensive grounds for the owner, the hôtels and the gardens became, at the same time, ornaments to the public space. Thus, the garden of the Hôtel Brunoy was not only a viewing point for the owner into the Champs Elysées, but it could in turn be viewed by the passers-by through the grille (Fig. 130); the main facade of the Hôtel de Salm (begun in 1783 by P. Rousseau) could be seen through a colonnaded screen (Fig. 138); and the Hôtel de Sainte-Foix would dominate public space from a prominent position on a podium (Fig. 136). In another example of the merging of public and private space, the Chinese pavilion in the garden of the Duc de Montmorency projected over the street (Fig. 141). Moreover, the hôtels facing the Seine could be viewed as a part of the river scene. Thus the garden facade of the Hôtel de Salm was so much a part of the riverscape

[35] Bachaumont, *Essai*, pp. 60-61: "A l'égard du projet formé par *Colbert* pour la partie droite des Champs Elysées, on pourroit y supplier, en laissant même subsister les Hôtels & Jardins qui remplissent aujourd'hui ce terrain. Il ne seroit question que de former ces Jardins par des Terrasses, des Fosses revêtus, ou des Grilles de fer peintes en verd; on en a usé à Londres dans le Parc de S. James, où cela fait un très bon effet: par ce moien la vûe ne seroit plus offusquée, & l'on jouiroit du spectacle de ces Jardins dont le plupart méritent les regards & l'admiration du Public."

[36] Mercier, *Tableau*, xi, p. 33: "L'art ensuite a tra-vaillé le fer pour l'unir à l'architecture, il s'est développé dans de superbes grilles, qui ont l'avantage d'orner le point de vue sans le détruire."

[37] For the Hôtel de Sainte-Foix, see J. Silvestre de Sacy, *Alexandre-Théodore Brongniart, 1739-1813*, Paris, 1940, pp. 32-33. For De Wailly's house, see Thièry, *Guide à Paris*, i, p. 78.

[38] De Croÿ, *Journal*, ii, p. 144, 6 May 1764: ". . . j'allai à Montmartre, monter sur le plus haut moulin, pour comparer les vues. On plonge mieux dans Paris, étant plus près, mais la mienne est plus étendue."

that one contemporary observer noted the beautiful effect during festivals of its illumination as it was reflected in the water (Fig. 139).[39] Similarly, the Maison Chevalier (built in 1783 by the Chevalier de Beauregard) was designed as a classical temple perched half-way up the hill of Chaillot (Fig. 140), and it must have provided a bright classical accent for spectators on the Seine.

There is no doubt that the most important residence and surely the most comprehensive example of the new style was Ledoux's Hôtel Thélusson (Figs. 142, 144, 145).[40] It is also the most comprehensive Parisian example of the integration of public and private space. The hôtel and garden were designed along an axial vista from the rue Cerutti (today, the rue Lafitte) down which the spectator might look through a gigantic triumphal arch into the private space. The arch, erected between the sunken center garden and the street, appeared to be partially buried, as were the arches in the antique Forum in Rome, so that the sunken garden achieved the appearance of a space remote in time and distance: the rocky grotto at the far end was, as it were, a reminder that the garden signified a more primitive period. The spectator was not only invited, but impelled to gaze into this fantastic world. The inclusion of the public into the private life of the wealthy and eccentric Parisian society could not go farther than this.

In addition to the picturesque contribution of the new houses to the Parisian cityscape, another element associated with gardens now appeared in Paris. The newly developed areas contained amusements and diversions which had been associated with private recreation and which now became an accepted part of the public life of the city. Buildings for tennis and riding and numerous pleasure gardens began to appear,[41] and there was a sudden mushrooming of theaters, mainly along the northern boulevards.[42] All this began to occur in the newly developed areas of Paris after the peace treaty with England in 1763.

The application of the principles of the picturesque garden to urban design is not discussed in eighteenth-century theory. But theorists on the picturesque garden, both in England and in France, were concerned after 1770 with a related problem: the extension of picturesque garden design beyond private and into public space. As we have already observed, Whately, in his *Observations on Modern Gardening*, was concerned with the garden element known as a "riding," or a carriage road designed to provide the greatest possible variety of picturesque effects as the spectator passed through different areas of the wider countryside and even villages. In France, Morel discussed the type of garden with a countryscape which he called the *pays* in his *Théorie des jardins de la nature*.[43] And Chambers carried this point of view to its ultimate conclusion when he stated that the purpose behind the writing of his *Dissertation on Oriental Gardening* was "to decorate kingdoms, even the World."[44]

The same group of theorists also had definite ideas about the type of garden that should be designed for a city. The Duc d'Harcourt wrote around 1775 that in a city garden fantasy must be the main goal in the decoration, so that all details would be of interest.[45] Chambers, in the second edition of his *Dissertation*, restricted the "richer and more artificial manner" of garden-

[39] Landon, *Annales du musée*, VIII, 1805, p. 112.

[40] O. Reutersvärd, "De sjunkna bågarna hos Ledoux, Boullée, Cellerier och Fontaine," pp. 98-117.

[41] See note 54 below.

[42] L. Hautecoeur, *Histoire de l'architecture classique*, IV, pp. 97-101; V, p. 191. Also see G. Bapst, *Essai sur l'histoire du théâtre*, Paris, 1893, pp. 430-459.

[43] Morel, *Théorie*, pp. 33-34.

[44] See chapter III, p. 54.

[45] Duc d'Harcourt, *Traité des jardins*, p. 110.

ing to the proximity of great cities and of elegant structures.[46] Even Walpole, who strongly condemned artificial gardening in his history of modern gardening, recommended artifices as proper "for the narrow spaces allotted to the gardens of a house in a capital city."[47] And he went on to comment that "Those treillages in the gardens at Paris, particularly on the Boulevard, have a gay and delightful effect.—They form light corridores (*sic*), and transpicuous arbours through which the sunbeams play and chequer the shade, set off the statues, vases and flowers, that marry with [the] gaudy hotels, and suit the galant and idle society who paint the walks between their parterres."[48]

If in theory the picturesque garden was extended into public space, and the artificial version of this garden—that is, the *jardin anglo-chinois*—was associated with the city, in practice the designing of these gardens is associated with many of the architects who designed the Parisian hôtels. Among them were not only Bélanger, who probably visited England twice, and whose sketchbook of his visit records his interest in the English picturesque garden,[49] but also other architects, such as J. F. Le Roy (who designed the English garden at Chantilly and worked at Betz), Soufflot (who worked at Menars and Chatou), Chalgrin (who is associated with Brunoy and Balbi), Brongniart (who was at Maupertuis), Ledoux (who was connected with Maupertuis and who designed many of the gardens for his Parisian hôtels), Boullée (who may have designed the early picturesque garden at Chauvry and who was responsible for the garden of the Hôtel Brunoy), P. A. Pâris (who designed gardens for many of his smaller hôtels), and even Lequeu (who worked at Chatou and who may have been connected with Monceau).[50] These architects, trained and experienced in considering vast spaces for their picturesque scenic effects, would surely apply their knowledge to the creation of picturesque effects within an urban context. For them the ideal cityscape would have been as varied, diverse, and full of surprises and theatrical effects as the *jardins anglo-chinois* which they also designed and in which many of the new Parisian hôtels were set.

In this fashion a new concept of cityscape emerged, one which incorporated some of the picturesque and artificial qualities of the *jardin anglo-chinois*. It is a concept certainly brought into play in the designing of the new Parisian residential quarters, but did it have a role also in the designing of monumental public spaces? It would have been quite easy for this concept to move from private into public design at a time when residential architecture was taking on a more and more public and monumental character. For example, after 1770 the colossal order was frequently used in the new hôtels. Blondel considered it suitable only for public monuments and palaces and criticized its use on residences, as applied to the facade of the Hôtel d'Uzès, which had been remodeled in 1768 by Ledoux.[51] And contemporary opinion

---

[46] See chapter III, p. 57.

[47] Walpole, "On Modern Gardening," p. 122. See also chapter III, p. 62 and n. 204.

[48] *Ibid.*, p. 123. However, Girardin, *Observations*, pp. 219-222, also considered planning a city as he would a garden.

[49] For the sketchbook, see chapter II, n. 57. Bélanger also taught a course on gardening at the Athenée des Etrangers (see *Journal des bâtiments*, IX, no. 224, I

brumaire, an II, pp. 143-144).

[50] Ganay, *Jardins à l'anglaise en France*, II, p. 592.

[51] Blondel, *Cours*, 1771, I, p. 110. The Uzès colossal order was also criticized by Blondel and J. F. Bastide in *L'Homme du monde éclairé par les arts*, I, pp. 255-266. See W. Herrmann, "The Problem of the Chronology in Claude-Nicolas Ledoux's Engraved Work," *Art Bulletin*, XLII, September 1960, pp. 191-210.

found the Hôtels de Salm and Thélusson to be in bad taste because they appeared to be suitable only for royalty.[52]

The residential area had become in a sense public in another way, too, for some of the hôtels, such as the Hôtel Thélusson, were opened for public viewing.[53] Finally, some of the larger Parisian estates were already so nearly public in function that they easily would be converted later into public pleasure gardens. Indeed, the urban and theatrical character of the Parisian *jardin anglo-chinois* made it ideally suited for transformation into public use. To be sure, gardens such as the first and second Vauxhalls, the Colisée (Fig. 147),[54] and the Paphos (Fig. 146),[55] were originally designed for their public role; the grounds of the Palais Royal (Fig. 148), which were extensively developed in the 1780s by the Duc de Chartres, had always been open to the public.[56] But the Duc de Chartres's private park, Monceau, was also open to the public by admission tickets, as were other fashionable private parks and gardens. Moreover, two of the three Tivolis were converted after the Revolution from large, fashionable residences—the estate of Boutin was opened in 1796 to the public,[57] and the estate of M. de La Boissière became the third Tivoli as late as 1826 (Fig. 149). A section of the Beaujon estate was acquired in 1801, and it remained open as a public garden (Fig. 150) from that time until 1825, when three streets were cut through it. Finally, the most popular and elegant of all the public gardens, Frascati, was converted from the estate of the Hôtel Bondy (designed by Brongniart in 1771), after its purchase by an Italian glass manufacturer in 1796, and it was opened to the public in 1800.[58]

Few public projects, however, can be considered to have been designed within the context of the picturesque garden. Those few might include the Granary (Fig. 151), with a plan derived from the Roman Coliseum[59] (and possibly related to the "Grand Circus" designed by John Wood for Bath in 1725),[60] and the Odéon (Fig. 152), with its twin bridges which look like sunken triumphal arches,[61] and its colonnaded front.[62] In particular, the planning of the area around the Odéon, follows the picturesque but symmetrical principles of Dézallier d'Ar-

[52] For the Hôtel Thélusson, see Legrand and Landon, *Description de Paris*, II, pp. 109-112; for the Hôtel de Salm, see *ibid.*, I, pp. 89-92. For the history of the Hôtel de Salm, see H. Thirion, *Le Palais de la Legion d'Honneur, ancien Hôtel de Salm*, Versailles, 1883.

[53] Oberkirch, *Mémoires*, I, p. 243, 31 May 1782.

[54] For the Paris Vauxhalls, see Gruber, "Les Vauxhalls parisiens," pp. 125-143.

[55] For the Paphos, see Landon, *Annales*, XIII, 1805, pp. 111-112, "Projet d'une Guinguette."

[56] For the Palais Royal, see E. Dupezard, *Le Palais-Royal de Paris*, Paris, 1911; Hautecoeur, *Histoire de l'architecture classique*, IV, pp. 369-419; M. J. A. D——, *Lettre à M——, sur le cirque qui se construit au milieu du jardin du Palais Royal*, Paris, 1787; F. Nash and J. Scott, *Picturesque Views of the City of Paris*, London, 1820-1823 (2v.): I, "The Galleries of the Palais Royal," and "The Garden of the Palais Royal": II, "The Palais Royal."

[57] See S. Blondel, *L'Art pendant la Révolution;*

beaux-arts, arts décoratifs, Paris [1887], pp. 101-102.

[58] See J. Hillairet, *Dictionnaire historique des rues de Paris*, I, p. 360. For contemporary descriptions of Frascati, see *Paris et ses curiosités*, Paris, 1802, pp. 111-112; *Paris et ses curiosités*, Paris, 1804, p. 172; and *Voyage à la Chaussée d'Antin*, Paris, 1804, pp. 130-132. The best description of the Frascati garden is in William Shepherd, *Paris in 1802 and 1814*, London, 1814 (2nd ed.), pp. 64-65.

[59] Wiebenson, "The Two Domes of the Halle au Blé in Paris," *Art Bulletin*, LV, June 1973, pp. 262-279.

[60] See J. Wood, *An Essay towards a Description of Bath*, London, 1765 (2v.): II, pp. 345-346, on the question of picturesque effects; p. 351, on the importance of prospects from the town into the country.

[61] A. Braham, "Charles de Wailly and Early Neo-Classicism," *Burlington Magazine*, CIV, October 1972, p. 682, n. 5.

[62] The Odéon is the first theater to be designed like a temple, according to Braham, *ibid.*, p. 682.

genville.[63] But surely the Surgical School (1769-1774) and its projected square (1771) cannot be considered apart from developments in picturesque garden design (Figs. 153-156).[64] It is to be noted that the architect, Gondoin, was the son of a gardener, and he would later design his own garden on his estate at Vives-Eaux near Melun, to which he retired after the Revolution.[65] Here, at the Surgical School, an early work, the colonnaded open facade provides a vista into the interior court in the same way that colonnades, grilles, and arches provided vistas into private gardens: the architect justified the openness of his design, first, on the basis of its derivation from antique prototypes; second, by the fact that a palatial appearance was necessary in order to suggest the School's royal patronage (Louis XV donated the funds for the construction, and the colonnaded open front was associated with royal garden pavilions); and, last and most important for our purposes, because the celebrity of the School, which accepted students from all nations, should be expressed visually, by an open and easy access.[66]

However, even more than the School itself, the square projected for it provides an illustration of the extent to which picturesque gardening ideas were carried over into the design of public urban spaces. The square was entered, not on axis, but obliquely from narrow, twisting medieval streets. Gondoin designed an asymmetrical area, consisting of the stark wall of a debtor's prison, facing the colonnaded entrance to the School and remodeled from an existing convent cloister; and he gave a temple facade to the projected parish church of the Carmelites which would have terminated the square. According to the architect, the prison was deliberately designed to form the greatest possible contrast to the School, as well as to express public security.[67] Its only ornament was a fountain opposite the entrance to the School, the design of which was based on the most primitive of orders, the Greek Doric.[68] The church facade, however, was decorated with the "most majestic" of orders,[69] the Roman Doric, so that it, too, contrasted with both the open, Ionic colonnade of the School, and with the stark prison wall. The heaping up of different "effects," the sudden entrance into the square at an oblique angle, and even a picturesque moonlit study of the School must surely be seen within the context of the picturesque garden.

Lemonnier used the term "megalomaniacal" when he described the style of Gondoin's project, which he related to projects by Boullée and Ledoux.[70] Lemonnier also compared this style to the engravings of Piranesi,[71] in particular, to Piranesi's fantastic reconstruction of the Appian Way, where pyramids, sepulchers, mausoleums, urns, statues, obelisks, columns, and temples

[63] See M. Steinhauser and D. Rabreau, "Le Théâtre de l'Odéon de Charles de Wailly et Marie-Joseph Peyre, 1767-1782."

[64] For the Ecole de Chirurgie, see J. Adhémar, "L'Ecole de Médecine; sa place dans l'architecture française du XVIIIe siècle," *L'Architecture*, XLVII, no. 3, 15 May 1934, pp. 105-108; J. Gondoin, *Description des Ecoles de Chirurgie*. For Gondoin, see Quatremère de Quincy, *Notice historique sur la vie et les ouvrages de M. Gondoin*, Paris, 1821.

[65] *Ibid.*, pp. 13-15.

[66] Gondoin, *Description*, p. 7.

[67] *Ibid.*, p. 8.

[68] G. E. L. Poisson, *Napoléon et Paris*, Paris, 1964, p. 87. The fountain was not erected until 1804-1807, was altered in 1832 and demolished in 1878.

[69] Gondoin, *Description*, p. 8.

[70] R. Lemonnier, "La Mégalomanie dans l'architecture." See also Wiebenson, "'L'Architecture terrible' and the 'Jardin anglo-chinois.'"

[71] Gondoin was closely enough acquainted with Piranesi to leave him his drawings for a project for the reconstruction of Hadrian's Villa at the end of his second Italian trip (Quatremère de Quincy, *Notice historique*, pp. 11-12).

—all elements as appropriate to rural as to urban design—proliferated (Fig. 157).[72] Chambers may have had Piranesi's engraving in mind when he specified in the second edition of his *Dissertation on Oriental Gardening* that in order to transform the "whole kingdom" into "one magnificent vast garden . . . ," highways should be decorated with mausoleums and public bridges should be adorned with triumphal arches, rostral pillars, bas-reliefs, statues and other indications of victory and the glorious achievements of war.[73]

Now, the idea of including antique references in city planning for their associational value was not limited to theoretical writings or to fanciful archeological reconstructions. In 1768, M. Dussausoy suggested the construction of a major avenue through Paris which he described in terms of a continuous series of views to public edifices and monuments.[74] This was in line with the picturesque gardening concepts of Dézallier d'Argenville and surely continued the early eighteenth-century picturesque urban concepts of Meissonnier and Delamair.[75] The architect Soufflot contemporaneously designed a project for a royal Parisian avenue where existing "gothic" edifices were to be demolished, and palaces and triumphal arches built on their ruins, symmetrically disposed in regularly ordonnated perspectives. Soufflot's biographer, Monval, commented on the design that the symbolic decoration, like that of a Classical forum, would turn the new avenue into a triumphal way for the king of France, who thus would represent his nation as a new Roman Caesar.[76]

The idea of Paris, transformed through "emblematic" decoration into a new Rome, symbolizing the power of the monarchy, was an established planning concept by the time of the competition for a public square for the equestrian statue of Louis XV, although it surely was rooted in earlier and traditional planning design.[77] But by the 1770s the type of urban monument to be associated with the glory of ancient Rome began to be overshadowed by one designed to recall, instead, nature and sentiment. Indeed, the physical appearance of contemporary Rome itself may have helped to inspire this new development, just as it had helped to inspire the concept of the city as an exhibition of ancient monuments recalling past empirical power. For Rome, more than any other eighteenth-century city in Europe, was literally invaded by nature. The French scholar, Focillon, in his monograph on Piranesi, describes movingly the appearance of the city in this period. Rome was, according to him, a city of lush vegetation, green and shaded, where the ancient ruins were enclosed by forests, covered by pasture land, and in some instances impenetrably overgrown. It was, a "city of gardens and of shadows," where undisciplined nature contributed much to the charm.[78] It is within this context that the *Lettres sur l'architecture* of Viel de Saint-Maux, published beginning in 1779, can be placed. In these letters the author maintained that the significance of architecture de-

[72] Lemonnier, "La Mégalomanie dans l'architecture," pp. 275-276; and see chapter v, n. 72.

[73] See chapter III, p. 55.

[74] M. Dussausoy, *Le Citoyen désinteressé*, part ii, pp. 8-9. See also P. Devillers, *L'Axe de Paris*.

[75] See Garms, "Projects for the Pont Neuf."

[76] Monval, *Soufflot*, p. 269.

[77] Laugier, *Essai*, pp. 250-251, contemporaneously called for triumphal arches at the entrances to the city to remind the spectator of the French monarchs whose exploits had filled all Europe by recalling the arches erected in honor of the Roman emperors. See also Laugier, *Observations*, pp. 226-250, where he suggests the erection of triumphal arches, public fountains, triumphal columns, monuments in memorial of illustrious men, and mausoleums.

[78] H. Focillon, *Giovanni-Battista Piranesi, 1720-1778*, Paris, 1918, pp. 150-151.

pended on its symbolic, and not on its formal values, but that the symbolism should be associated with agriculture rather than with political power. By 1792 even a major public monument in Paris could be interpreted as a garden structure: the critic G. Kersaint, in his *Discours sur les monuments publics*, suggested that the portico of the unfinished Madeleine inspired "noble thoughts" and "melancholy sentiments," so that the architect himself would "not know if he had created a temple or a ruin."[79]

The architectural form which best represents the new associations attached to public monuments is the colonnade. For the colonnade as for the general concept of city planning, the new associations based on nature seem to have superseded the traditional formal and symbolic ones around 1770. Earlier, when mid-eighteenth century critics—Saint-Yves in 1748, Voltaire in 1749, and Bachaumont in 1751—called for the completion of the work on the colonnade of the east front of the Louvre (Fig. 158), they focused attention on the symbolic references in the monument to the reign of Louis XIV.[80] When in the late 1760s, however, work was resumed on the disengagement of the facade,[81] a new analysis of the colonnade was made by the architect J. D. Le Roy, a friend of Chambers and an admirer of both of his works on gardening. In the second edition of his *Les Ruines des plus beaux monumens de la Grèce*, published in 1770, Le Roy described the colonnade as suggestive not of royalty or national glory, but of nature, as if it were itself an element of landscape, constantly changing with the times of the day, the weather, and the seasons, and with different points of view. To Le Roy, it was: ". . . the most beautiful piece of architecture in Europe . . . Not only does the spectator not exhaust in several hours the pictures that the Louvre [colonnade] is able to offer, but also the different moments of the day furnish him with new ones. Each new location of the sun creates response in the shadows of the columns . . . ,"[82] and he compared rows of free-standing columns to allées of trees.

Colonnades—for porticos, to screen buildings, to frame streets—played a considerable role in the concept of the cityscape during the last quarter of the eighteenth century. Most urban transformations of the period such as the projects of the students of the Academy of Architecture,[83] and Boullée's *Architecture, essai sur l'art* (an unpublished manuscript probably written during the 1780s, in which the author emphasized the role of the seasons, of light, and of the landscape setting in architecture) remained simply projects. But it is against the background of these partial expressions of a pre-Revolutionary concept of the picturesque that we must see such often cited post-Revolutionary examples of the use of the colonnade as the rue des Colonnes and Brongniart"s Bourse.

[79] A. G. Kersaint, *Discours sur les monuments publics*, p. 34.

[80] Saint-Yves, *Observations*; Voltaire, "Des Embellissements de Paris"; Bachaumont, *Essai*, p. 81.

[81] For a history of the Louvre colonnade, see Hautecoeur, *L'Histoire des châteaux du Louvre et des Tuileries*, Paris, 1927, pp. 72-76; *Histoire de l'architecture classique*, IV, pp. 92-93; and Monval, *Soufflot*, pp. 151ff.

[82] Le Roy, *Les Ruines . . . de la Grèce*, p. viij. Le Roy also read Burke: his "combinaison des objets simples" (columns) (*idem.*), is surely a variation on Burke's artificial infinite, which was produced by a "colonnade of uniform pillars in a right line" (Burke, *Enquiry*, pp. 139-141).

[83] See H. Rosenau, "The Engravings of the *Grands Prix* of the French Academy of Architecture," *Architectural History*, III, 1960, pp. 15-180 (reprint and catalog of A. P. Prieur and P. L. van Cléemputte, *Collection des prix que la ci-devant Académie d'Architecture proposoit et couronnoit tous les ans*, Paris, 1787-c. 1796.

The role of England in this development in urban planning cannot be overlooked. At the same time that concepts of picturesque gardening design were entering into the Parisian cityscape, English rural planning also was absorbed into French urban design. We know that the Comte d'Artois's speculative Parisian development which was to be called Nouvelle Londres (1778) was based on the English village square,[84] and the garden village at Maupertuis, designed by Ledoux (after 1780?) (Fig. 159),[85] surely has an English rural prototype. On the other hand, there are indications from guidebooks and critical essays that some of the characteristics of the picturesque garden were absorbed into English city planning. As early as 1771, James Stuart criticized picturesque planning in his *Critical Observations on . . . London* when he advised that "a garden in a street is not less absurd than a street in a garden: and he that wishes to have a row of trees before his door in town, betrays almost as false a taste as he that would build a row of houses for an avenue to his seat in the country." Stuart also criticized the fact that Grosvenor Square was planted with trees and shrubs, and he ridiculed the attempt to "excite pastoral ideas" at Cavendish Square by "cooping up a few frightened sheep,"[86] suggesting that the effect was similar to that of the automated garden at Lunéville. By 1785 Sir Joshua Reynolds seems to have fully accepted picturesque planning in cities, for he noted that "The forms and turnings of the streets of London, and other old towns, are produced by accident, without any original plan of design; but they are not always the less pleasant to the walker or spectator, on that account. On the contrary, if the city had been built on the regular plan of Sir Christopher Wren, the effect might have been as we know it is in some parts of the town, rather unpleasing; the uniformity might have produced weariness, and a slight degree of disgust."[87]

How much of the interest in rural and informal planning in urban London was the result of Parisian influence cannot be known now. One work suggesting a possible tie with Parisian planning is Nash's scheme for the development of London. In his design for Regent Street, Nash proposed a curved peristyle. Now, Summerson has observed that the use of a colonnade in English planning is unusual at this time.[88] And, indeed, detailed justification of the scheme which Nash submitted with his proposal suggests that he expected to meet strong opposition. The bases for the defense of his project ranged from the "grand and striking effect" the columns would produce, to the practical desirability of the colonnade as a shelter for walking, and he included a provision for lighting the shops and even a defense of the round columns as prohibiting the committing of "nuisances."[89] Surely Nash was thinking of the fashionable, picturesque colonnaded Parisian street when he proposed his own picturesque design.

When Nash designed Regent's Park, he utilized concepts which appear to be at least as French as they are English. In the proposal submitted in 1811 for the Regent's Park development, he described the park's amenities: there would be open space, free air, the scenery of nature, and the possibility of exercise. Moreover, there would be inducements to the wealthy to establish

[84] For Nouvelle Londres, see Thièry, *Guide à Paris*, I, p. 74; Métra, *Correspondance secrète.* XIV, pp. 236-238, 10 April 1783 (the most complete description of the project); and Stern, *Bélanger*, pp. 97-98.

[85] For the village at Maupertuis, see C. Rivière, *Un Village de Brie*, p. 53.

[86] Stuart, *Critical Observations*, pp. 12-13.

[87] J. Reynolds, *Discourses on Art*, London, 1966 (1st ed., 1778), Discourse Thirteen, pp. 210-211, and p. 213.

[88] J. Summerson, *John Nash, Architect to King George IV*, London, 1935, p. 125.

[89] *Ibid.*, p. 126.

themselves there: markets and all the conveniences essential to the comforts of life would be included in the area. And the park would be self-contained—the terraces would face inward toward the park, and the original fifty-six villas (reminiscent of the excessive garden structures in some of the French *jardins anglo-chinois*), intended to be located there, would be designed so that each "should appear to possess the whole park and yet be invisible to the others." A larger villa—or *ginguette*, a name given to public and private pleasure houses in French parks and gardens—was to be situated at the center of the complex.[90]

One direct connection of the Regent's Park scheme with France can be suggested. Illustrations of Paris by architects and artists had, on occasion, shown Parisian houses and public monuments arranged like garden architecture within a parklike setting. This method of presentation was used by Chambers in several of his Parisian sketches made in May 1774 (Fig. 161),[91] and by an unknown artist in sketches of Parisian hôtels, probably done in the 1780s (Fig. 162).[92] Again, a set of early nineteenth-century panels of wallpaper by Dufour,[93] shows Parisian monuments grouped together within a park (Fig. 165). In 1810 the two large panels of villas in a landscape which were designed to promote Nash's Regent's Park scheme depicted Parisian architecture, both public and private, within a parklike setting (Figs. 166a-f). As it was noted in chapter v, it has been suggested that these panels were designed by a French artist.[94]

Regent's Park is often said to be the first "garden city." However, picturesque urban planning did not continue in this form directly into the nineteenth century. The landscape garden remained in the public domain, but it was restricted to parks and cemeteries. It is fitting that one of the latest developments of the *jardin anglo-chinois* would be Brongniart's Père Lachaise cemetery. (Fig. 164), which was derived from the late eighteenth-century memorial garden of Alexander Le Noire (Fig. 163). This is designed on an irregular, hilly terrain, full of unexpected views, and, with its many differently styled tombs, creates the greatest possible variety.[95]

Not until the publication of Camillo Sitte's book on planning at the end of the nineteenth century did picturesque planning again achieve a place within an urban context. From that time on the picturesque garden would be associated with the garden cities which, initiated by Ebenezer Howard and promoted by Sir Raymond Unwin under the influence of Sitte's work, assumed an important position in urban planning of the twentieth century.

[90] For the description of the Regent's Park proposal, see *First (Third) Report of His Majesty's Commissioners of Woods, Forests and Revenues*, London, 1812-1819, Appendix 12 (B): "Report of *Mr. John Nash, Architect in the Department of Woods, with Plans for the Improvement of Mary-le-Bone Park*," pp. 89-90. Also see Appendix G, pp. 113-114: "An Additional Report of Mr. Nash, with the PLAN of Mary-le-Bone Park."

[91] J. Harris, "Sir William Chambers and his Parisian Album," *Architectural History*, VI, 1963, pp. 54-90. The Album is deposited in the Prints and Drawings Collection of the Royal Institute of British Architects.

[92] *Idem.* The drawings are deposited in the British Museum, King's Maps, CXXIV, Suppl. See R. Middle-

ton, review of J. Harris, *Sir William Chambers, Architectural Design*, April 1971, pp. 248-249, for a discussion of Chambers' connection with these drawings.

[93] See Hautecoeur, *Histoire de l'architecture classique*, V, pp. 387-388. Among the Dufour wallpapers are also a related series on the Jardin de Bagatelle and on the *Plaisirs de la Campagne*.

[94] See chapter v, n. 47.

[95] See A. F. Brongniart, *Plan du palais de la Bourse de Paris et du cimetière Mont-Louis*, Paris, 1814, for the Père Lachaise cemetery. For Alexandre Le Noire's garden, see L. Réau, "Le Jardin-Elysée," with bibliographical references.

Bibliography

PRIMARY SOURCES

Addison, J. "The Pleasures of the Imagination," *Spectator*, nos. 411-422, 21 June-4 July 1712; and no. 477, 6 September 1712 (ed. D. F. Bond, Oxford, 1965 [5v.], III, pp. 535-586; IV, pp. 188-192).

——. *Remarks on Several Parts of Italy &c. in the Years 1701, 1702, 1703.* London, 1705.

Attiret, J. D. *Lettres édifiantes et curieuses, écrits des Missions étrangères de la Compagnie de Jésus*, XXVII, 1749 (ed. L. Patouillet), letter of 1 November 1743, pp. 7-43 (English translation, H. Beaumont [J. Spence], *A Particular Account of the Emperor of China's Gardens near Pekin.* London, 1752).

Bachaumont. *See* Petit de Bachaumont.

Bastide. *See* Blondel.

Baumgärtner, F. G. *Neue Gartenbaukunst, oder Sammlung neuer Ideen zur Verzierung der Gärten und Parks.* Leipzig, 1818-1824.

Beaumont. *See* Attiret.

Blaikie, T. *Diary of a Scotch Gardener at the French Court at the End of the Eighteenth Century.* London, 1931 (ed. F. Birrell).

Blondel, J. F. *Architecture françoise.* Paris, 1752-1756 (4v.).

——. *Cours d'architecture.* Paris, 1771-1777 (9v.).

——. *De la distribution des maisons de plaisance, et de la decoration des édifices en general*, Paris, 1737-1738.

——. *L'Homme du monde éclairé par les arts.* Amsterdam, 1774 (2v.) (ed. J. F. de Bastide).

——. *Maisons de Plaisance.* Paris, 1736 (2v.).

Boccage. *See* Fiquet du Boccage.

Boitard, P. *Traité de la composition et de l'ornement des jardins.* Paris, 1825 (3rd ed.).

Boullée, E. L. *Architecture, Essai sur l'art.* Paris, 1968 (ed. Pérouse de Montclos).

——. *Boullée's Treatise on Architecture.* London, 1953 (ed. H. Rosenau).

Briseux, C. E. *L'Art de bâtir les maisons de campagne.* Paris, 1743.

Brongniart, A. F. *Plan du Palais de la Bourse de Paris et du cimetière Mont-Louis.* Paris, 1814.

Burke, E. *A Philosophical Enquiry into the Origin of our Ideas of the Sublime and the Beautiful.* London, 1958 (1st ed. 1757).

Cambry, J. de. *De Londres et de ses environs.* Amsterdam, 1788 (2nd ed. *Promenades d'automne en Angleterre.* Paris, 1791).

——. *See* Bibliography. Individual Gardens: Ermenonville.

Carrogis, L. (Carmontelle) *Jardin de Monceau, pres de Paris.* Paris, [1778], Prospectus.

——. *Jardin de Monceau, près de Paris, appartenant à S.A.S. Mgr. le duc de Chartres.* Paris, 1779.

Castell, R. *The Villas of the Ancients Illustrated.* London, 1728.

Caylus. *See* Tubières de Grimoard de Pestels de Levis.

de Chabanon, M. P. G. *Epitre sur la manie des jardins anglois.* Paris, 1775.

Chambers, W. *Designs of Chinese Buildings, Furniture, Dresses, Machines and Utensiles . . . to which is annexed a Description of their Temples, Houses, Gardens.* London, 1757.

——. *Dissertation on Oriental Gardening.* London, 1772 (2nd ed. 1773, . . . To which is annexed, an explanatory discourse, by Tan Chet-qua, of Quang-chew-fa).

——. *Plans, Elevations, Sections and Perspective Views of the Gardens and Buildings at Kew in Surrey.* London, 1763.

Cochin, C. N. *Recueil de quelques pièces concernant les arts, extraites de plusieurs Mercures de France.* Paris, 1757.

Cooper, A. A. (Lord Shaftesbury). "The Moralists," *Characticks of Men, Manners, Opinions, Times*, 1711-1727 (3v.), II, pt. v, pp. 181-443.

Croÿ, E. de. *Journal inédit du Duc de Croÿ 1718-1784.* Paris, 1906 (4v.) (ed. Vte. de Grouchy and P. Cottin).

Curten, M. *Essai sur les jardins.* Lyon, 1807.

Darly. *See* E. Edwards.

Decker, P. *Chinese Architecture, Civil and Ornamented.* London, 1759.

——. *Gothic Architecture Decorated.* London, 1759.

De La Coste. *See* La Coste.

De Ligne. *See* Ligne.

De Lille, J. *Les Jardins, ou l'art d'embellir les paysages: poème.* Paris, 1782.

Dézallier d'Argenville, A. J. *La Théorie et la pratique du jardinage.* Paris, 1709 (English translation, J. James, *The Theory and Practice of Gardening.* London, 1712).

Duchesne, A. N. *Sur la Formation des jardins.* Paris, 1775.

Dufresny. *See* Rivière du Fresny.

Du Hamel de Monceau. *See* Tull.

Dulaure, J. A. *Nouvelle Description des curiosités de Paris*. Paris, 1785 (2 pts.).

———. *Nouvelle Description des environs de Paris.* Paris, 1786 (2 pts.).

Dussausoy, M. *Le Citoyen désinteressé, ou divers idées patriotiques concernant quelques établissemens et embelissemens utiles à la ville de Paris*. Paris, 1767, 1768.

Edwards, E. and M. Darly. *A New Book of Chinese Designs*. London, 1754.

Essay on the Different Natural Situations of Gardens. London, 1774.

Evelyn. *See* Rapin.

Félibien des Avaux, J. F. *Les Plans et les descriptions de deux des plus belles maisons de campagne de Pline le consul*. Paris, 1699.

Ferri de San-Constante, J. L. *Londres et les Anglois*. Paris, an xii [1803] (4v.).

Fiquet du Boccage, M. A. *Le Paradis Terrestre, poème imité de Milton*. London, 1748.

———. *Recueil des oeuvres de Madame du Boccage*. Lyon, 1762 (2v.) (English translation, *Letters Concerning England, Holland and Italy*. London, 1770, 2v.).

Fischer von Erlach, J. B. *Entwurff einer Historischen Architectur*. Vienna, 1721.

Gallien de Salmorenc. *Le Spectacle de la Nature, poème didactique en quatre chants*. Liège, 1770.

Gandy, J. *Designs for Cottages, Cottage Farms, and Other Rural Buildings*. London, 1805.

———. *The Rural Architect, Consisting of Various Designs for Country Buildings*. London, 1806.

Gerard, A. *An Essay on Taste*. London, 1759 (French translation, *Essai sur le goût*. Paris, 1766).

Gilpin, W. *Three Essays: on Picturesque Beauty; on Picturesque Travel; and on Sketching Landscape: to which is added a Poem, on Landscape Painting*. London, 1794 (2nd ed.).

Girardin, R. L. de. *De la Composition des paysages, ou des moyens d'embellir la nature autour des habitations, en joignant l'agréable à l'utile*. Geneva, 1777 (English translation, D. Malthus, *An Essay on Landscape; or, on the means of improving and embellishing the country round our habitations*. London, 1783).

Gondoin, J. *Description des Ecoles de Chirurgie*. Paris, 1780.

Grimm, F. M. *Correspondance litteraire, philosophique et critique par Grimm, Diderot, Raynal, Meister, etc.* Paris, 1877-1882 (16v.) (ed. M. Tourneux).

Grohmann, J. G. *See Ideenmagazine*.

Grosley, P. J. *Londres*. Lausanne and London, 1770 (3v.), III, pp. 105-129.

———. *Nouveaux Mémoires, ou observations sur l'Italie*. London, 1764 (3v.) (2nd ed. *Observations sur l'Italie et sur les Italiens*. London, 1770).

Halfpenny, W. *Six New Designs for Convenient Farm-Houses*. London, 1751-1752.

———. *Useful Architecture in 21 New Designs*. London, 1752.

Halfpenny, W. and J. *Chinese and Gothic Architecture properly ornamented*. London, 1752.

———. *New Designs for Chinese Temples, Triumphal Arches, Garden Seats, Palings, etc.* London, 1750-1752.

———. *Rural Architecture in the Gothick Taste*. London, 1752.

———. *Rural Architecture in the Chinese Taste*. London, 1750-1752.

d'Harcourt, F. H. *Traité de la décoration des dehors des jardins et des parcs*. Paris, 1919 (ed. E. de Ganay) (written ca. 1774).

Hartig, F. de P. A. von. *Lettres sur la France, l'Angleterre, et l'Italie*. Geneva, 1785.

Héré, E. *Plans et élévations de la Place Royale de Nancy, et des autres édifices qui l'environment*. Paris and Nancy, 1753.

———. *Recueil des plans, élévations, et coupes tant générales qu'en perspective des châteaux, jardins et dépendances que le Roi de Pologne occupe en Lorraine*. Paris and Nancy, 1753 (pt. i); *Suite des plans, élévations et coupes des châteaux que le Roi de Pologne occupe en Lorraine*. Paris and Nancy, 1756 (pt. ii).

Hirschfeld, C. C. L. *Theorie der Gartenkunst*. Leipzig, 1779-1785 (5v.) (published simultaneously in French as *Théorie de l'art des jardins*).

Home, H. (Lord Kames). *Elements of Criticism*. Edinburgh, 1762 (3v), III, chap. xxiv: "Gardening and Architecture," pp. 294-350.

———. *The Gentleman Farmer*. Edinburgh, 1776.

Huet, P. D. *Huetiana; ou, pensées diverses de M. H. Evesque d'Avranches*. Paris, 1722 (ed. J. T. d'Olivet).

Ideenmagazine für Liebhaber von Gärten. Leipzig, 1796-1811 (nos. 1-60).

Kersaint, A. G. *Discours sur les monuments publics*. Paris, 1792.

Knight, R. P. *The Landscape, a didactic poem*. London, 1794.

Krafft, J. C. *Plans de plus beaux jardins pittoresques de France, d'Angleterre et d'Allemagne*. Paris, 1809-1810 (2v.).

———. *Recueil des plus jolies maisons de Paris et de ses environs*. Paris, 1809.

——— and N. Ransonnette. *Plans, coupes, élévations des plus belles maisons & des hôtels construits à Paris & dans les environs*. Paris, 1801-1802.

Laborde, A. L. J. de. *Description des nouveaux jardins de la France, et de ses anciens chateaux*. Paris, 1808-1815.

Laborde, J. B. de. *Description générale et particulière de la France*. Paris, 1781-1796 (12v.) (after v. IV, the title becomes *Voyage pittoresque de la France*).

———. *Tableaux de la Suisse*. Paris, 1784-1788 (12v.).

Lacombe, F. *Observations sur Londre et ses environs*. London, 1777.

La Coste, [de]. *Voyage philosophique d'Angleterre fait en 1783 et 1784*. London, 1786 (2v.).

Lalos, J. *De la Composition des parcs et jardins pittoresques*. Paris, 1817.

Landon, C. P. *Annales du Musée et de l'Ecole Moderne des Beaux-Arts*. Paris, 1800-1822 (42v.).

————. *See* Legrand.

Langley, B. *Ancient Architecture, restored, and improved, by a great variety of grand and useful designs, entirely new in the gothick mode, for the ornamenting of buildings and gardens.* London, 1742.

————. *New Principles of Gardening.* London, 1728.

Latapie. *See* Whately.

Laugier, M. A. *Essai sur l'architecture.* Paris, 1753.

————. *Observations sur l'architecture.* The Hague, 1764.

Le Blanc, J. B. *Lettres d'un François.* The Hague (3v.) (English translation, *Letters on the French and English Nations,* London, 1747, 3v.).

Le Camus de Mezières, N. *Le Génie de l'architecture, ou l'analogie de cet art avec nos sensations.* Paris, 1780.

————. *See* Bibliography. Individual Gardens: Chantilly.

Lecreulx, F. M. *Discours sur le goût, appliqué aux arts et particulièrement à l'architecture.* Nancy, 1778.

Ledoux, C. N. *L'Architecture considérée. . . .* Paris, [1802], Prospectus.

————. *L'Architecture considérée sous le rapport de l'art, des moeurs et de la législation.* Paris, 1804, 1846 (2v.).

Legrand, J. G., and C. P. Landon. *Description de Paris et de ses édifices.* Paris, 1806-1809 (2v.).

Le Rouge, G. L. *Curiosités de Londres et d'Angleterre.* Bordeaux, 1766.

————. *Détails des nouveaux jardins à la mode* (cahier i, n.d.); *Jardins anglo-chinois à la mode* (cahiers ii; iii; iv, 1776; v [1776]; vii, 1779; viii; x [1783]; xi, 1784; xii, 1785; xvii); *Serrail et jardins du Grand Seigneur* (cahier vi); *Jardins chinois* (cahier ix, 1781; xiv; xv, 1786; xvi, 1786); *Cahier des jardins* (Cahier xii [1784]); *Jardins anglais* (cahier xviii [1787]; xix [1787]; xx, 1788).

Le Roy, J. D. *Les Ruines des plus beaux monuments de la Grèce.* Paris, 1770 (2v.) (2nd ed., aug.).

Lezay-Marnésia, C. F. A. de. *Essai sur la nature champêtre.* Paris, 1787.

Ligne, C. J. E. de. *Coup d'oeil sur Beloeil.* Paris, 1922 (ed. E. de Ganay from 1786 Brussels ed.) (1st ed. 1781).

Lubersac de Livron, C. F. de. *Discours sur les monumens publics de tous les âges et de tous les peuples connus.* Paris, 1775.

L. L. G. D. M. *Lettre sur les jardins anglois.* Paris, 1775 (rev. and abr. in *Journal Encyclopédique,* October 1775, VIII, pp. 132-142).

Malthus. *See* Girardin.

Mariette, J. *L'Architecture française.* Paris, 1727-1738 (reprint with introduction, ed. L. Hautecoeur, 1927-1929).

Mason, G. *An Essay on Design in Gardening.* London, 1768.

Mason, W. *The English Garden.* London, 1772-1779 (French translation, M. Masson [*sic*], *Le Jardin anglais,* Paris, 1788).

————. *An Heroic Epistle to Sir William Chambers.* London, 1772.

————. *An Heroic Postscript to the Public, occasioned by their favourable reception of a late Heroic Epistle to Sir W. Chambers.* London, 1773.

————. *Satirical Poems published anonymously by William Mason, with notes by Horace Walpole, now first printed from his manuscript.* Oxford, 1926 (ed. P. Toynbee) (written in 1779).

Mercier, L. S. *Tableau de Paris.* Amsterdam, 1782-1788 (12v.).

Métra, F. *Correspondance secrète, politique et littéraire.* London, 1787-1790 (9v.).

Middleton, C. *The Architect and Builder's Miscellany, or Pocket Library: containing picturesque designs in architecture.* London, 1812.

————. *Decorations for Parks and Gardens.* London, 1800.

————. *Picturesque and Architectural Views for Cottages, Farmhouses and Country Villas.* London, 1793.

Miller, J. *The Country Gentleman's Architect.* London, 1787.

Morel, J. M. *Théorie des jardins.* Paris, 1776 (2nd ed. aug., an xi [1802], 2v.).

Morris, R. *The Architectural Remembrancer: being a collection of New and Useful Designs, of Ornamental Buildings and Decorations for Parks, Gardens, Woods, &c.* London, 1751.

————. *Rural Architecture: Consisting of Regular Designs of Plans and Elevations for Buildings in the Country.* London, 1750 (pub. as *Select Architecture* in 1757).

Neufforge, J. F. de. *Recueil élémentaire d'architecture.* Paris, 1757-1768 (8v. and Supplement, 1780).

Nieuhoff, J. *Het Gezantschap der Neërlandtsche Oost-Indische Compagnie.* Amsterdam, 1665.

Nourse, T. *Campania Felix: or, a Discourse of the Benefits and Improvements of Husbandry.* London, 1700.

d'Oberkirch, *Mémoires de la Baronne d'Oberkirch.* Paris, 1853 (2v.) (English translation, *Memoires of the Baroness d'Oberkirch,* London, 1852).

d'Olivet. *See* Huet.

Over, C. *Ornamental architecture in the Gothic, Chinese and Modern Taste.* London, 1758.

Panseron, P. *Recueil de jardinage.* Paris, 1783.

Patte, P. *Mémoires sur les objets les plus importans de l'architecture.* Paris, 1769.

————. *Monumens érigés en France à la gloire de Louis XV.* Paris, 1765.

Petit de Bachaumont, L. *Essai sur la peinture, la sculpture, et l'architecture.* Paris, 1751.

————. *Mémoires secrets pour servir à l'histoire de la république des lettres en France.* London, 1777-1789 (36v.).

Peyre, M. J. *Oeuvres d'architecture.* Paris, 1765.

Phlipon Roland de la Platière, M. J. *Oeuvres de J. M. Phlipon Roland de la Platière.* Paris, 1800 (3v.) (English translation, *The Works of J. M. Phlipon Roland,* London, 1800).

Pluche, N. A. *Le Spectacle de la Nature.* Paris,

1732ff. (9v.) (English translation, *Spectacle de la Nature*, London, 1736-1739, 4v.).

Poncet de la Grave, G. *Projet des embellissemens de la ville et faubourgs de Paris*. Paris, 1756 (3 parts).

Pope, A. *Guardian*, number 173, 29 September 1713.

Price, U. *An Essay on the Picturesque as Compared with the Sublime and the Beautiful*. London, 1794-1798 (2v.).

——. *A Dialogue on the Distinct Characters of the Picturesque and the Beautiful. In answer to the Objections of Mr. Knight*. London, 1801.

——. *A Letter to H. Repton . . . on the Application of the Practice as well as the Principles of Landscape-Painting to Landscape-Gardening*. London, 1795.

Prieur, A. P. *Petites maisons de Paris*. Paris [179?].

M. L. R. *Les Curiosités de Paris, de Versailles, de Marly, de Vincennes, de Saint-Cloud et des environs*. Paris, 1771 (2nd ed.) (1st ed. Paris, 1716).

Rapin, R. *Hortorum libri quattuor*. Paris, 1665 (English translation, J. Evelyn, *Of Gardens*. London, 1673).

Rea, J. *Flora, seu de Florum Cultura*. London, 1665.

Repton, H. *An Enquiry into the Changes of Taste in Landscape Gardening*. London, 1806.

——. *Fragments on the Theory and Practice of Landscape Gardening*. London, 1816.

——. *Observations on the Theory and Practice of Landscape Gardening*. London, 1803.

——. *Sketches and Hints on Landscape Gardening*. London, 1794.

Richard de Saint-Non, J. C. *Voyage pittoresque ou description des royaumes de Naples et de Sicile*. Paris, 1781-1786 (5v.).

The Rise and Progress of the Present Taste in Planting. London, 1767.

Rivière du Fresny, C. de la. *Oeuvres*. Paris, 1731 (6v.), I, "Avertissement," pp. 11-17.

Roland. *See* Phlipon Roland de la Platière.

Rosset, P. F. de. *L'Agriculture, poème*. Paris, 1774-1782 (2 pts.).

Rousseau, J. J. *Lettres de deux amants, habitans d'une petite ville au pied des Alpes: Julie, ou la Nouvelle Héloïse*. Amsterdam, 1761 (6v.) (English translation, *Eloisa: or, a Series of Original Letters*, Dublin, 1761).

——. *Oeuvres complètes*. Paris, 1788-1793 (38v.) (ed. L. S. Mercier, G. Brizard, and F. Il. S. de L'Aulnaye).

——. *Oeuvres complètes*. Paris, 1959-1964 (3v.) (ed. B. Gagnehin and M. Raymond).

Saint-Lambert, J. F. de. *Les Saisons et les jours, poème*. Amsterdam, 1764.

Saint-Non. *See* Richard de Saint-Non.

Saint-Yves. *Observations sur les arts*. Leyden, 1748.

Scott, J., and F. Nash. *Picturesque Views of the City of Paris and its Environs*. London, 1820-1823 (2v.).

Shaftesbury. *See* Cooper.

Shenstone, W. *The Works in Verse and Prose of W. Shenstone*. London, 1764 (2v.) (ed. R. Dodsley), II, pp. 77-91: "Unconnected Thoughts on Gardening."

Spence. *See* Attiret.

[Stuart, J.]. *Critical Observations on the Buildings and Improvements of London*. London [1771].

Switzer, S. *Ichnographia, or The Nobleman, Gentleman, and Gardener's Recreation*. London, 1715 (2nd ed., rev. and enl., *Ichnographia Rustica . . .*, London, 1718, 3v.).

Temple, W. *Five Miscellaneous Essays by Sir William Temple*. Ann Arbour, 1963 (ed. S. Monk), "Upon the Gardens of Epicurus: or, Of Gardening, in the Year 1685," pp. 1-36; "Of Heroic Virtue," pp. 107-123.

Testard, F. M., Le Campion, Sergeant, Roger, etc. *Paris et la province ou choix des plus beaux monuments d'architecture en France*. Paris [1790?].

Thièry, L. V. *Guide des amateurs et des étrangers voyageurs aux environs de Paris*. Paris, 1788.

——. *Guide des amateurs et des étrangers voyageurs à Paris*. Paris, 1787 (2v.).

Thouin, G. *Plans raisonnés de toutes les espèces de jardins*. Paris, 1820.

Titon du Tillet, E. *Description du Parnasse François*. Paris, 1727.

——. *Le Parnasse François*. Paris, 1732 (2nd ed., aug., 1734).

Tubières de Grimoard de Pestels de Levis, A. C. P. de (Comte de Caylus). *Recueil d'antiquités egyptiennes, étrusques, romaines et gauloises*. Paris, 1752-1767 (7v.).

Tull, J. *The New Horse-Houghing Husbandry: or, an Essay on the Principles of Tillage and Vegetation*. London, 1731 (French translation H. L. Du Hamel de Monceau, *Traité de la culture des terres, suivant les principes de M. Tull*. Paris. 1750-1761, 6v.).

d'Urfé, H. *L'Astrée, ou, par plusieurs histoires, et souz personnes de bergers et d'autres, sont deduits les divers effets de l'honneste amitié*. Rouen, 1647 (5v.) (first complete edition).

Vergnaud, N. *L'Art de créer les jardins*. Paris, 1835.

Viel de Saint-Maux, J. L. *Lettres sur l'architecture*. Brussels, 1779-1784.

Voltaire, F. M. A. de. *Oeuvres complètes de Voltaire*. Paris, 1877-1885 (54v.) (ed. Garnier), "Epitre IV: Au Prince Royal de Prusse," [1738], X, pp. 306-308; "Des embellissements de Paris," [1749], XXIII, pp. 297-304; "Des embellissements de la ville de Cachemire," [1756], XXIII, pp. 473-478.

Walpole, H. "On Modern Gardening," *Anecdotes of Painting in England*. Strawberry Hill, 1762-1771 (4v.), IV, pp. 117-151.

——. *The Letters of Horace Walpole, fourth Earl of Orford*. Oxford, 1903-1925 (19v.) (ed. P. Toynbee).

——. *See* Mason.

Ware, I. *A Complete Body of Architecture*. London, 1756.

Watelet, C. H. *Essai sur les jardins*. Paris, 1774.

Whately, T. *Observations on Modern Gardening*. London, 1770 (French translation, F. de P. Latapie, *L'Art de former les jardins modernes*. Paris, 1771).

Wimpffen, A. S. de. *Lettres d'un voyageur*. Amsterdam, 1788.

Wood, J. *An Essay towards a Description of Bath.* Bath, 1734 (2v.).

Wood, J. *A Series of Plans for Cottages or Habitations of the Labourer.* London, 1792.

The World, London, 4 January 1753 - 30 December 1756 (nos. 1-201).

Worlidge, J. *Systema agriculturae, the Mystery of Husbandry discovered.* London, 1669.

Wrighte, W. *Grotesque Architecture, or rural amusement.* London, 1767.

Young, A. *Travels in France during the Years 1787, 1788 & 1789.* Bury St. Edmunds, 1792-1794.

SECONDARY SOURCES

Allen, R. S. *Tides in English Taste: 1619-1800. A Background for the Study of Literature.* Cambridge, Mass., 1937 (2v.).

d'Ariste P., and M. Arrivetz. *Les Champs-Elysées, la Place de la Concorde.* Paris, 1913.

Bald, R. C. "Sir William Chambers and the Chinese Garden," *Journal of the History of Ideas,* II, no. 3, June 1959, pp. 287-320.

Baltrušaitis, J. *Abberations: Quatre essais sur la légende des formes.* Paris, 1957.

Bardet, G. *Naissance et méconnaissance de l'urbanisme.* Paris, 1951.

Biver, M. L. *Le Paris de Napoléon.* Paris, 1963.

Bjurström, P. *Giacomo Torelli and Baroque Stage Designs.* Stockholm, 1961.

——. "Servandoni, décorateur de théâtre," *Révue de la société d'histoire du théâtre,* VI, 1954, pp. 150-159.

Blunt, A. "The Hypnerotonmachia Poliphili in Seventeenth-Century France," *Journal of the Warburg and Courtauld Institutes,* I, 1937-1938, pp. 117-137.

Bourde, A. *Agronomie et agronomes en France au XVIIIe siècle.* Paris, 1967 (3v.).

——. *The Influence of England on the French Agronomes: 1750-1789.* Cambridge, 1953.

Carpechot, L. *Les Jardins de l'intelligence.* Paris, 1912.

Chase, I. W. U. *Horace Walpole: Gardenist.* Princeton, 1943.

——. "William Mason and Sir William Chambers' *Dissertation on Oriental Gardening," Journal of English and Germanic Philology,* XXXV, no. 4, October 1936, pp. 517-529.

Choppin de Janvry, O. "Les Jardins promenades au XVIIIe siècle," *Les Monuments historiques de la France,* 1976, no. 5, pp. 7-15.

Clark, H. F. "Eighteenth-Century Elysiums: The Role of 'Association' in the Landscape Movement," *Journal of the Warburg and Courtauld Institutes,* VI, 1943, pp. 165-189.

——. *The English Landscape Garden.* London, 1948.

Clarke, G. "The Gardens of Stowe," *Apollo,* XCVI, June 1972, pp. 18-25.

——. "Grecian Taste and Gothic Beauty," *Apollo,* XCVI, June 1972, pp. 26-31.

Clifford, D. *A History of Garden Design.* London, 1962.

Connolly, C. V., and J. Zerbe. *Les Pavillons. French Pavilions of the Eighteenth Century.* London, 1962.

Coussillan, A. A. *Dictionnaire historique des rues de Paris.* Paris, 1968 (2v.).

Devillers, P. *L'Axe de Paris et André Le Nôtre, grand jardinier de France.* Paris, 1959.

Dennerlein, I. *Die Gartenkunst der Régence und des Rokoko in Frankreich.* Bamberg, 1972.

Fortair, S. de. *Discours sur la vie et les ouvrages de Jean-Marie Morel.* Paris, 1813.

Gallet, M. *Demeures Parisiennes: L'Epoque de Louis XVI.* Paris, 1964.

——. *Stately Mansions.* London, 1972.

Ganay, E. de. *Beaux jardins de France.* Paris, 1959.

——. *Bibliographie de l'art des jardins.* 1942 (typescript on deposit at the Bibliothèque des Arts Décoratifs, Paris).

——. "Fabriques aux jardins du XVIIIe siècle," *Révue de l'art ancien et moderne,* LXIV, June-December 1933, pp. 49-74.

——. "Fabriques aux jardins du XVIIIe siècle," *Gazette des beaux-arts,* XLV, May-June 1955, pp. 287-298.

——. "Le Goût du moyen âge et des ruines dans les jardins du XVIIIe siècle," *Gazette des beaux-arts,* VIII, October 1932, pp. 183-197.

——. *Les Jardins à l'anglaise en France au dix-huitième siècle (de 1750 à 1789).* 1923 (2v.) (manuscript on deposit at the Bibliothèque des Arts Décoratifs).

——. *Les Jardins à la française en France au XVIIIe siècle.* Paris, 1943.

——. *Les Jardins de France et leur décor.* Paris [1949].

——. "Les Rochers et les eaux dans les jardins à l'anglaise," *Révue de l'art ancien et moderne,* LXVI, June-December 1934, pp. 63-80.

——. See also articles cited under Bibliography. Individual Gardens.

Garms, J. "Projects for the Pont Neuf and Place Dauphine in the First Half of the Eighteenth Century," *Journal of the Society of Architectural Historians,* XXVI, May 1967, pp. 102-113.

Gaxotte, P. *Paris au XVIIIe siècle.* Grenoble, 1968.

Gothein, M. L. *Geschichte der Gartenkunst.* Jena, 1914 (2v.) (English translation, *A History of Garden Art,* London, 1928, 2v.).

Granet, S. *Images de Paris: La Place de la Concorde.* Paris, 1963.

Green, D. *Gardener to Queen Anne: Henry Wise (1653-1738) and the Formal Garden,* London, 1956.

Grimal, P. *L'Art des jardins*. Paris, 1954.

Gruber, A. C. *Les grandes Fêtes et leurs décors à l'époque de Louis XVI*. Geneva and Paris, 1972.

————. "Les Vauxhalls Parisiens au XVIIIe siècle," *Bulletin de la Société de l'Histoire de l'Art Français*, 1971, pp. 127-143.

Guimbaud, L. *Saint-Non et Fragonard, d'après des documents inédits*. Paris, 1928.

Harris, E. "*Designs of Chinese Buildings* and the *Dissertation on Oriental Gardening*," in J. Harris, *Sir William Chambers*, London, 1970, pp. 144-162.

Hautecoeur, L. *Histoire de l'architecture classique en France*. Paris, 1943-1957 (7v.), v: *Revolution et Empire; 1792-1815*, 1953, pp. 3-50.

————. *Les Jardins des dieux et des hommes*. Paris, 1959.

Hazard, P. *La Crise de la conscience européene: 1680-1715*. Paris, 1935 (English translation, *The European Mind: 1680-1715*. London, 1953).

Herrmann, W. *Laugier and Eighteenth-Century French Theory*. London, 1962.

Hersey, G. L. "Associationism and Sensibility in Eighteenth Century Architecture," *Eighteenth Century Studies*, IV, 1970, pp. 71-89.

Hillairet. *See* Coussillan.

Honour, H. *Chinoiserie: The Vision of Cathay*. London, 1961.

Hunt, J. D. "Emblem and Expression in the Eighteenth-Century Landscape Garden," *Eighteenth Century Studies*, IV, 1971, pp. 294-317.

Hussey, C. E. C. *English Gardens and Landscape: 1700-1750*. London, 1967.

————. *The Picturesque, Studies in a Point of View*. London, 1927.

Jardins en France, 1760-1820. Pays d'illusion. Terre d'expériences, Paris, 1977 (exhibition catalog).

Les Joies de la nature au XVIIIe siècle. Paris, 1971 (exhibition catalog).

Kimball, S. F. *The Creation of the Rococo*. Philadelphia, 1943.

————. "Les Influences anglaises dans la formation du style Louis XVI," *Gazette des beaux-arts*, v, January 1931, pp. 27-44.

Lang. S. *See* Pevsner.

Langner, J. "Architecture pastorale sous Louis XVI," *L'Art de France*, III, 1963, pp. 170-186.

————. "Ledoux und die 'Fabriques': Voraussetzungen der Revolutionsarchitektur im Landschaftsgarten," *Zeitschrift für Kunstgeschichte*, XXVI, 1963, pp. 1-36.

Lavedan, P. "Le IIe Centenaire de la Place de la Concorde," *La Vie Urbaine*, July-September 1956, pp. 161-176.

————. *Histoire de l'urbanisme: Renaissance et temps modernes*. Paris, 1941.

————. "La Place Royale de Nancy et son influence," *La Vie Urbaine*, October-December 1952, pp. 250-262.

Lemonnier, H. "La Mégalomanie dans l'architecture à la fin du XVIIIe siècle," *L'Art moderne (1500-*

1800): Essais et esquisses, Paris, 1912, pp. 272-289 (originally published in *L'Architecte*, v, December 1910, pp. 92-97).

Loisel, G. *Histoire des ménageries de l'antiquité à nos jours*. Paris, 1912 (3v).

Manwaring, E. W. *Italian Landscape in the Eighteenth Century: A Study chiefly of the Influence of Claude Lorraine and Salvator Rosa on the English Taste*. London and New York, 1925.

Marie, A. *Jardins français classiques des XVIIe et XVIIIe siècles*. Paris, 1949.

————. *Naissance de Versailles, le château, les jardins*. Paris, 1968 (2v.).

Martial, A. P. *Ancien Paris*. Paris, 1866.

Matthews, W. H. *Mazes and Labyrinths; A General Account of their History and Development*. London, 1922.

Mondain-Monval, J. *Soufflot. Sa vie.—Son oeuvre.—Son esthétique; 1713-1780*, Paris, 1918.

Monk, S. H. *The Sublime: A Study of Critical Theories in XVIII-Century England*. New York, 1935.

————. *See* Bibliography. Sources: Temple.

Mornet, D. *Le Sentiment de la nature en France; de J. J. Rousseau à Bernardin de Saint-Pierre*, Paris, 1907.

Neumayer, A. "Monuments to Genius in German Classicism," *Journal of the Warburg and Courtauld Institutes*, II, 1938-1939, pp. 156-163.

Nyberg, D. "Meissonnier: An Eighteenth-Century Maverick," *Oeuvre de Juste Aurèle Meissonnier*, New York, 1969 (reprint), pp. 6-43.

Pérouse de Montclos, J. M. "L'Architecture à l'antique et la Revolution," *Art de France*, IV, 1964, pp. 325-327.

————. *Etienne-Louis Boullée: 1728-1799, De l'Architecture classique à l'architecture révolutionnaire*. Paris, 1969.

————. "De la villa rustique d'Italie au pavillon de banlieve," *Révue de l'art*, 1976, no. 3, pp. 23-36.

————. *See* Bibliography. Sources: Boullée.

Pevsner, N., and S. Lang. "The Genesis of the Picturesque," *Architectural Review*, XCVI, November 1944, pp. 139-146.

————. "Sir William Temple and Sharawaggi," *Architectural Review*, CVI, December 1940, pp. 391-393.

Poisson, G. E. L. "L'Art de la Révolution à Paris: architecture et décors," *Gazette des beaux-arts*, LXXVI, December 1970, pp. 337-358.

————. *Napoléon en Paris*. Paris, 1964.

Rabreau, D. *See* Steinhauser.

Réau, L. "Le Jardin-Elysée de Musée de Monuments français," *Beaux-Arts, Révue d'information artistique*, 1 January 1924, pp. 1-3.

Reutersvaard, O. "De 'sjunkande' cenatofierna hos Moreau, Fontaine, Boullée och Gay," *Konsthistorisk Tidskrift*, III-IV, 1959, pp. 110-126.

Robinson, J. M. "Model Farm Buildings of the Age of Improvement," *Architectural History*, XIX, 1976, pp. 17-31.

Rosenau, H. *Social Purpose in Architecture: Paris and London Compared. London,* 1970.

——. *See* Bibliography. Sources: Boullée.

Røstvig, M. S. *The Happy Man: Studies in the Metamorphosis of a Classical Ideal.* I: *1600-1700,* II: *1700-1760,* Oslo, 1954-1958.

Siren, O. *China and Gardens of Europe of the Eighteenth Century.* New York, 1950.

Soulier, L. "Les jardins dans la ville de la fin du XVIIIe siècle à nos jours," *Les monuments historiques de la France,* 1976, no. 5, pp. 20-27.

Stein, R. *Les Jardins de France, des origines à la fin du XVIIIe siècle.* Paris, 1913.

Steinhauser, M., and D. Rabreau, "Le Théâtre de l'Odéon de Charles de Wailly et Marie-Joseph Peyre, 1767-1782," *Révue de l' art,* 1973, no. 19, pp. 9-49.

Thacker, C. "Voltaire and Rousseau: Eighteenth-Century Gardeners," *Studies on Voltaire and the Eighteenth Century,* XC, 1972, pp. 1595-1614.

Wiebenson, D. " 'L'Architecture terrible' and the 'Jardin Anglo-Chinois,' " *Journal of the Society of Architectural Historians,* XXVII, May 1968, pp. 136-139.

——. "Le Parc Monceau et ses 'Fabriques'," *Les Monuments historiques de la France,* 1976, no. 5, pp. 16-19.

Wittkower, R. "English Neo-Palladianism, the Landscape Garden, China, and the Enlightenment," *L'arte,* XI, no. 6, June 1969, pp. 18-35.

INDIVIDUAL GARDENS

AUTEUIL

Guillois, A. "Les Boufflers à Auteil," *Bulletin de la Société Historique d'Auteuil et de Passy,* I, 1892, pp. 238-247.

BAGATELLE

Scott, B. "Bagatelle: Folie of the Comte d'Artois," *Apollo,* June 1972, pp. 478-485.

Stern, J. *A l'Ombre de Sophie Arnould. François-Joseph Bélanger.* Paris, 1930 (2v.), I, pp. 66-72.

Thiéry. *Guide à Paris.* I, pp. 26-30 (for complete reference, *see* Primary Sources, above).

Villeneuve (ed.). *Vues pittoresques* (for complete reference, *see* Ermenonville, below).

BALBI

Scott, B. "Madame's Pavillon de Musique," *Apollo,* May 1972, pp. 390-399.

BELLEVUE

Biver, P. *Histoire du Château de Bellevue.* Paris, 1933.

Ganay, E. de. "Les Jardins à l'anglaise de Mesdames de France: à Bellevue et Versailles," *Révue de l'art ancien et moderne,* L, June-December 1926, pp. 215-228.

BELOEIL

Album-Souvenir avec notice historique du parc et du Château de Beloeil. Beloeil, n.d.

Guide de Beloeil. Beloeil, 1914.

See Primary Sources: Ligne.

BETZ

"Description historique du Château de Betz," *Société d'histoire et d'archéologie de Senlis. Mémoires,* 1907, X, pp. 180-262.

Cérutti, M. *Le Jardin de Betz.* Paris, 1792 (written 1785).

Ganay, E. de. "Les Jardins de Betz," *Figaro artistique,* no. 124, 14 October 1926, pp. 3-6.

Hallays, A. *A Travers la France: Autour de Paris.* Paris, 1910, pp. 222-252.

Macon, G. *Les Jardins de Betz.* Senlis, 1908.

Ségur, P. M. M. H. de. *La Dernière des Condé, Louise-Adélaïde de Condé, Marie-Catherine de Brignole, Princesse de Monaco.* Paris, 1899.

CHANTELOUP

Edouard-André, R. "Documents inédits sur l'histoire du château et des jardins de Chanteloup," *Bulletin de la Société de l'Histoire de l'Art Français,* 1935, pp. 21-39.

Hallays, A., R. E. André, and R. Engerand. *Chanteloup.* Tours, 1928.

d'Orliac, J. *La Vie merveilleuse d'un beau domaine français, Chanteloup du XIIIe siècle au XXe siècle.* Paris, 1929.

CHANTILLY

Broglie, R. de. "Le Théâtre de Chantilly," *Gazette des beaux-arts,* LVII, March 1961, pp. 155-166.

——. "Le Hameau et la laiterie de Chantilly," *Gazette des beaux-arts,* XXXVII, December 1950, pp. 309-324.

Chambry, J. work cited under Ermenonville.

Ganay, E. de. *Chantilly au XVIIIe siècle.* Paris, 1925.

——. "Chantilly au XVIIIe siècle d'après le jeu de cavagnole du Musée Condé," *Révue de l'art ancien et moderne,* LIII, January-June 1928, pp. 93-110.

——. *Chantilly. Notice historique et descriptive.* Paris, 1962.

——. "Les Jardins de Chantilly sous la restauration," *Révue de l'art ancien et moderne,* LXX, July 1936, pp. 19-21.

——. "Les Jardins de Chantilly au XVIIIe siècle," *Gazette illustrée des amateurs de jardins,* 1923, pp. 10-15.

[Girardin, S.] *Promenades ou itinéraire des jardins de Chantilly.* n.p., 1791 (Mérigot engr.).

Hallays, A. *Autour de Paris.* pp. 253-284 (for complete reference, *see* Betz, above).

Le Camus de Mezières, N. *Description des eaux de Chantilly et du Hameau.* Paris, 1783.

Macon, G. *Chantilly. Le château, le parc, les écuries.* Paris [1927].

Trois Jours en voyage. For complete reference, *see* Ermenonville.

Recueil des plans des châteaux, parcs et jardins de Chantilly, levé en 1784: Album exécuté par ordre du Prince de Condé et envoyé à la grande Catherine en 1784 (ms. deposited at the Musée Condé, Chantilly).

"Les Voyages d'Antoine Nicolas Duchesne à Ecouen, Chantilly, Ermenonville, Choisy, Brunoy, etc. en 1780, 1786, et 1791," *Révue de l'histoire de Versailles (et de Seine-et-Oise)*, January-March 1921.

ERMENONVILLE

Boulenger, J. *Au Pays de Gérard de Nerval.* Paris, 1914.

Cambry, J. *Description du département de l'Oise.* Paris, 1803 (2v.), II.

Ganay, E. de. "Le Jardin d'Ermenonville," *Gazette illustrée des amateurs de jardins*, 1925, pp. 1-18.

[Girardin, S.] *Promenade ou itinéraire des jardins d'Ermenonville.* n.p., 1788 (Mérigot engr.).

Martin-Decaen, A. *Le dernier Ami de J. J. Rousseau: Le Marquis René de Girardin (1735-1808).* Paris, 1912.

Mathieu, R. *Le Parc d'Ermenonville,* n.p., n.d. (publication of the Touring-Club de France).

Thiébaut de Berneaud, A. *Voyage à Ermenonville.* Paris, 1819.

A Tour to Ermenonville. London, 1785.

Trois Jours en voyage, ou guide du promeneur à Chantilly, Mortefontaine et Ermenonville. Paris, 1828.

Valenciennes, P. H. de. *Elémens de perspective pratique.* Paris, an viii [1800], chap. VII: "Des Jardins," pp. 344-373.

Villeneuve (ed.), *Vues pittoresques, plans, &c. des principaux jardins anglois qui sont en France, accompagnés de leurs descriptions, Ermenonville, Trianon, Bagatelle,* n.p., n.d. (c. 1785, according to Ganay, *Beaux jardins de France,* p. 135. Ganay, *Jardins à l'anglaise,* II, p. 615, notes that Bruel, author of the catalog of the collection of Vinck, attributes the engravings to Laurent Guyot after drawings by A. F. Sergant-Marceau).

Volbertal, J. H. *Aux Environs de Paris: Un domaine célèbre, Ermenonville, ses sites, ses curiosités, son histoire.* Senlis, 1923.

FERNEY

Bavoux, E. *Voltaire à Ferney.* Paris, 1858.

Beer, G. de. and A. M. Rousseau. "Voltaire's British Visitors," *Studies on Voltaire*, XLIX, 1967, pp. 7-201.

Brailsford, H. N. *Voltaire.* London, 1963, chap. VII: "He cultivates his Garden," pp. 94-103.

Caussy, F. *Voltaire, seigneur de village.* Paris, 1912.

Crouvezier, G. *La Vie de Voltaire.* Paris, 1937, chap. XII: "Le Patriarche de Ferney," pp. 119-124.

Sherlock, M. *Lettres d'un voyageur anglais.* London, 1779.

Thacker, C. "The Misplaced Garden? Voltaire, Julian and Candide," *Studies on Voltaire*, XLI, 1966, pp. 189-202.

FRANCONVILLE

Le Prieur, J. C. *Description d'une partie de la vallée de Montmorency et de ses plus agréables jardins.* Paris, 1784.

LABRÈDE

Barrière, P. F. *Un grand Provincial, Charles Louis de Secondat, Baron de la Brède et de Montesquieu.* Bordeaux, 1946.

Baurein, J. *Variétés bordelaises.* Bordeaux, 1784-1786 (5v.), V, pp. 40-41.

Desgraves, L. *Le Château de La Brède et Montesquieu.* Bordeaux, 1953.

Pesne, G. *En flânant chez Montesquieu à La Brède.* Bordeaux, 1936.

LE RAINCY

Chavard C., and O. Stemler. *Recherches sur Le Raincy 1238-1848.* Paris, 1884.

Gaulard M., and J. J. A. Bougon. "Le Parc du Raincy," *En Aulnaye jadis*, 1974, no. 3, pp. 16-38.

LIANCOURT

Dreyfus, F. *Un Philanthrope . . . La Rochefoucault-Liancourt.* Paris, 1903.

Mantil, E. "La Rochefoucauld Liancourt, un novateur français dans la pratique agricole du XVIIIe siècle," A. Rigaudière, E. Rilberman, R. Mantil, *Etudes d'histoire économique rurale au XVIIIe siècle,* Paris, 1965, pp. 150-206 (no. 5 of *Travaux et recherches de la Faculté de Droit et des Sciences Economiques de Paris,* série "Sciences historiques").

LUNÉVILLE

Baldensperger, F. "Le Kiosque de Stanislaus à Lunéville: décor et suggestion d'Orient," *Révue de la littérature comparée*, XIV, 1934, pp. 183-187.

Boyé, P. *Les Châteaux du Roi Stanislaus en Lorraine.* Nancy, 1910.

Héré, E. *Recueil des plans, élévations . . . ,* (for complete reference, *see* Primary Sources, above).

Ostrowski, J. "Nurt egzotyczny w architekturze Stanislawa Lesczynskiego w Lotharyngh," *Kwartalnik Architeckturyi Urbanistyki,* XVII, 1972, pp. 161-175.

——. "Rocher, teatr automatow Stanislawa Lesczynskiego w Lunéville," *Pamiectnik Teatralny,* XXI, 1972, no. 2, pp. 187-198.

——. "Le Rocher, théâtre des automats," *Le Pays Lorrain,* LIII, 1972, no. 4, pp. 175-184.

——. "Tschifflik, Maison de Plaisance Stanislawa Lesczynskiego w Zweibrückewi," *Biuletyn Historii Sztuki,* XXXIV, 1972, pp. 309-315.

Rau, J. (Gräfin v.d. Schulenberg). *Emmanuel Héré: Premier Architect von Stanislaus Leszcynski in Lothringer (1705-1763).* Berlin, 1973.

MAUPERTUIS

Rivière, C. *Un Village de la Brie au XVIIIe siècle, Maupertuis.* Paris, 1939.

MENARS

Ganay, E. de. "Les Jardins de Menars," *Révue de l'art ancien et moderne*, April 1935, suppl. 2, pp. 157-174.

Marigny, F. L. "Ménars, le château, les jardins," *Mémoires de la Société des Sciences et Lettres de Loire-et-Cher*, XX, 1912.

Mosser, M. "Monsieur de Marigny et les jardins: projets inédits des fabriques pour Menars," *Bulletin de la Société de l'Histoire de l'Art Français*, 1972, pp. 269-293.

MÉRÉVILLE

Bernois, C. *Histoire de Méréville et de ses seigneurs*. Orléans, 1903.

Cayeux [Cailleux], J. de. "Hubert Robert dessinateur des jardins et sa collaboration au Parc de Méréville," *Bulletin de la Société de l'Histoire de l'Art Français*, 1968, pp. 127-133.

Choppin de Janvry, O. "Méréville," *L'Oeil*, December 1969, pp. 39-40, 83, 96.

Ganay, E. de. "L'Art des jardins, dans les jardins de Jeurre," *Révue de l'art ancien et moderne*, L, June-December 1926, pp. 310-316.

Lefèvre, J. E. "Méréville," *Gazette illustrée des amateurs de jardins*, 1921, pp. 1-20.

Petit de Bachaumont, L. *Mémoires secrètes*, XXXI, pp. 270-273, 20 April 1786.

MEUDON

Biver, P. *Histoire du château de Meudon*. Paris, 1923.

MONCEAU

Britsch, A. *La Jeunesse de Philippe-Egalité*. Paris, 1926.

Carmontelle, L. *See* Primary Sources, above.

Dacier, E. "Le Jardin de Monceau avant la Révolution," *Publication de la Société d'Iconographie Parisienne*, VI, 1910, pp. 49-64.

Mareuse, "Le Parc Monceau, allocation prononcée le 20 mars 1902," *Bulletin de la Société Historique du VIIIe Arrondissement*," I, 1902, pp. 18-27.

Roué, G. *Les Squares de Paris—Le Parc de Monceau*. Paris, 1864 (3rd ed.).

MORTEFONTAINE (MORFONTAINE)

Cambry, J. *See* Ermenonville, above.

Guerard, C. J. *Promenade de Mortefontaine et vues pittoresques*. Paris, n.d.

Volbertal, J. H. *Les Domaines célèbres. Mortefontaine, le domaine de Vallières, ses sites, ses curiosités, son histoire*. Senlis, 1924.

Trois Jours en voyage. For complete reference, *see* Ermenonville, above.

MOULIN-JOLI

Dézallier d'Argenville, A. N. *Voyage pittoresque des environs de Paris*. Paris, 1779 (4th ed.), pp. 9-12.

Dulaure, J. A. *Nouvelle Description des environs de Paris*. Paris, 1786 (2v.) II, pp. 123-131.

Henriot, M. "Un Amateur d'art au XVIIIe siècle, l'académicien Watelet," *Gazette des beaux-arts*, VI, 1922, pp. 173-194.

Hirschfeld, C. C. L. *Théorie de l'art des jardins*, I, pp. 45-54.

Hofer, P. "Venuta in Roma," *Harvard Library Bulletin*, X, no. 2, Spring 1956.

———, *A Visit to ROME in 1764*. Cambridge, Mass., 1956.

Laruelle, R. "Marguerite Le Comte," *Bulletin de beaux-arts*, 1885, III, pp. 130-135.

Poisson, G. *Evocation du Grand Paris: La banlieu Nord-Ouest*. Paris, 1960, pp. 388-390.

Portalis, E. *Les Dessinateurs d'illustrations au 18e siècle*. Paris, 1877 (2v.), I, p. 90.

Portalis, E., and H. Beraldi. *Les Graveurs du dix-huitième siècle*. Paris, 1882 (3v.), III, pts. 1, 2.

Quénéhen, L. *Histoire de Colombes à travers les âges*. Paris, 1937, pp. 378-392, chap. XIV: "Watelet et Moulin-Joli."

Saint-Aubin, P. *Dictionnaire historique typographique et militaire de tous les environs de Paris*. Paris, 1816, pp. 462-466.

Serouille, A. *A la Ronde du Grand Paris: Bezons à travers les âges*. Paris [1944], pp. 145-149.

Thièry, L. V. *Guide aux environs de Paris*. pp. 295-299.

Vicq-d'Azyr, F. "Eloge de Watelet," *Oeuvres de Vicq-d'Azyr*, Paris, *an xiii* [1805] (6v.), II, pp. 63-93.

Vigée Lebrun, L. E. *Souvenirs*, Saint-Amand, 1867 (2v.), II, pp. 150-153 (1st ed. 1835-1837, 2v.; English translation, *Souvenirs of Madame Vigée Le Brun*, London, 1879, 2v.).

Watelet, C. H. *Essai sur les jardins*. Paris, 1774, pp. 138-160: "Le jardin françois."

———. *La Maison de campagne à la mode, ou la Comédie d'après Nature*. Paris, 1784.

RAMBOUILLET

Lenôtre, G. *Le Château de Rambouillet*. Paris, 1930.

Longnon, H. *Le Château de Rambouillet*. Paris, 1909.

Lorin, F. *Rambouillet. La Ville, le château, ses hôtels*. Paris, 1907.

Moutié, A. *Notice historique sur le domaine et le château de Rambouillet*. Rambouillet, 1850.

Tesier, M. *Notice relative à l'établissement d'économie rurale de Rambouillet*. Paris, 1805.

RETZ

Choppin de Janvry, O. "Le Désert de Retz," *Bulletin de la Société de l'Histoire de l'Art Français*, 1970, pp. 125-153.

———. "Avant que disparaisse à jamais le Désert de Retz," *L'Oeil*, September 1967, pp. 151-153.

Colette and Izis-Bidermanas. *Paradis Terrestres*. Paris, 1953, pp. 59-82.

Lécuyer, R., and J. C. Morevux. "Le Désert de M. de Monville," *L'Amour de l'art*, XIX, no. 3, April 1938, pp. 119-126.

Lefève, L. E. "Le Jardin anglais et la singulière habitation du Désert de Retz," *Bulletin de la Commission des Antiquités et des Arts de Seine et Oise*, 1917, pp. 62-69.

———. 'Maison construite dans le jardin nommé *le*

désert près la forêt de Marly par le propriétaire M. de Monville," *Bulletin de la Commission des Antiquités et des Arts de Seine et Oise*, 1917, pp. 70-71.

Siren, O. "Le Désert de Retz," *Architectural Review*, CVI, November 1949, pp. 327-332.

FOLIE DE SAINTE-JAMES

Bouillet, A. *La Folie de Sainte-James à Neuilly.* Paris, 1894.

Ganay, E. de. "L'Art des jardins: Les jardins de Sainte-James," *Révue de l'art ancien et moderne*, January-June 1922, pp. 392-398.

Stern, J. *Bélanger*, I, pp. 133-147.

THURY-HARCOURT

Ganay, E. de. "L'Art des jardins: les jardins d'Harcourt," *Révue de l'art ancien et moderne*, XLIII, January-June 1923, pp. 59-64.

VERSAILLES. *Jardin anglais* and *Hameau*.

Desjardins, G. *Le Petit-Trianon, histoire et description*. Versailles, 1885.

Gromort, G. *Le Hameau de Trianon*. Paris, 1928.

Nolhac, P. de. *Le Trianon de Marie-Antoinette*. Paris, 1914.

Villeneuve (éd.), *Vues pittoresques*. For complete reference, *see* Ermenonville, above.

INDEX

Illustrations

1 Richmond, Royal Park. From Campbell, *Vitruvius Britannicus*, IV

2 Versailles, *Bosquet des Sources*.
Detail of late seventeenth-century plan.
Bibliothèque Nationale, Paris

3 Versailles, Trianon de Porcelain. Engraving between 1668 and 1689. Bibliothèque Nationale, Paris

4   Versailles, Colonnade. Engraving after 1686. Bibliothèque Nationale, Paris

5   Versailles, Kiosk, elevation and plan.
    Archives Nationales, Paris

6   Versailles, Kiosk, elevation and plan.
    Archives Nationales, Paris

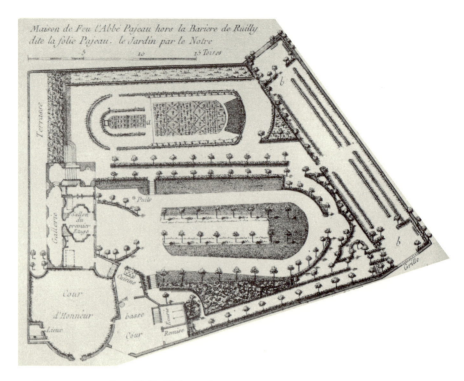

7 Vincennes region, Folie Pajou, plan.
Detail from Le Rouge, *Nouveaux jardins*, cahier 1

8 Lunéville, Kiosk, elevation. From Héré, *Chateaux en Lorraine*

9   Lunéville, Trèfle, elevation. From Héré, *Chateaux en Lorraine*

10   Kew, House of Confucius, elevation. From Chambers, *Gardens of Kew*

11 Lunéville, Chartreuses. Detail of mid-eighteenth-century painting. Musée de Lunéville

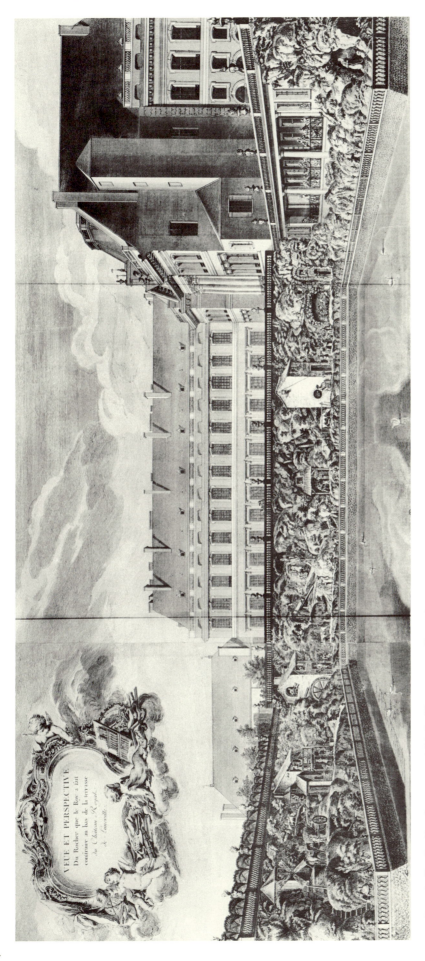

VEUE ET PERSPECTIVE
Du Rocher que le Roy a fait
construire au bas de la terrasse
du Chateau Royale
de Luneville

12 Lunéville, *Le Rocher*. From Héré, *Chateaux en Lorraine*

13 Malgrange, Château, garden front. Detail of mid-eighteenth-century painting. Musée Historique de Lorrain, Nancy

14 Einville, Château, view of grounds. Detail of mid-eighteenth-century painting. Musée de Lunéville

15 Chanteheux, Château. Detail of mid-eighteenth-century painting. Musée de Lunéville

16 *Maison de campagne*, perspective view.
From Ledoux, *L'Architecture*

17 Rural scene. Lithograph by Watelet.
Bibliothèque Nationale, Paris

18 Rural scene. Lithograph by Watelet.
Bibliothèque Nationale, Paris

19 Moulin-Joli. Title sheet to set of six etchings. Saint-Non after Le Prince, 1755.
Bibliothèque Nationale, Paris

20 Moulin-Joli. Etching by Saint-Non after Le Prince, 1755. Bibliothèque Nationale, Paris

21 Moulin-Joli. Etching by Saint-Non after Le Prince, 1755. Bibliothèque Nationale, Paris

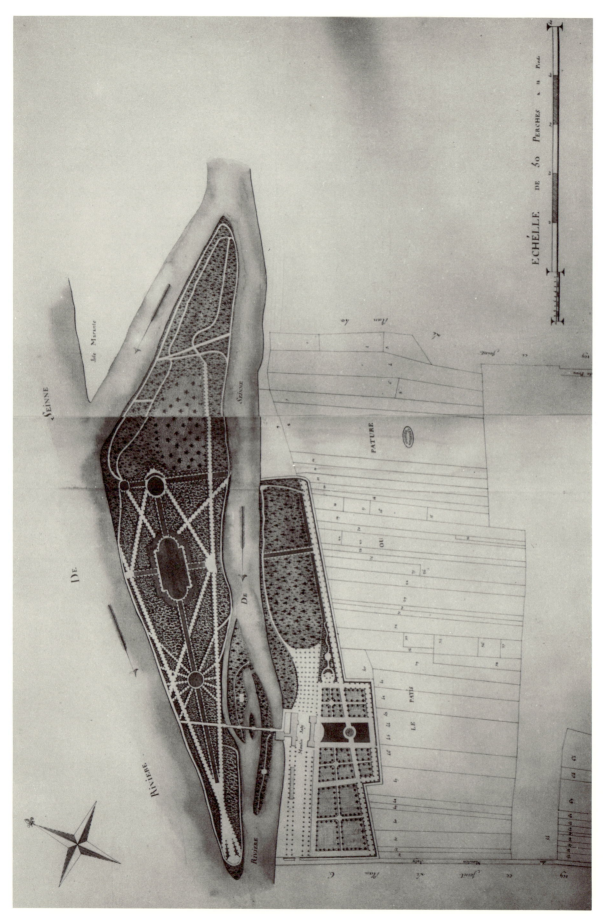

22 Moulin-Joli, plan, before 1786. Archives Nationales, Paris

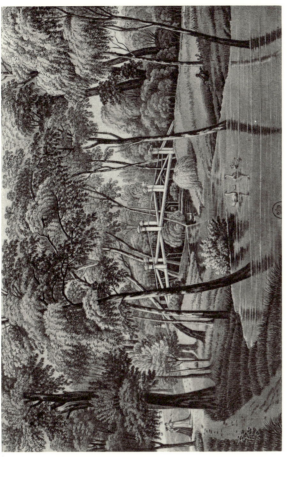

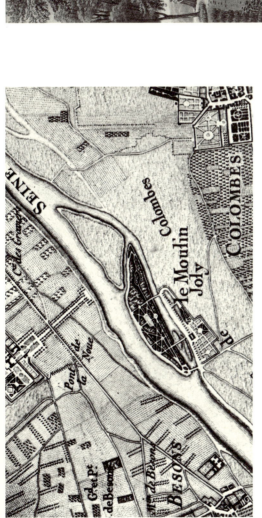

25 Moulin-Joli, Chinese bridge.
From Berthault, *Jardins anglais*, early nineteenth century

24 Moulin-Joli, view of west tip of island with mill and bridge.
Painting by Hubert Robert, 1780. Private collection

23 Environs of Versailles, map (Carte des Chasses), ca. 1785,
detail showing Moulin-Joli. Bibliothèque Nationale, Paris

26 Moulin-Joli, court and kitchen (originally dairy). Wash drawing, late eighteenth-century. Bibliothèque Nationale, Paris

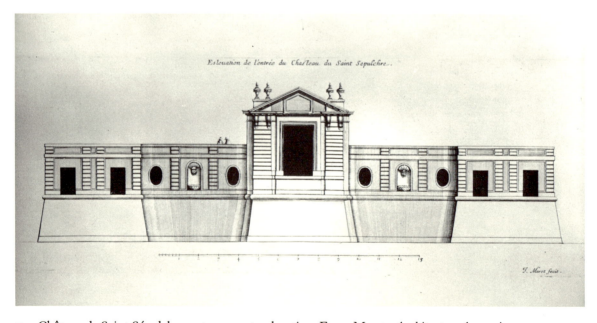

27 Château de Saint-Sépulchre, entrance gate, elevation. From Marot, *Architecture françois*

28 Moulin-Joli. Etching by Saint-Non after Le Prince, 1755. Bibliothèque Nationale, Paris

29 Moulin-Joli, mill. Drawing by Robert, after 1759. Musée de Valence

30 Moulin-Joli. Etching by Saint-Non after Le Prince, 1755. Bibliothèque Nationale, Paris

31 Moulin-Joli, Watelet's house. Etching by Watelet and Marguerite Le Comte, 1765.
Bibliothèque Nationale, Paris

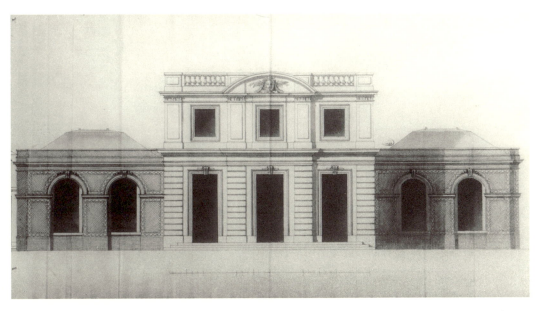

32   Fontainebleau, Hermitage, ca. 1748, elevation. Garnier de l'Ile (?). Archives Nationales, Paris

33   Evening Landscape. Painting by Boucher, 1743. Bowes Museum, Barnard Castle

34 Château de Ferney, view from garden. Engraving by Queverdo. Bibliothèque Nationale, Paris

35 Richmond, Merlin's Cave, section. From Vardy, *Designs of Kent*

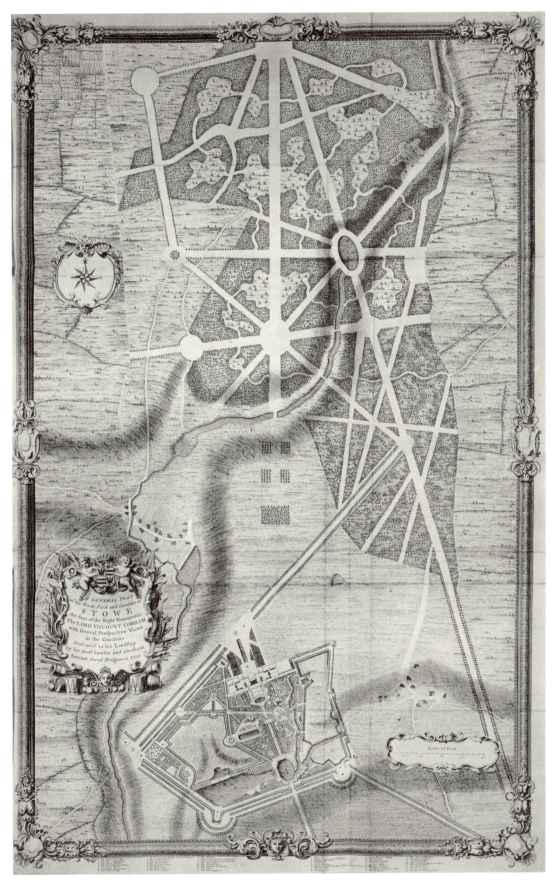

36 Stowe, gardens, plan. Engraving by Rigaud, 1738. Metropolitan Museum of Art, New York

37 Studies of rocks. From Le Rouge, *Nouveaux jardins*, cahier XII

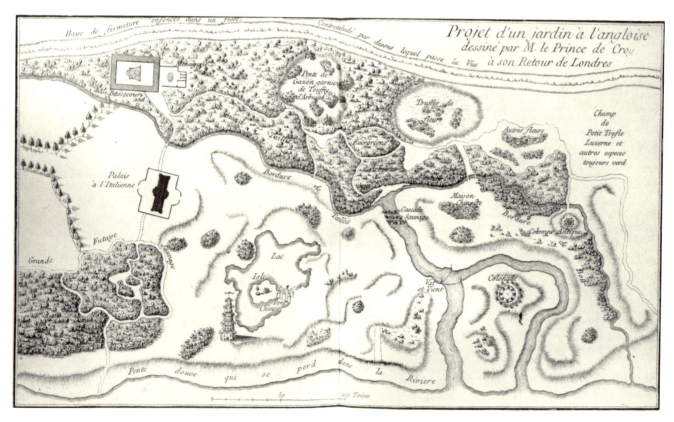

38 Project for a *jardin anglais*, plan, attributed to the Prince de Croÿ. From Le Rouge, *Nouveaux jardins*, cahier I

39 Chiswick, The Exedra. Wash drawing by Kent ca. 1730.
Devonshire Collection, Chatsworth

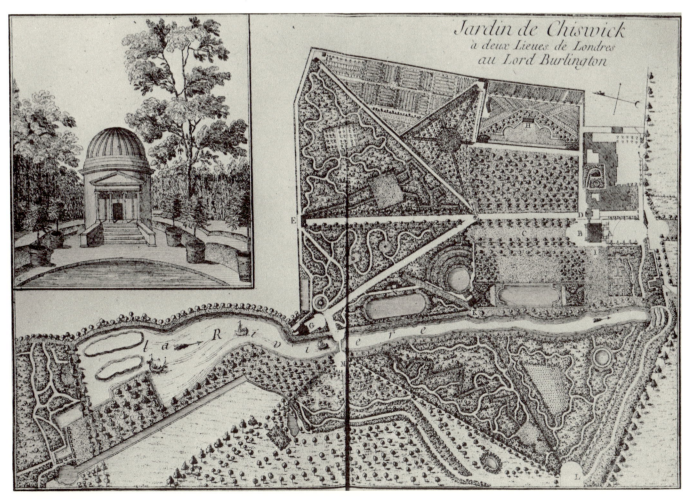

40 Chiswick, garden, plan. From Le Rouge, *Nouveaux jardins*, cahier 1

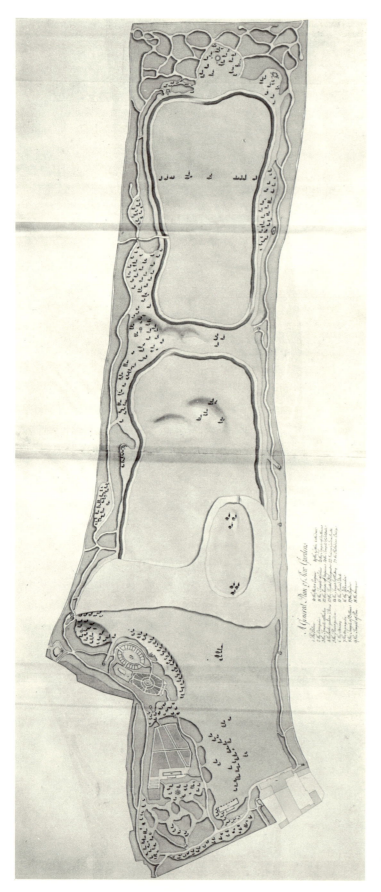

41 Kew, gardens, plan. Drawing by Chambers, before 1763. Metropolitan Museum of Art

42 Kew, gardens, view of the Wilderness, including the Moorish pavilion, pagoda and mosque. From Chambers, *Gardens of Kew*

43 Kew, gardens, view of lake, island and pagoda. From Chambers, *Gardens of Kew*

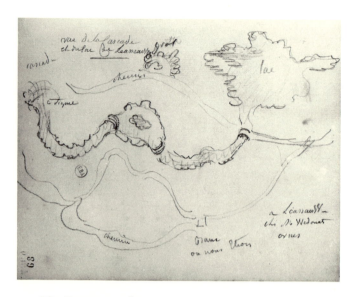

44 The Leasowes, plan

45 The Leasowes, cascade

46 Stowe, Doric temple

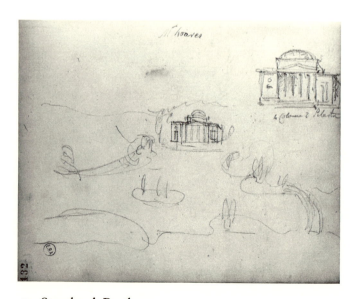

47 Stourhead, Pantheon

44-47 From Bélanger, "Croquis d'un voyage en Angleterre."
Ecole Nationale Supérieur des Beaux-Arts, Paris

48 Wilton, House and bridge

49 Unidentified garden

50 Dovedale, rocks

48-51 From Bélanger, "Croquis d'un voyage en
Angleterre."
Ecole Nationale Supérieur des Beaux-Arts, Paris

51 Matlock Baths

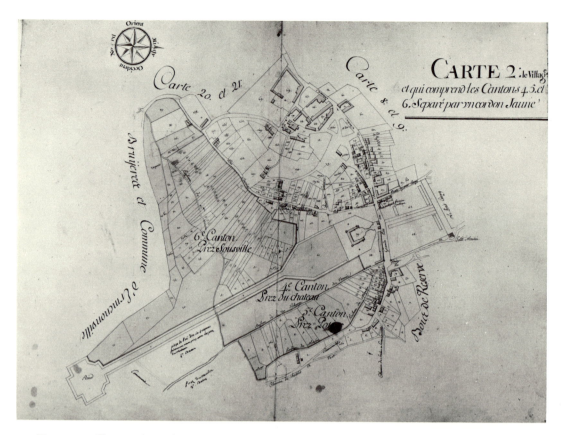

52 Ermenonville, north garden before 1760, plan (read north to left). Musée Jacquemart-André, Château de Châalis

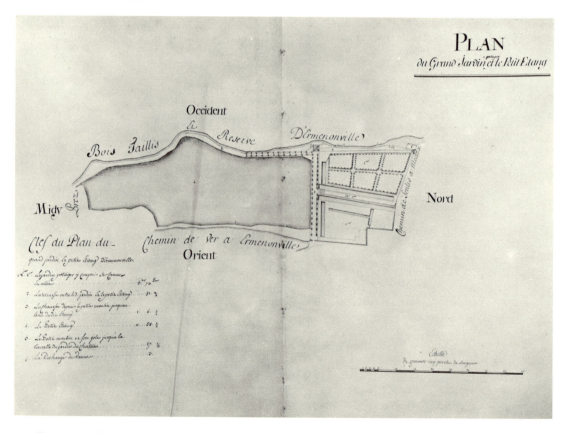

53 Ermenonville, south garden before 1760, plan (read north to right).
Musée Jacquemart-André, Château de Châalis

LES JARDINS
D'ERMENONVILLE
Levés sur les Lieux
par le Rouge Ing.^r
en 1775.

a Cascade
b Grotte
c Billiard et
   Brasserie
d le jardinier Ruiné
e Tombeau de J.J. Rousseau

50   100   200 T^s

54   Ermenonville, gardens, plan. From Le Rouge, *Nouveaux jardins*, cahier III

55 Ermenonville, village. From A. Laborde, *Description*

56 Decoration for a pastoral opera. Oil sketch by François Boucher, 1743.
Musée de Picardie, Amiens

57 Ermenonville, south garden. From Girardin, *Guide*

58 Ermenonville, north garden. From A. Laborde, *Description*

59 Ermenonville, Philosopher's Pyramid.
From A. Laborde, *Description*

60 Ermenonville, Hermitage. From Girardin, *Guide*

61 Ermenonville, Cascade under the Grotto. From Girardin, *Guide*

62 Ermenonville, Monuments of Old Loves. From Girardin, *Guide*

63 Ermenonville, The Wilderness. From A. Laborde, *Description*

64 Ermenonville, Philosopher's Hut.
From Le Rouge, *Nouveaux jardins*, cahier III

65 Ermenonville, Rustic temple. From Girardin, *Guide*

66 Charcoal-maker's hut, elevation. From Ledoux, *L'Architecture*

67 Ermenonville, Grange. From Girardin, *Guide*

68   Ermenonville, Arcadian Fields. From Girardin, *Guide*

69   Ermenonville, Farm. From A. Laborde, *Description*

70 Ermenonville, Rousseau's cottage. Painting by Mayer.
From *Gazette illustrée des amateurs des jardins*, 1925

71 Rural scene. Painting by François Boucher, ca. 1740's.
Musée des Beaux-Arts, Orléans

72 Ermenonville, Temple of Modern Philosophy. Wash drawing by S. Gobelain.
Bibliothèque Nationale, Paris

73 Temple of the Sibyl at Tivoli. Drawing by Fragonard, 1759. Musée des Beaux-Arts, Besançon

74 Ermenonville, Brasserie,
view from rear.
From A. Laborde, *Description*

75 Ermenonville, view of Mill. Drawing by Hubert Robert, after 1759.
Musée de Valence

76 Cypresses at the Villa d'Este.
Drawing by Fragonard, 1759.
Musée des Beaux-Arts, Besançon

77 Ermenonville, Brasserie, view of entrance.
From A. Laborde, *Description*

78 Italian Park. Painting by Hubert Robert.
Fundacão Calouste Gulbenkian, Lisbon

79 Ermenonville, Tower of Gabriel. From A. Laborde, *Description*

80 Ermenonville, Italian Mill. From A. Laborde, *Description*

82 Ermenonville, Island of Poplars.
From Girardin, *Guide*

81 Ermenonville, Keeper's Lodge. Aquatint by Guirard. Bibliothèque Nationale, Paris

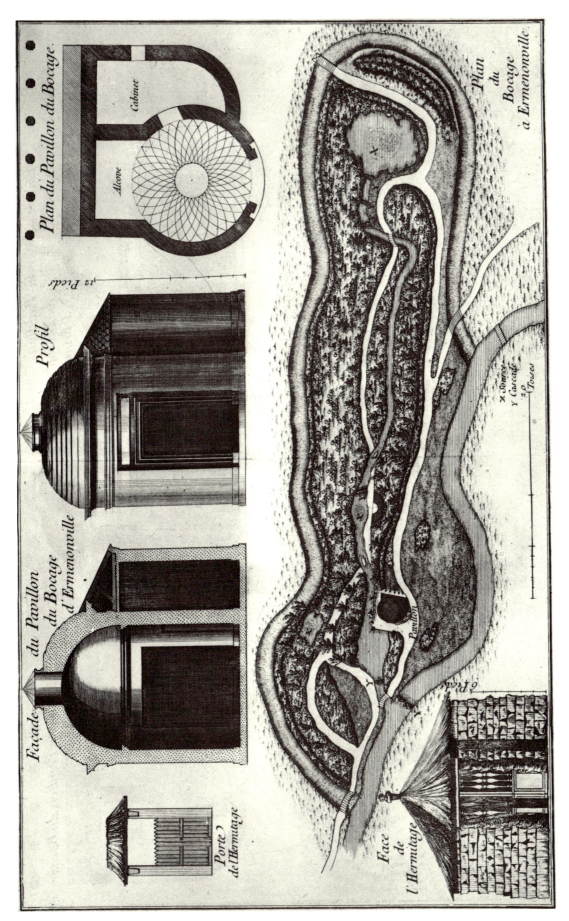

83   Ermenonville, *Bocage*, plan. From Le Rouge, *Nouveaux jardins*, cahier II

84 Paris, Hôtel of the Baronne Neubourg. Wash drawing by Maréchal, 1786.
Bibliothèque Nationale, Paris

85 Paris, house on the Hosten estate, elevation.
From Ledoux, *L'Architecture*

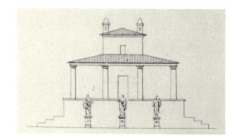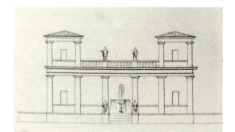

86 Designs for porticos. From Durand, *Précis des leçons*, part II

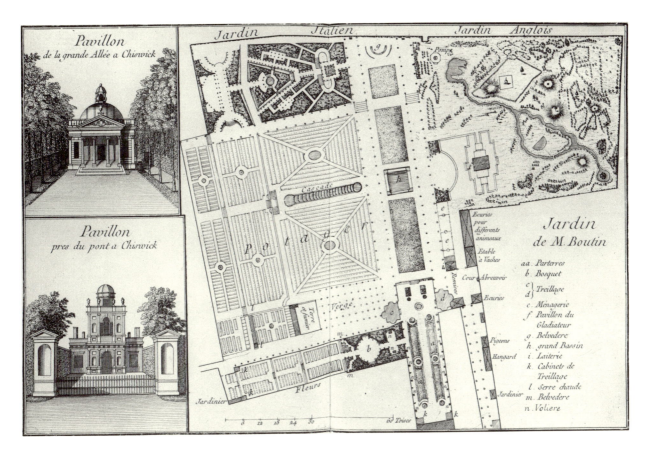

Pavillon
de la grande Allée a Chiswick

Pavillon
pres du pont a Chiswick

Jardin   Italien   Jardin   Anglois

Jardin
de M. Boutin

aa. Parterres
b. Bosquet
c. } Treillage
d. }
e. Ménagerie
f. Pavillon du
   Gladiateur
g. Belvedere
h. grand Bassin
i. Laiterie
k. Cabinets de
   Treillage
l. Serre chaude
m. Belvedere
n. Voliere

87   Paris, Boutin's garden "Tivoli," plan. From Le Rouge, *Nouveaux jardins*, cahier 1

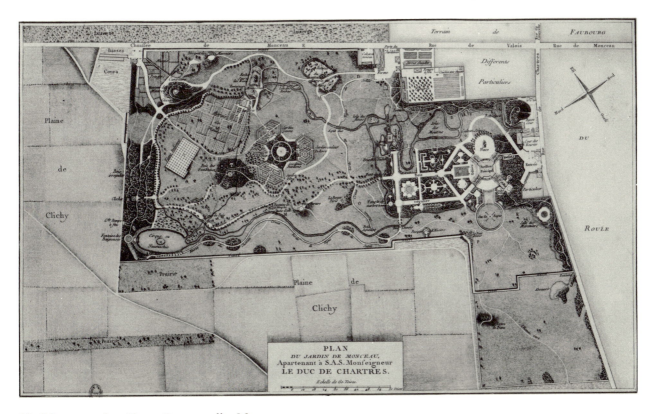

PLAN
DU JARDIN DE MONCEAU,
Apartenant à S.A.S. Monseigneur
LE DUC DE CHARTRES.

88   Monceau, plan. From Carmontelle, *Monceau*

89   Monceau, view of farm. From Carmontelle, *Monceau*

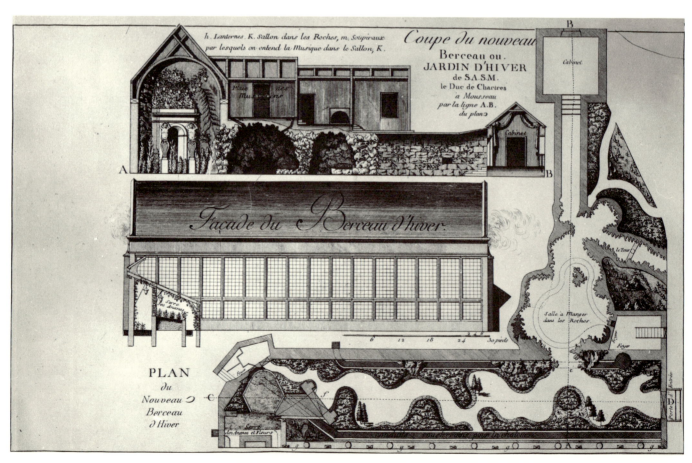

90   Monceau, *jardin d'hiver*. From Le Rouge, *Nouveaux jardins*, cahier x

91　Monceau, Island of Rocks. From Carmontelle, *Monceau*

92　Monceau, Minaret. From Carmontelle, *Monceau*

93   Monceau, Naumachia. From Carmontelle, *Monceau*

94   Monceau, Turkish Tent. From Carmontelle, *Monceau*

95 Monceau, Gothic ruins and watermill. From Carmontelle, *Monceau*

96 Monceau, *Jeu de bague*. From Carmontelle, *Monceau*

97   Monceau, Wood of Tombs. From Carmontelle, *Monceau*

98   Fantastic ruins.
     From Legeay, *Rovine*. Bibliothèque Nationale, Paris

99 Fantastic monuments.
From Cuvilliès, *fils, Architecture bavaroise.* Bibliothèque Nationale, Paris

100 Egyptian pyramids. From Fischer von Erlach, *Historischen Architectur*

101   Residence of the King of Siam. From Fischer von Erlach, *Historischen Architectur*

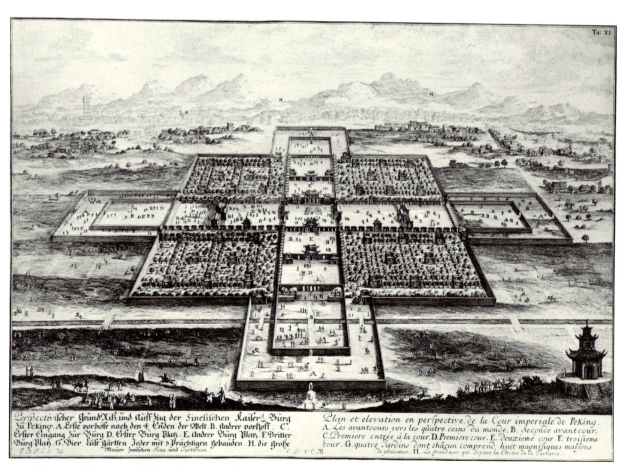

102   Imperial Court at Peking. From Fischer von Erlach, *Historischen Architectur*

103 Monceau, ruins of the Temple of Mars. From Carmontelle, *Monceau*

104 Ruins of Palmyra. From Fischer von Erlach, *Historischen Architectur*

HAMEAU

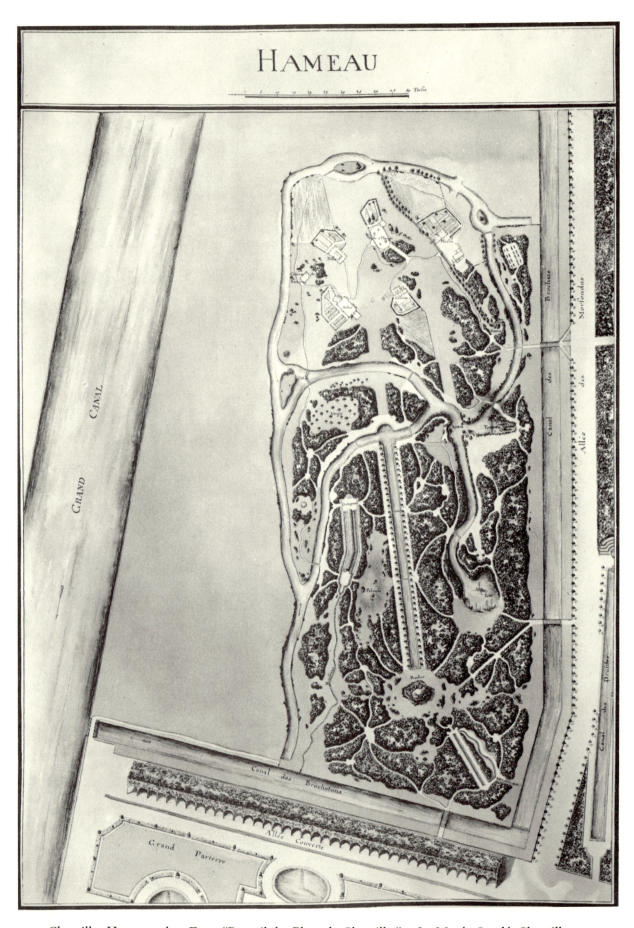

105   Chantilly, *Hameau*, plan. From "Recueil des Plans de Chantilly," 1784. Musée Condé, Chantilly

106   Chantilly, *Hameau*, elevations, sections and plans.
       From "Recueil des Plans de Chantilly," 1784. Musée Condé, Chantilly

107 Bellevue, farm. From Bacler d'Albe, *Promenades*

108 Franconville, Swiss village. From Le Prieur, *Montmorency*

Vue du Caffé Restaurateur du Reinci
Dans le gout Russe à 2 lieues ½ de Paris, par la Porte St. Martin et Pantin.
Dans le Jardin Anglais de M. D'orléans.
Ce Lieu charmant est tenu par le St. ESSE Restaurateur, on trouve Chez lui des provisions de bouche
de toute espece, de toute Sorte de Vins et servis très proprement. on y parle françois et anglois.
toutes les Fêtes et Dimanches Il y à des Bals Champêtres.

109 Le Raincy, Russian village. Engraving, late eighteenth century.
Bibliothèque Nationale, Paris

111 Rambouillet, entrance to farm
(now Centre d'Enseignement
Zootechnique). From Rambouillet
postcard

110 Liancourt, factories. From photograph of
late eighteenth-century wash drawing
by Vaurelle. Bibliothèque Nationale, Paris

112 Méréville, mill. From A. Laborde, *Description*

113 Méréville, view of temple and château. Painting by Hubert Robert, after 1786. Private collection

114 Méréville, grand cascade. Painting, late eighteenth century. Musée de Sceaux, Ile de France

115 Méréville, hut and bridge. Painting by Robert, after 1786. Nationalmuseum, Stockholm

116 Bridge over rapids of Moulins. From J. B. Laborde, *Tableaux de la Suisse*, II

117 View of chapel. From J. B. Laborde, *Tableaux de la Suisse*, II

118 Mountains of Lugarno. From J. B. Laborde, *Tableaux de la Suisse*, II

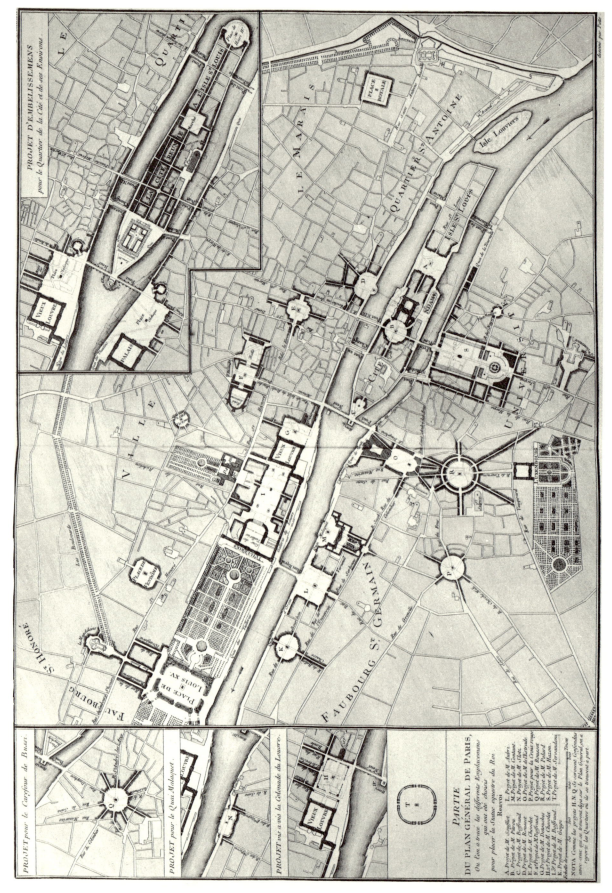

119 Projects for Place Louis XIV, Paris. From Patte, *Monumens*

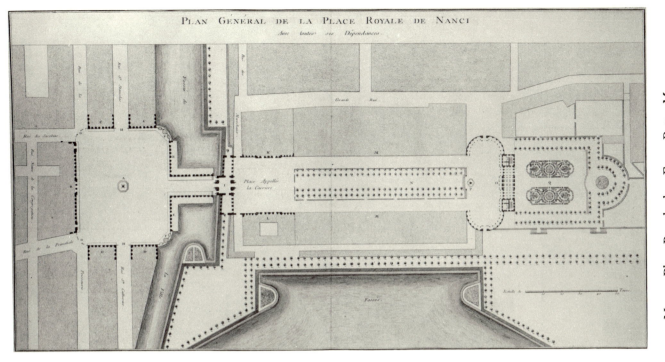

PLAN GÉNÉRAL DE LA PLACE ROYALE DE NANCI
Avec toutes ses Dépendances

121 Nancy, Place Royal, plan. From Patte, *Monumens*

120 Boffrand's project for Place Louis XV, Paris, plan.
From Patte, *Monumens*

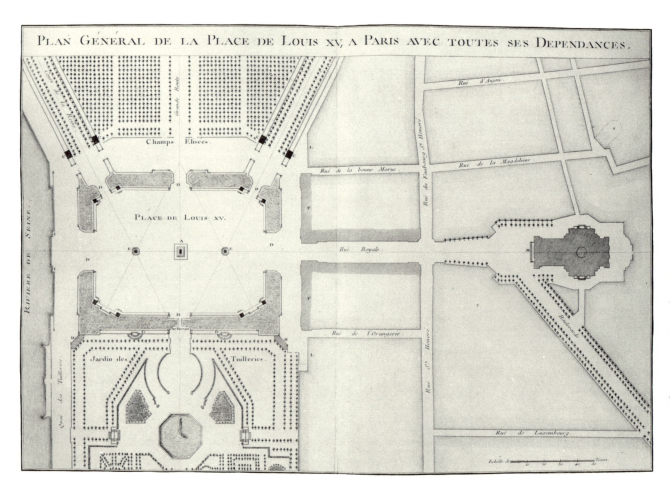

DEVELOPPEMENT D'UNE GUERITE.
Vüe du Côté de la Place.

Vüe du Côté.

du Fossé.

Plan.

trottoir.

Echelle de

123   Paris, Place Louis XV, sentry box, elevation. From Patte, *Monumens*

PLAN GÉNÉRAL DE LA PLACE DE LOUIS XV, A PARIS AVEC TOUTES SES DEPENDANCES.

Champs Elisees.

PLACE DE LOUIS XV.

RIVIERE DE SEINE.

Jardin des   Tuilleries.

Quai des Tuilleries.

Rue d'Anjou.

Rue de la bonne Moruë.

Rue de la Magdeleine.

Rue du Faubourg St Honoré.

Rue Royale.

Rue de l'Orangerie.

Rue St Honoré.

Boulevard.

Rue de Luxembourg.

Echelle de

122   Paris, Place Louis XV, plan. From Patte, *Monumens*

124　Paris, Place Louis XV, wash drawing. Bibliothèque Nationale, Paris

125 Paris, plan by Maire, 1808.
From N. M. Maire, *La Topograpie de Paris*

126 Paris, Beaumarchais garden, plan. From Gosselin, *Les Quartiers de Paris*

128 Paris, Beaumarchais garden, watercolor by Bélanger, after 1790.
Bibliothèque Nationale, Paris

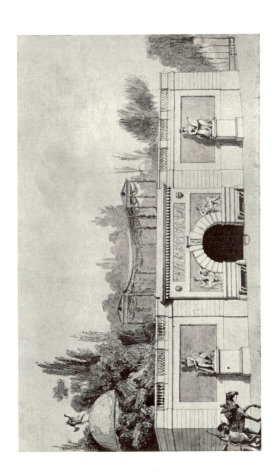

127 Paris, Beaumarchais garden, watercolor by Bélanger, after 1790.
Bibliothèque Nationale, Paris

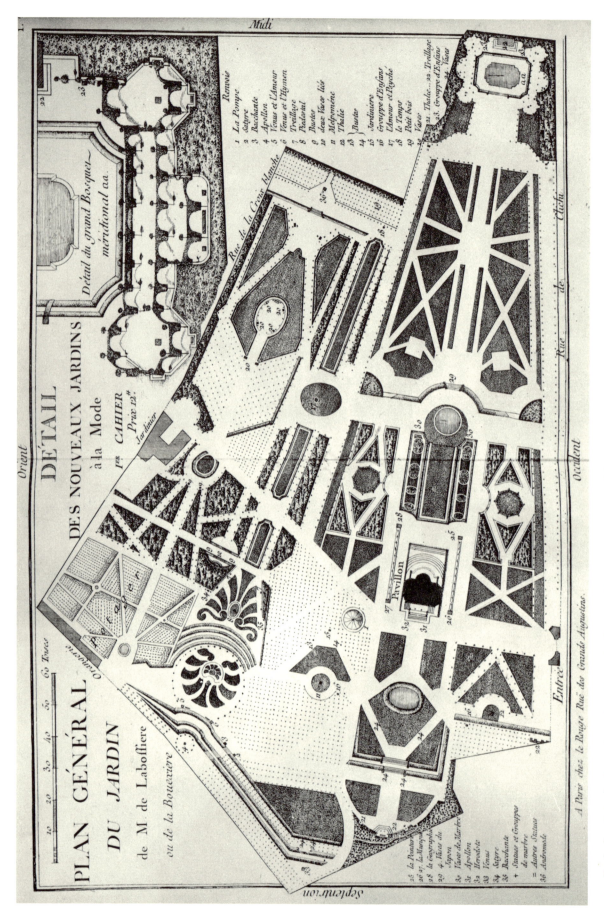

129 Paris, La Boissière's garden, plan. From Le Rouge, *Nouveaux jardins*, cahier 1

130 Paris, Hôtel Brunoy. Wash drawing by Maréchal, after 1774. Bibliothèque Nationale, Paris

131 Paris, Hôtel Tamnay. Wash drawing on engraving by Prieur. Musée Carnavalet, Paris

132 Paris, Maison Olivier, entrance. From Krafft and Ransonnette, *Plans des plus belles maisons à Paris*

133 Désert de Retz, entrance from the Forest of Marly. From Le Rouge, *Nouveaux jardins*, cahier XIII

134 Project for house in Paris, street elevation. Engraving attributed to Ledoux, early nineteenth century. From Raval, *Ledoux*

135 Chinese house, elevation. From Chambers, *Designs*

136 Paris, Hôtel Sainte-Foix, view from street. Wash drawing, after 1775. Bibliothèque Nationale, Paris

137 Paris, Hôtel Sainte-Foix, view from the terrace. Wash drawing, after 1775. Musée Carnavalet, Paris

138 Paris, Hôtel de Salm, view from street. Wash drawing after 1783. Bibliothèque Nationale, Paris

139 Paris, Hôtel de Salm, view from river. From Testard, *Paris*

140 Paris, house of M. Le Chevalier, facade. From Testard, *Paris*

141 Paris, The Duc de Montmorency's Chinese pavilion. From Testard, *Paris*

142 Paris, Hôtel Thélusson, plan. From Ledoux, *L'Architecture*

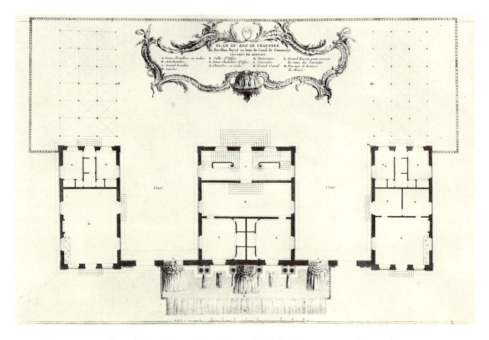

143 Commercy, Royal Pavilion, plan. From Héré, *Chateaux en Lorraine*

144 Paris, Hôtel Thélusson, view of arch from street. Wash drawing, after 1780. Bibliothèque Nationale, Paris

145 Paris, Hôtel Thélusson, view of arch from garden. Wash drawing, after 1780. Bibliothèque Nationale, Paris

146 Paris, Paphos, view of ball
room and garden. From
Martial, *Ancien Paris*
(etching from early nineteenth-
century illustration)

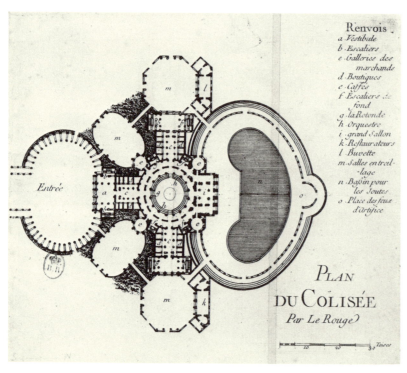

147 Paris, Colisée, plan.
From Le Rouge, *Description du Colisée*

148 Paris, Palais Royal, court.
Engraving by Née after Meunier,
early nineteenth century.
Bibliothèque Nationale, Paris

149 Paris, Tivoli III (originally
Pavillon de La Boissière).
Engraving, early nineteenth-
century. Musée Carnavalet, Paris

150 Paris, Beaujon estate transformed
into a Vauxhall. Print, 1817.
Musée Carnavalet, Paris

151. Paris, Granary, view from
street. Wash drawing by Maréchal,
1786.
Bibliothèque Nationale, Paris

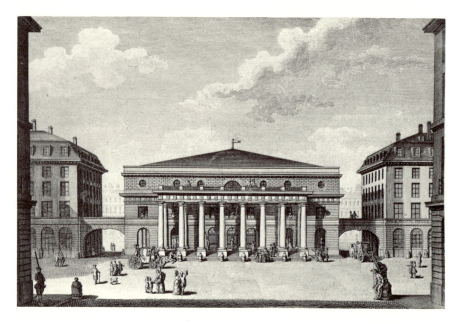

152 Paris, Odéon, elevation.
Bibliothèque Nationale, Paris

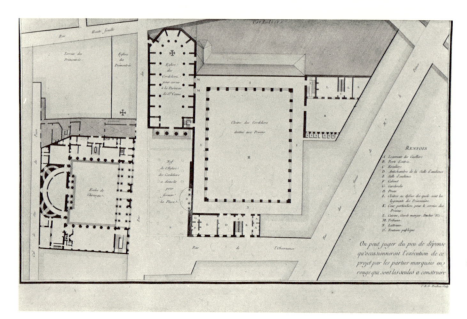

153 Paris, School of Surgery, plan of
square. Detail from Gondoin,
*Description des Ecoles
de Chirurgie*

154 Paris, School of Surgery, portico
and court. Drawing by
Ransonnette, late eighteenth
century.
Bibliothèque Nationale, Paris

155 Paris, School of Surgery, view of
square. From Gondoin,
*Description des Ecoles de
Chirurgie*

156 Paris, School of Surgery, late
eighteenth-century view.
Bibliothèque Nationale, Paris

157   Fantastic reconstruction of the Appian Way. From Piranesi, *Antichità Romane*, II

158 Paris, restoration of the Louvre colonnade. Drawing after 1763. Bibliothèque Nationale, Paris

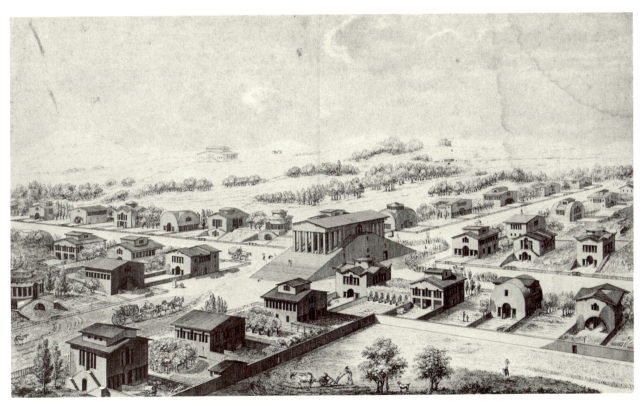

159 Maupertuis, project for a village. Contemporary print. Archives de Seine-et-Marne, Melun

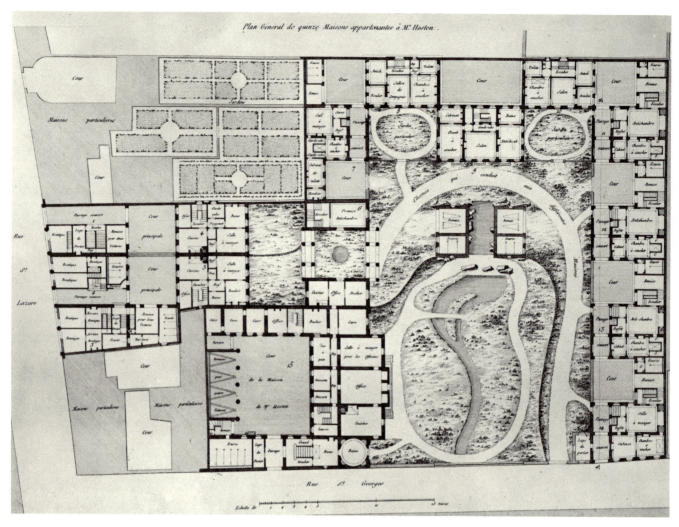

160   Paris, Hosten estate, plan. From Ledoux, *L'Architecture*

161 Marly and Paris, Pavilions of Louveciennes and Duc de Chartres. Drawings by Chambers, ca. 1773.
From Chambers's Paris sketchbook, Royal Institute of British Architects,
Prints and Drawings Collection, London

162 Paris, Hôtels Guimard and Montmorency. Drawing, late eighteenth century.
From anonymous Paris sketchbook, British Museum Map Room, London

163 Paris, Memorial Gardens of the Museum of French Monuments. Painting by Hubert Robert. Musée Carnavalet, Paris

164 Paris, Père La Chaise cemetery. From Martens, *Vues de Paris*

165 "Monuments de Paris," wallpaper by J. Dufour, 1814.
The Henry Francis du Pont Winterthur Museum, Winterthur, Delaware

a

166a-f London, promotion drawings for Regent's Park, ca. 1810. Public Record Office, London

b

c

d

e

f